In this thoroughly researched volume, Ross Hastings offers a crackling compendium of fundamental theological criteria by which Christians may guide their ethical reflection. The ideas contained within these covers resonate with clear thinking as well as an intriguing engagement with other leading modern theologians, public controversies as well as the biblical sources.

—PAUL ALLEN, academic dean and professor of theology, Corpus Christi College

Ethics is never autonomous but always arises from a particular narrative. Hastings cogently argues that Christian ethics must be theological and therefore is Trinitarian, biblical, ecclesial, and missional. A significant contribution to both Christian ethics and theology.

—DENNIS P. HOLLINGER, president emeritus and senior distinguished professor of Christian ethics, Gordon-Conwell Theological Seminary

Ross Hastings argues convincingly that Christian ethics must be restored to its status as a profoundly *theological* discipline. In making the case he offers us excellent perspectives on specific topics in ethics—including some very pressing ones in contemporary life. And there is more: refreshing insights on Trinitarian thought, the church as the locus of moral reflection, the need for grounding theology in careful biblical exposition, and the relationship of morality to spirituality. An impressive and refreshing book!

—RICHARD J. MOUW, president emeritus, Fuller Theological Seminary

One of the most damaging legacies of modernity is the extent to which Christian theologians have lost their evangelical nerve when it comes to "Christian" ethics. Fear of questioning universal epistemic access to the moral law, confused accounts of the conditions for repentance, and a concern to ratify accounts of the state and its laws independently of the gospel have distracted theologians from the recognition at the heart of the faith, namely, that Jesus Christ is the key to understanding the totality of God's purposes for human beings and thereby every facet of their relationship to God and to each other.

In this remarkable book, Ross Hastings has the courage to think through the totality of Christian ethics from its centre in the triune God and his radical and liberating engagement with the contingent order in Jesus Christ. Rather than defining ethics with reference to generic assumptions about human purposiveness, it focuses on the one who alone mediates God's creative purposes to humanity and who alone is the true image of God the Father. Consequently, rather than turning to some perceived natural order for guidance, Hastings interprets our obligations in the light of our participation in the new creation and in the life of the new humanity to which the resurrection bears witness. The result is an approach to ethics that is grace-oriented, liberating, and inspirational rather than legalistic—that refuses to reduce Christian ethics to secular humanism in religious guise. This is a courageous, cogent, and convincing account of the radical and distinctive nature of Christian ethics. Not only will it challenge, but it will inspire and excite students, pastors, and theologians alike. What it reminds us is that theological ethics is never more relevant than when it actively witnesses to the gospel of Jesus Christ and interprets its grounds accordingly.

—ALAN J. TORRANCE, emeritus professor,
University of St. Andrews

THEOLOGICAL ETHICS

THEOLOGICAL ETHICS

The Moral Life of the Gospel
in Contemporary Context

———

W. ROSS HASTINGS

ZONDERVAN
ACADEMIC

ZONDERVAN ACADEMIC

Theological Ethics
Copyright © 2021 by W. Ross Hastings

Requests for information should be addressed to:
Zondervan, *3900 Sparks Dr. SE, Grand Rapids, Michigan 49546*

Zondervan titles may be purchased in bulk for educational, business, fundraising, or sales promotional use. For information, please email SpecialMarkets@Zondervan.com.

ISBN 978-0-310-11195-5 (hardcover)

ISBN 978-0-310-12457-3 (audio)

ISBN 978-0-310-11196-2 (ebook)

Cover design: Tammy Johnson
Cover image: Bequest of Harry G. Friedman, 1965 / Metropolitan Museum of Art
Interior Design: Kait Lamphere

Printed in the United States of America

20 21 22 23 24 25 26 27 28 29 30 /TRM/ 15 14 13 12 11 10 9 8 7 6 5 4 3 2 1

Contents

To my supervisor and friend,
master theological ethicist
Alan Torrance

Acknowledgments

I must acknowledge the theologians of ethics referenced in this book who have shaped my way of thinking about theological ethics. To four contemporary theologians I am particularly indebted: Alan Torrance, for his portrayal of a deeply Trinitarian ontology that shapes ethics, one that entails the crucial notion that the church as the image of the Trinity must reflect inner and outward expressions of justice (*communio* in *ekstasis*), a notion that is profoundly evangelical and public in its approach; Oliver O'Donovan, whose masterly work *Resurrection and Moral Order* brings out the crucial reality that the resurrection of Jesus is the reaffirmation of creation, and with it an evangelical and textured creational approach to ethics that does have a place in the public square; Stanley Hauerwas, for his emphasis, following that of Karl Barth, on the theological nature of ethics and on the role of narrative virtue formation of the church as God's primary ethical community; and Dennis Hollinger, whose work *Choosing the Good* is both an eloquent and accessible (!) introduction to Trinitarian worldview ethics that gave me confidence in a Trinitarian approach and specifically in the assertion that the category of *persons* (in relation) is a larger one than even that of *character* in theological ethics.

I am thankful for colleagues at Regent College who have given me helpful feedback on various chapters, including Iain Provan, Jeff Greenman, Paul Spilsbury, Bruce Hindmarsh, Grace Liang, Craig Gay, George Guthrie, Iwan Russell-Jones, Diane Stinton, and Jonathan Wilson. My research teaching assistants Jennifer Wotochek, Chris Agnew, and Jacob Raju provided helpful feedback, as well as editing and providing indices. I am extremely grateful for the work of my editors at Zondervan, Katya Covrett and Matthew Estel.

I am profoundly thankful for the unstinting support and encouragement of my wife, Tammy. Her sunny disposition and prayers lift my spirits in the midst of the ups and downs of writing a book such as this one. The birth of a beautiful granddaughter, Ada, during the time of its writing, adding to seven other lovely grandchildren we have, has also added a joy of a surprising nature and the hope that there may be an ongoing legacy of Christian theology in the clan!

CHAPTER 1

Theological Ethics
Are *Theological*

On the first Sunday after I had begun writing the first chapter of this book, the sermon of our Kiwi pastor, Aaron Roberts, resonated with some of the themes of my writing in a remarkable way. It was an excellent exposition of Paul's sermon at the Areopagus in Athens, the intellectual and cultural capital of the ancient world, recorded in Acts 17. The similarities between Paul's task that day, in that culture, and the task I face in writing this book, in our time, are striking. These are some of those common assumptions shared between modern/postmodern/ fragmented Western culture and the culture of Athens: pantheism is prominent, as seen in phrases like nature is "mother earth" and the "universe has given you this musical gift"; multicultural tolerance and equal rights are highly valued; religion is suspect, but a fuzzy kind of spirituality is honoured; self-sufficiency is praised; there is a great love of sports (the Olympics began there), fashion, and material wealth . . . and perhaps there is a God, but he is distant and inaccessible.

THEMES IN THEOLOGICAL ETHICS FROM
ATHENS TO CONTEMPORARY CULTURE

Passionate Intellect

The *first* thing to notice about Paul's approach to his speech to the intellectual elite of Athens is the *state of the heart* that fuelled it. Paul is "greatly distressed" (Acts 17:16; Gk. παρωξύνετο, which sounds like the English noun *paroxysm*), indeed "outraged" (an alternative translation) by the idolatry of the city of Athens, in which there were many temples to many gods. His words to that city's intellectuals are not just cognitively brilliant; they are also carefully contextualized, so much so that he uses their own Greek poetry twice (17:28). Paul's sermon is also emotively *energized by a passion for the supremacy and glory of the one true God.*

1

Paul knows that calling for change begins with a change of mind about God and who the one real God really is. Change is first theological. We must know it, and then we must *feel* it.

In a similar vein, the instincts that guide this book are more than merely cognitive, for the approach of any theological ethicist begins with the heart. As our pastor lamented, "We do not speak as Paul spoke because we don't feel what Paul felt."[1] And so I write as someone who is deeply distressed, even outraged, about the moral state of the world and especially of the church that is so deeply enculturated in the narratives of society. Not that we must speak with uncontrolled emotion and thin substance. Paul speaks calmly and lucidly. His emotions are under control, but at a deep level he is motivated affectively by a desire for the glory of God, and he knows that change of any kind, the repentance that he preaches, is not possible without a change of mind about who God is. Christian ethics is theological! It cannot be separated from theology.

The Upending of Narratives

Second, Paul's approach within this masterly sermon was to "*flip the narratives*"[2] of the Athenian people, as our pastor put it—to stand them on their heads. He does this in four ways, which form the structure of the sermon. The four ways correspond to four things the Athenians thought were true about the gods and thus the new God they were hearing about, yet in each case the opposite was true. First, Paul observes their incurably religious hunger despite their cynicism about religious matters. He indicates that in sightseeing around Athens, he "found an altar with this inscription: TO AN UNKNOWN GOD. So you are ignorant of the very thing you worship—and this is what I am going to proclaim to you" (17:23). What narrative is Paul upending here? These Epicurean and Stoic philosophers subscribed to a narrative of religious pluralism accompanied by agnosticism ("ignorance") that assumes nothing can be known with any certainty (in a way that resembles postmodern deconstruction). Epicureanism specifically is "an elite philosophy in the ancient world which taught that even if the gods exist they are a long way away and never concern themselves with our world, and that our world simply makes itself as it goes along, evolving under its own steam."[3]

---

1. Aaron Roberts, evening sermon St. John's Vancouver, June 2, 2019.
2. Aaron Roberts, evening sermon St. John's Vancouver, June 2, 2019.
3. N. T. Wright, "Wouldn't You Love to Know? Towards a Christian View of Reality," lecture,

It has survived into the Enlightenment period as the dualism and materialistic deism of modernity. Stoicism is best known for its pantheism, the equating of the cosmos with God. Paul is clearly upending both of these narratives by speaking of God as the Creator who is distinct from his creation, yet who is also profoundly and lovingly engaged with his creation.

Paul's interlocutors seem to be assuming that the best humans can do is to make up gods to serve their needs. These gods were in fact robbing them of life, however. Paul upends this by asserting that there is a God who has made himself known by revelation. We don't create him to meet our needs. He in fact created us, and when we find life in him, we find in him the answer to our core needs as human persons. Western culture today is also incurably religious, characterized by great idolatry, and made by the gods of power and success and pleasure. These gods may be subtler than those of ancient Greece, but they are therefore much more powerful, robbing us of life and of ethical clarity. Novelist David Foster Wallace reflects a deep understanding of idolatry in human experience:

> If you worship money and things—if they are where you tap real meaning in life—then you will never have enough. Never feel you have enough. It's the truth. Worship your own body and beauty and sexual allure and you will always feel ugly, and when time and age start showing, you will die a million deaths before they finally plant you. Worship power—you will feel weak and afraid, and you will need ever more power over others to keep the fear at bay. Worship your intellect, being seen as smart—you will end up feeling stupid, a fraud, always on the verge of being found out. And so on.[4]

One modern narrative that needs to be upended is the one that says only some humans are religious. Humans are incurably religious. Everybody worships. There is no such thing as someone without a god. Atheism is, on this account, actually a myth. In contemporary Western culture a popular narrative that is proclaimed is that people

the Grasping the Nettle project, sponsored by the John Templeton fund, Glasgow, September 1, 2016, p. 5.
4. David Foster Wallace, *This Is Water: Some Thoughts, Delivered on a Significant Occasion* (New York: Little, Brown, 2009), 107–10.

can be "spiritual" without being religious. The narrative goes a little bit like this: "There is great doubt about whether there can be one God and whether any one religion can be right, and religions have been oppressive . . . so I want to be spiritual but not religious." For some there is the fragmented approach that affirms the good in all religions, and with this comes strong condemnation of any form of Christianity that affirms the exclusivity of Jesus as the only Saviour and of ethical stances expressed in the light of divine revelation. The proclamation, not argumentation, of the reality that God is the Creator and that he has revealed himself in Jesus and in the Christian Scriptures is still needed to upend the cultural narrative of pluralism, which, ironically, is itself a dogma.[5]

Next Paul flips the narrative of the Athenians with respect to what is real about their gods and God. Verses 24 and 26 may be summed up in these words: "You are trying to make temples for God, when in fact, he made the whole world. You don't need to build a house for the real God; he built the whole world for you. You don't make a home for God; he makes a home for you."[6] Furthermore, you don't sustain God (they were seeking to sustain their gods with food and rituals); he sustains *your* every breath, moment by moment, until you die (v. 25). And lastly, if God is the Creator of all and not created at all, that is, if he is not a tribal deity with a limited scope of interest, then you can't reduce him to something you have created and can hold in your hands, and therefore your greatest aim is being with him, in intimate relationship with him (v. 29). Paul then speaks of judgment in what could be called another upending. The Greeks assumed they were in a position to judge the gods, including the one Paul has been presenting in the marketplace and now in the lecture theatre. Paul turns the tables once again: God will judge *you*, and not the other way around. Paul gives them a theology proper, a doctrine of God, and then calls them to repent, to change their minds about God so their lives can begin to change.

---

5. By *pluralism*, I mean the view that all religions are equal, and none can claim to be better than the rest. This is different from a religious pluralism in society, which says that on the basis of the image of God, all persons in any nation have the right of their own religion and religious practices, provided they do not violate the civil law. Tolerance is a Christian virtue not always observed in the history of the church!

6. Aaron Roberts, evening sermon St. John's Vancouver, June 2, 2019.

The Proclamation of Resurrection

The *third* thing Paul does that is instructive for a text on theological ethics is that he closes the lecture in verse 31 by *proclaiming resurrection*: "He has fixed a day on which he will have the world judged in righteousness by a man whom he has appointed, and of this he has given assurance to all by raising him from the dead" (NRSV). Paul's justification of judgment in the world to come is grounded in the One who has already entered that world to come. Although Paul uses the word *assurance* to verify the assertion of divine judgment, it seems clear that he does not actually seek to prove the resurrection in this discourse. He simply proclaims it. He does not engage in rationalistic apologetics to make his case. He trusts the Spirit to convince his hearers, having presented it as a *fait accompli*. This is important for how the church is to be a witness and how it can influence culture. The church is a *witness* to resurrection. It does not employ logical positivism as its mode of proclamation, but rather it is a witness to it in a way that may be better described as critical realism. Pointing to the historical evidence for the resurrection has validity, and apologetics may remove some obstacles for some seeking people in a helpful way, but ultimately it is the community that is the witness and the Spirit that does the convincing. Beyond the method of the church's witness, it is vital to notice that Paul majors on the resurrection rather than the death of Jesus in this context. Why is this so? Perhaps it has to do with asserting the identity of Jesus as Son of God, God the Son. Perhaps it has to do with presenting resurrection as a sign of completed atonement, in a manner reflected in other sermons in Acts. Most likely it is because the discourse is largely on the doctrine of creation. Paul's doctrine of the resurrection not only asserts that it demonstrates the identity of Jesus as God, reveals the one true God as the self-revealing triune God, and signals that God's just judgment has, by his atoning work, been satisfied with respect to the idolatry and sin of humanity. But it also *reaffirms God's created order.* It signals in an eloquent way that the one and only supreme and sovereign God of creation is the God revealed in Jesus Christ, his Son, and that in the Son a new humanity has begun, one that includes all nations and enables humans to become fully human, image bearers in the One who is the image of the invisible God, and God's covenant people stewarding reconciled creation.

So Paul apparently thought that it is worth speaking passionately in the public square about these matters, and that it is valid to upend cherished cultural narratives and bear witness to the risen Jesus and who he has revealed God to be. Paul knows that there can be no call to repent, no change of mind, no change of heart, no epistemic transformation, no change of lifestyle apart from this gospel of resurrection. No real resurrection, no real God, no real gospel, no real church, no real ethics—that is how Paul thinks. This book intends to point to the triune God of the risen Christ as essential for theological ethics, indeed indispensable and interconnected with it. We will point also to the body of the risen Christ as the community of covenant and *torah* and worship in which moral formation and ethics are done. We will point toward how the church as a community in *ekstasis* spills over in love to the public square—*from* the church, the true home of ethics, *to* the world. In this discussion of ethics, there will often be a need to upend the narratives of an idolatrous culture.

This is not to say that there is no good in culture. Human cultures reflect evidence of both the image of God and fallenness. We do not wish to deny a universal *sensus moralis* as a vestige of God's creative purpose or the image of God in fallen humanity, one that keeps societies in some semblance of moral order (Romans 2:14–15 and 1 Timothy 1:8–10 allow for that, I think). It is to say, however, over against moral theologies grounded in the natural reason or conscience of humans, based in the Thomistic *analogia entis*, that an *analogia relationis* (Bonhoeffer) or *communionis* (Alan Torrance) will be preferred. As Alan Torrance states, a more certain "access to God's purpose will involve access to God's expressly disclosed and endorsed purpose, namely, his covenant purposes for humanity as these are defined in the *kaine diatheke*, the New Covenant, and which is the fulfilment of all that may *properly* be described as 'law' (*Torah*), that is, as the divinely declared objective will of God."[7] Torrance actually upends the concepts of *syntērēsis* (a term used in scholastic moral philosophy to refer to a natural capacity or disposition [*habitus*] of practical reason in all humanity to understand intuitively what are the universal first principles of human action) and *syneidēsis* (conscience) as they were understood within moral philosophy by retrieving their true theological intent. When "theologically conceived," these concepts "must properly refer to our reconciled

---

7. Alan Torrance, "On Deriving 'Ought' from 'Is,'" in *The Doctrine of God and Theological Ethics*, ed. Alan J. Torrance and Michael Banner (London: T&T Clark, 2006), 170–71.

participation *en Christo* (in Christ) as this includes the subjective epistemic transformation that attends and characterizes this."[8] In other words, a new humanity is required to be birthed before theological ethics—indeed, any ethics—can be done. An ecclesial community that has been "transformed and reconciled and reconstituted in and through that event of epistemic at-one-ment between God and humanity—an at-one-ment of mind which is Christ's and which is only realized in us as we are recreated by the Spirit to participate *en Christo*,"[9] the last or *eschatos* Adam. This is the ecclesial community that is caught up in the grand narrative of God and his being for the world and that shares that story with the world. This is also expressed eloquently by New Testament scholar Richard Hays in *The Moral Vision of the New Testament*:

> In sum, Paul sees the community of faith being caught up into the story of God's remaking of the world through Jesus Christ. Thus, to make ethical discernments is, for Paul, simply to recognize our place within the epic story of redemption. There is no meaningful distinction between theology and ethics in Paul's thought, because Paul's theology is fundamentally an account of God's work of transforming his people into the image of Christ.[10]

FOUNDATIONS OF THEOLOGICAL ETHICS

The foundations of this book's approach should be clear: to show that theological ethics must be theological and, given that this is *Christian* theology, must be Trinitarian. They must be christological. They must be pneumatological. They also must be biblical in the sense that the Torah is the concrete expression of ethics within the covenantal grace of God, given and expounded in the Old Testament, and appropriated and expounded in the New. And given that the gospel of this triune God of grace forms a covenantal community in union with Christ by

---

8. Torrance, "On Deriving 'Ought' from 'Is,'" 171. Throughout this book, *participation* is understood as a relation of "in-ness" between divine and human persons without confusion, in a manner that reflects the thrust of the gospel as expressed by Paul, especially in his frequently used prepositional phrase "in Christ" and the Old Testament roots. Thus use of *participation* is in contrast with the Platonic concepts of *methexis* and *symplokē eidon*, which compromise the divine-human and God-creation distinction.

9. Torrance, "On Deriving 'Ought' from 'Is,'" 171.

10. Richard Hays, *The Moral Vision of the New Testament: A Contemporary Introduction to New Testament Ethics* (Edinburgh: T&T Clark, 1997), 45–46.

the Spirit, theological ethics also must be ecclesial. But given the nature and purpose of the body of Christ to be the new humanity and to be missional to all of humanity, theological ethics will also be missional, being shared not hoarded, even when the church suffers in doing so.

Theological Ethics Are Theological

At the risk of stating the glaringly obvious, our first contention is that theological ethics are just that: *theological*. It is a mistake to seek and express ethical judgments, that is, what is right or wrong, apart from the deep and wide context of the gospel of the gracious unconditional covenant of God with humanity. Ethical obligation can only be understood in the light of God's engagement with humanity in Jesus Christ. Only as we know *who* God is and what he has done can we know *how* we ought to be and do. In fact, there is "no dichotomy between the Being and the Act of God, between God's Being and God's Being-toward-humanity in Christ—to speak of the Being of God is to speak of God's Self-identification. It is thus to speak of Christ and the Spirit."[11] We must derive "ought" from "is," therefore. The "ought" of ethical obligation lies in the "is" of grace, which is the self-revelation of God in Jesus Christ as being for the world, and in being incorporated into the covenant community, the *koinōnia* that is God's church, the body of his Son (the moral conscience, as we shall see, is ecclesial, not individualistic).

Seeking ethical judgments (the "ought") apart from relationship with God (the "is") was, in fact, the primal sin made by the first humans, who wanted to know good and evil apart from communion with God. It is fascinating to listen to popular media and, despite the profoundly relativistic nature of post-Christian secular society, to hear people express with great conviction, "That's just wrong!" On what basis, we may ask? Chat shows and various forms of social media abound with explicit and implicit opinions about what is wrong in the realm of sexual ethics, for example. Most of what is most definitely *wrong* in this area and what would cause an outrage is having an opinion that might run contrary to the individual autonomy and "freedom" of any person to be who they *feel* they are or want to be. Sex is seen as good when it is accompanied by love, irrespective of marital status or gender. The irony of the firmness of these absolute-sounding moral convictions is that their absoluteness

---

11. Torrance, "On Deriving 'Ought' from 'Is,'" 175–76.

contradicts the generally cherished relativism implicit in their opinions about what is right or wrong in sexual ethics and the rights of others to express opinions to the contrary. The ethical response of some Western Christians in this relativistic ethical milieu is either to appeal to reason on the assumption that the human moral conscience gives everyone universal access to the divine will or law, a kind of innate conscience based on natural law, or to invoke divine propositional revelation and speak unevangelically in condemnation. But to appeal to moral reason or revelation or *torah* outside the context of the gospel is simply to perpetuate and complicate the problem by answering modernity in a modern way. To appeal to revelation using apologetics without a gospel context and apart from a visible community is similar. If this is true, then perhaps Christians should not speak about ethics in the public square. How then can the church speak evangelically in public? This will be the topic of chapter 9.

The Relationship between Dogmatics and Ethics

The immediate point at hand is that, actually, Christian ethics does not even *exist* in Christian theology apart from theology or apart from its communal context and practices in the church. One could say that ethics is the other half of systematic theology, which is thus made up of dogmatics and ethics. On the one hand, one could lament that the subdiscipline of ethics always seems to be invisible, or at best peripheral, in theological texts. The paucity of ethics courses in the curricula of many theological institutions is evidence. Yet ethics is moral *theology*. On the other hand, the failure to separate or distinguish ethics from theology may, in fact, be a good thing. For ethics without theology is a nonstarter, for "dogmatics itself is ethics,"[12] as Karl Barth said. Alan Torrance affirms that "Christian doctrine is 'ethics-laden' and Christian ethics is 'doctrine-laden,'" since both "articulate the triune grammar of our covenantal participation in Christ. . . . The imperatives of ethical law derive from, repose upon, and witness to, the indicatives of grace. The Christian ethicist *must* derive 'ought' from 'is.'"[13]

Stanley Hauerwas, reflecting Karl Barth in this regard, expresses similar sentiments. One of Hauerwas's greatest accomplishments has been

---

12. Karl Barth, *Church Dogmatics*, ed. G. W. Bromiley and T. F. Torrance (London: T&T Clark, 1969–1989), I/2, 793 (hereafter designated CD).
13. Torrance, "On Deriving 'Ought' from 'Is,'" 185.

his critique of Christian theology as it has come under the influence of modernity.[14] "At one time," Hauerwas asserts, "Christian ethics did not exist."[15] He means that "before the Enlightenment Christian theologians did not distinguish between the ethical and theological dimensions of Christian living."[16] This explains, for example, why ethics is interspersed throughout Barth's *Church Dogmatics* without a discrete section in it. The Enlightenment signalled "modernity's quest to find a secure basis for action that was independent of the contradictory claims of religious traditions," one very prominent example of which was Immanuel Kant's attempt to "secure ethics by reason alone"[17] through his formulation of the Categorical Imperative: "Act only according to that Maxim by which you can at the same time will that it should be a universal law."[18] The divorcing of what one believes from what one does led many Protestant theologians "to view theology as just a type of metaphysics, which can or cannot be dispensed with, depending upon one's metaphysical inclinations."[19] Christian theologians, finding the "metaphysical" claims of Christianity "harder to justify, responded to this challenge in one of two ways, both of which Hauerwas thinks distorted Christianity." Some emulated Kant in "turning to the subject" so that theology might be grounded in the security of the existential. This, for Hauerwas, means that "Christianity only makes sense as a disguised humanism."[20] The so-called ethical dimension of the kingdom of God overshadowed any interest in the atonement of Jesus on the part of Protestant liberal theologians.

If theologians with more liberal leanings appealed to reason, the more conservative theologians turned to natural theology in seeking a foundation for faith on which special revelation could be built. An example of this is the expressed intent of the Gifford Lectures (which Hauerwas actually delivered in 2001), through which Lord Gifford directed the

---

14. This has been summarized well by Derek Michaud, incorporating material from Josh Reeves, "Stanley Hauerwas (1940–)," in *Boston Collaborative Encyclopedia of Western Theology*, 2005, http://people.bu.edu/wwildman/bce/hauerwas.htm.

15. Stanley Hauerwas, *The Hauerwas Reader*, ed. J. Berkman and Michael G. Cartwright (Durham, NC: Duke University Press, 2001), 37.

16. Hauerwas. *Hauerwas Reader*, 40.

17. Michaud and Reeves, "Stanley Hauerwas (1940–)."

18. Cited in Hauerwas, *Hauerwas Reader*, 45.

19. Michaud and Reeves, "Stanley Hauerwas (1940–)," referring to Hauerwas, *Hauerwas Reader*, 47.

20. Hauerwas, *Hauerwas Reader*, 64.

lecturers to treat religion "as a strictly natural science, the greatest of all possible sciences, indeed, in one sense, the only science, that of Infinite Being, without reference to or reliance upon any supposed special exceptional or so-called miraculous revelation."[21] The underlying concern here is that "without a secure epistemological base, beliefs can only be 'arbitrary' and 'dogmatic.'"[22]

Hauerwas expresses the opinion that in fact both of these responses to modernity were reactive and unsuccessful. He believes that promoting Christianity as purely rational was to promote its demise. Why do Protestant liberals even need Christianity if they do not need theological claims to support their ethics? And reliance on natural theology simply threatens the particularity of Christianity.

Karl Barth, Hauerwas's mentor in this regard at least, reacted to both of these alternatives by affirming a distinctively Christian ethic. Trevor Hart confirms this when he states,

> For Barth, the distinctively Christian ethic, i.e. the gospel which the church proclaims and the "moral ontology" (borrowed from Charles Taylor) which unfolds from within its logic, provides a quite distinct context and purpose for ethical reflection. This is why for Barth, dogmatics and ethics stand and fall together.[23]

Theological Ethics in Modernity

Hauerwas's conclusion therefore was that "if Christianity is in fact true, it cannot accept the intellectual terms of modernity."[24] So what is Hauerwas's alternative to these options? In the absence of a logical positivism by which universal assent could be attained to remove all doubt, the Christian community was to bear witness, not to what they know, but to *whom* they know, God as revealed, God as Father, Son, and Holy Spirit. The church bears witness not so much "about what universally has to be, but what historically has been."[25] This is a critically realistic approach. Christians are witnesses to a "story" of the revealed God, one that "describes the particularity—of God's redemptive intervention into

---

21. Hauerwas, *Hauerwas Reader*, 26.
22. Michaud and Reeves, "Stanley Hauerwas (1940–)."
23. Trevor Hart, *Regarding Karl Barth: Essays toward a Reading of His Theology* (Carlisle, UK: Paternoster, 1999), 75.
24. Michaud and Reeves, "Stanley Hauerwas (1940–)."
25. Michaud and Reeves, "Stanley Hauerwas (1940–)."

the world. And stories, precisely because they are about the particular, cannot be universalized to meet modernity's criteria of rational belief."[26]

Critics of Hauerwas's approach claim that it is fideistic and tries to evade the challenges offered by science and pluralism. Hauerwas summarizes a critique of this kind offered by James Gustafson: "[Hauerwas's theology] cannot but result in a fideistic stance that legitimates a tribalistic understanding of Christianity. . . . It has the unfortunate effect of 'isolating Christianity from taking seriously the wider world of science and culture and limits the participation of Christians living in the ambiguities of moral and social life in the patterns of interdependence in the world.'"[27] In other words, it is a theology and an ethic "that ceases to submit its claims to public debate and possible revision becomes irrational and dangerous."[28]

Hauerwas responds by exposing the limits of reason. He employs Alasdair MacIntyre's "traditioned" account of rationality[29] to deconstruct the presuppositions in Gustafson's account. Since rationality is not monolithic, since the claims of modernity to a neutral or value-free rationality are spurious, and since modernity is itself a particular tradition, Hauerwas suggests that Christians, who "do not inhabit the world in the same way non-Christians do," need not "submit theological claims to non-theological standards."[30] It must be stressed that although Hauerwas believes his approach "rightly unveils the contradictions found in modernity," he does not ascribe to the "anything goes" approach of postmodernity either.[31]

The implications of Hauerwas's approach regarding engagement of the Christian and the church in the public square will be discussed later. For now it will suffice to say that his approach with regard to theology and ethics is to be thoroughly commended. Ethics and theology are interdependent. Ethics is theological or it is not ethics. Hauerwas's answer to Christian public engagement is that engagement is through the church's witness, and not until the Holy Spirit works to bring people into that community can they understand and live its ethics. People are initiated

---

26. Michaud and Reeves, "Stanley Hauerwas (1940–)."
27. Hauerwas, *Hauerwas Reader*, 93.
28. Michaud and Reeves, "Stanley Hauerwas (1940–)."
29. Alasdair MacIntyre, *Three Rival Versions of Moral Enquiry* (Notre Dame, IN: University of Notre Dame Press, 1990).
30. Michaud and Reeves, "Stanley Hauerwas (1940–)."
31. Michaud and Reeves, "Stanley Hauerwas (1940–)."

into the Christian church not by being "reasoned" into Christianity but by means of the change of heart that leads to a change of mind. Only God redeems the world and the human heart, and thus "witness and argument are the work of the Holy Spirit."[32] Theology, or the gospel, and ethics belong inextricably together because "the very content of Christian connections requires the self be transformed if we are adequately to see the truth of [its] convictions."[33]

Hauerwas seeks to "shift the epistemic burden placed on Christianity by modernity" by affirming that "Christians are within their epistemic rights to hold to their religious beliefs," even though "there is no way fully to justify them to those who have not been transformed." The Spirit "makes the argument to unbelievers," and the role of the community is not to convince but to be and bear witness in the power of the Spirit, "because the very fact that the community exists counts as evidence that the claims of Christianity are true."[34] Crucially for Hauerwas, "Christianity is unintelligible without witnesses, that is, without people whose practices exhibit their committed assent to a particular way of structuring the whole."[35] In Hauerwas's view, "the purpose of the church is not to prove that Christianity is true, but to demonstrate what the world is like if it is true. And because the church is a foretaste of the coming community of God, to be a Christian witness is, as the title of Hauerwas's Gifford Lectures suggests, to be working 'with the grain of the universe.'"[36]

Theological Ethics and Human Capacity

There is an important divide in theological ethics precisely on the assumptions of Hauerwas, Barth, and Bonhoeffer that ethics needs theology in order to be ethics, not a futile pursuit condemned from the outset to failure, drowned in the hubris of human autonomy. The crux of the issue has to do with human capacity and whether some sense of natural law that can guide society's ethics persists in fallen humanity. Undergirding this in turn is whether *metaphysics* is, in light of

---

32. Stanley Hauerwas, *With the Grain of the Universe: The Church's Witness and Natural Theology* (Grand Rapids: Brazos, 2001), 211.
33. Hauerwas, *Hauerwas Reader*, 100.
34. Michaud and Reeves, "Stanley Hauerwas (1940–)."
35. Hauerwas, *With the Grain of the Universe*, 214.
36. Michaud and Reeves, "Stanley Hauerwas (1940–)," reflecting Hauerwas, *With the Grain of the Universe*, 214.

the doctrine of creation, an irresistible reality. This conflict is evident, for example, in an article by William J. Meyer.[37] The opening abstract has Hauerwas in its sights, as well as his belief that "Christian ethics has lost its theological voice because it has accommodated itself to the secular assumptions of modern philosophical ethics." Hauerwas believes this "fateful accommodation" is the result of theology seeking to "translate its insights into a nontheological idiom" in order to be "publicly intelligible and relevant." On the contrary, Meyer argues that Hauerwas rightly identifies that there *has* been a fateful accommodation, but it lies not "in theology's attempt to be publicly intelligible and credible." Rather, it is in theology's "widespread acceptance of the modern denial of metaphysics."[38] This approach elevates the capacity of human conscience and reason based in the creation, but minimizes the effects of the fall. It also relativizes and devalues the revelation of God to his covenant people as the source for ethics, both in his personal revelation in Jesus Christ and in the Holy Scriptures. The assertion of belief in an innate conscience, or "with-knowing," has its roots in the Greek Fathers (especially Chrysostom) and not the New Testament, as Oliver O'Donovan has shown.[39] It became prevalent in the medieval period and again in the seventeenth and eighteenth centuries in both the Catholic and scholastic Reformed traditions. Conscience may be defined as that moral capacity of humanity to understand intuitively the universal first principles of ethical action. It is a capacity that remains "essentially intact even after the fall of man, as the *a priori* intellectual and volitional basis of all activity of conscience."[40] It is, by way of example, evident in Thomas Aquinas's definition of *synteresis* as the "permanent natural *habitus* of the primary moral principles."[41] This of course makes redemption of the critical ethical faculty unnecessary. This debate will be revisited in later chapters. Advocates of conscience believe themselves to be true to a doctrine of creation in which something rather than nothing has been created—and a creation analogous to its Creator.

---

37. William J. Meyer, "On Keeping Theological Ethics Theological: An Alternative to Hauerwas's Diagnosis and Prescription," *The Annual of the Society of Christian Ethics* 19 (1999): 21–45, https://www.jstor.org/stable/23560074?read-now=1&seq=1#page_scan_tab_contents.

38. Meyer, "On Keeping Theological Ethics Theological," 21.

39. Oliver O'Donovan, *Resurrection and Moral Order: An Outline for Evangelical Ethics* (Grand Rapids: Eerdmans, 1986), 115.

40. Rudolf Hofmann, "Conscience," in *Sacramentum Mundi: An Encyclopedia of Theology*, ed. Karl Rahner, vol. 1 (London: Burns and Oates, 1968), 413.

41. Hofmann, "Conscience," 413.

There is no doubt about where Dietrich Bonhoeffer would have been in this controversy, unsurprising in light of the outworking of reason and a natural view of human conscience in his country in the "German Christians" and the Nazis. The opening sentences of *Ethics*—a compilation of Bonhoeffer's reflections on ethics, some of which were tucked away in garden hiding places before he was arrested on April 5, 1943—make for startling reading: "The knowledge of good and evil seems to be the aim of all ethical reflection. The first task of Christian ethics is to invalidate this knowledge."[42] In the opening chapter again and again, Bonhoeffer makes the point from the first three chapters of Genesis that the primal sin of humanity was to seek to have knowledge of good and evil apart from relationship with God.

> Man at his origin knows only one thing: God. It is only in the unity of his knowledge of God that he knows of other men, of things, and of himself. He knows all things only in God, and God in all things. The knowledge of good and evil shows that he is no longer at one with this origin. . . . The knowledge of good and evil is therefore separation from God.[43]

Ethics Needs Participation

So, in essence, ethics does not exist. Yet Bonhoeffer still has a book called *Ethics*, and a discipline in Christian theology is called theological ethics. Bonhoeffer's point is that ethics is not a legitimate field apart from knowing God, apart from seeking to see him, and it is not the knowledge of good and evil apart from participation in the life of God: "Only against [the backdrop of and the context of life in] God can man know good and evil."[44] The essence of the fall was a pursuit of ethics in "a stolen way," as Bonhoeffer calls it.[45] Adam and Eve were made in the image of God to see good and evil as God sees it, but they stole a "likeness to God" and made themselves creator and judge: "What God had given man to be, man now desired to be through himself." Humanity's origin in God constituted the gift of knowing good and evil

---

42. Dietrich Bonhoeffer, *Ethics*, ed. Eberhard Bethge, trans. Neville Horton (London: Macmillan, 1955), 21.
43. Bonhoeffer, *Ethics*, 21–22.
44. Bonhoeffer, *Ethics*, 22.
45. Bonhoeffer, *Ethics*, 22.

in God's way. Humanity desired to know good and evil their own way, which really constituted "a complete reversal of man's knowledge."[46] As Bonhoeffer confirms, "Instead of knowing only the God who is good to him, he now knows himself as the origin of good and evil."[47]

Bonhoeffer speaks of God's knowledge of good and evil with "extreme reserve." Even God, who is the origin of choice and eternal election, speaks of this with reticence. How he does this is "the secret of him in whom there is no disunion because he is himself the one and eternal origin and the overcoming of all disunion."[48] God gave those who bore his image the gift of making moral choices. His image bearers chose to seek the knowledge of good and evil on their own. Thus the first Adam was disbarred from God's presence by the cherubim and a flaming sword, which guarded the way to the tree of life. God in his holy otherness distances himself from those who seek to practise ethics on the basis of self-knowledge.

Isaiah's God and Ethics

How then are fallen humans ever to be justified and morally formed and able to make ethical judgments in participation with God? Along with the Genesis narrative, Isaiah 6 offers a solution that is more fully unfolded in the New Testament. It is without doubt the fullest revelatory event in the Old Testament and reveals the holiness of God in an unrivalled way. Isaiah 6 reveals God's *majestic* holiness as the One who is "high and lifted up" (KJV), the One who, when the mostly stable but finally vulnerable king Uzziah dies, shows himself to be the King who never dies. The *aesthetic* nature of the holiness of Yahweh is also conveyed in the beauty of the train of his robe. What's more, the New Testament reception of this passage, that this vision event revealed Jesus (John 12:41), leads us to see that this revealed God is none other than the triune God of the New Testament, the God who is and who defines beauty in his Trinitarian being in relation, three persons in supreme harmony. He is the God who is *morally* holy, for his presence causes the seraphim to cover their faces lest they see God and be consumed. But the human person in this vision narrative, Isaiah, is also deeply exposed and cries out, "Woe is me!" God's moral holiness is revealed by his

---

46. Bonhoeffer, *Ethics*, 22.
47. Bonhoeffer, *Ethics*, 23.
48. Bonhoeffer, *Ethics*, 23.

covenant faithfulness, signified by the fact that God is called the Holy One of Israel twenty-eight times in the book of Isaiah (a title present only forty times in the Old Testament). This is the amazing grace of Isaiah's prophecy: God is not just the Holy One; he is the Holy One *of Israel*, the God who chooses not to be without his covenantal people despite their idolatry and failures, the God who is faithful when they are not. But how can this be? How has the barrier between God and sinful humanity, depicted in the expulsion of the first Adam, been so overcome that Isaiah enters the presence of God, the Holy One *of Israel*?

This passage communicates a revealedness and a hiddenness about God. Even if he is the God of his people, he is not to be treated lightly. Even the seraphim cover themselves. Even the great prophet is exposed. Isaiah's vision is reticent in its revelation of the face and nature of God. His glory, the outward manifestation of inward excellence, is revealed, but there is much that is concealed. For this is a fear-evoking revelation. But here is the crucial gospel revelation of this event: God's otherness and transcendence actually cleanse and anoint human lips so that they might speak of his justice and mercy to Israel and then the nations.

Much conjecture has been expressed on why God addresses and cleanses the prophet's lips in particular. No doubt it is a form of synecdoche, where the part represents the whole person. Isaiah 1:5–6 expresses the extensiveness of Judah and Jerusalem's sin: "Your whole head is injured, your whole heart afflicted. From the sole of your foot to the top of your head there is no soundness." However, the choice of the lips to represent the whole is not accidental. Isaiah needed clean lips because he, along with his people with whom he was identified, had duplicitous lips: "These people draw near with their mouths and honor me with their lips, while their hearts are far from me" (Isa. 29:13 NRSV). There is more than one withering exposé in Isaiah of the insincere worship of the people with their lips. They failed to love God, and their failure corresponded to and was symptomatic of a failure in justice—in ethics, if you like. Isaiah 1:11–15 illustrates this by expressing God's displeasure with their worship:

> "The multitude of your sacrifices—
>   what are they to me?" says the LORD.
> "I have more than enough of burnt offerings. . . .
> Stop bringing meaningless offerings!

> Your incense is detestable to me.
> New Moons, Sabbaths and convocations—
>   I cannot bear your worthless assemblies. . . .
> When you spread out your hands in prayer,
>   I hide my eyes from you;
> even when you offer many prayers,
>   I am not listening."

And the reason for this displeasure is exposed in verses 16–17:

> "Wash and make yourselves clean.
>   Take your evil deeds out of my sight;
>   stop doing wrong.
> Learn to do right; seek justice.
>   Defend the oppressed.
> Take up the cause of the fatherless;
>   plead the case of the widow."

There can be no question that Isaiah and his people needed a lip cleansing. But beyond need, there is *purpose* behind the cleansing of the *lips* of Isaiah. Isaiah 6 describes his call to be a prophet. His lips are cleansed by a "live coal," and although the text makes it clear that this was atoning, there is an implicit commissioning dimension. The sheer grace of this moment is that Isaiah the sinner is now near enough to God to hear the consultation going on in the Godhead: "Then I heard the voice of the Lord saying, 'Whom shall I send? And who will go for us?'" (v. 8). So the transcendent God of otherness and purity has drawn near to him to cleanse and then to commission him to speak for God. And Isaiah, silenced a moment earlier, is now free to speak in the majestic presence of God. The barrier between God and humanity described in Genesis 3 is gone. Not only that, the grace of God in atoning and reconciliation has evoked a response of grace in Isaiah, and he expresses his surrender to the purposes of God: "And I said, 'Here am I. Send me!'" (v. 8). Alec Motyer's commentary on this is priceless: "He finds that being joined to God means joining a missionary society."[49] The moral

---

49. J. Alec Motyer, *Isaiah: An Introduction and Commentary* (Downers Grove, IL: IVP, 1999), 72.

and spiritual formation of Isaiah, in significant part through this divine encounter, was robust enough to carry him through what would be a ministry of the proclamation of gospel and justice with very little success. Faithfulness, not success, was to be the criterion that assessed his ministry of gospel proclamation. But Isaiah provides ample evidence that ethics must be grounded in the divine encounter and relationship—that is, in a theology that lives. Isaiah communicates the wonder of the gospel that makes theological ethics possible, that rules out ethics without theology. God comes to humanity as he did in Isaiah 6, and although there is no denying his transcendence, there is a merciful immanence. His "veiled otherness is used to transform us"[50] and then to commission the whole people of God. In the New Testament, the prophetic has been democratized (Acts 2), and every Christian is called to live in God and to speak for God in every culture. And, as was the case with Isaiah, Christians must do so expecting rejection of the message and messenger and, with that, possible suffering and persecution. Exactly *how* we are to do that is the subject of another chapter.

New Testament Ethics within Theology

The New Testament gives the fullest revelation of how an estranged humanity that is obsessed with what is right and wrong can be reconciled to God, enter into participation with him, and find an ethics within theology. It happens because God becomes one with us in the incarnation and acts for us, standing in our place, as the last Adam. As the image of the invisible God, Christ can discern between good and evil because he is in perfect union with the Father by the Spirit. His vicarious life and the offering up of his life in death are the basis of our justification, our rightness before God. Through faith we are brought into union with Christ (*unio Christi*) and therefore into the twin graces (*duplex gratia*) of justification and sanctification. Barth added a third grace, vocation, which is bearing witness or mission understood in its broadest sense, in participation with the missional God. *Justification*—being justified in Christ, our being rather than a state, our being in that place of acceptance and freedom—grants the freedom and safety of being able to pursue moral formation and ethical discernment knowing that our formation will be imperfect until the fulness of the eschaton.

---

50. Matthew Lynch, lecture on Isaiah 6, Regent College, June 4, 2019.

Justification engenders a contemplative rather than introspective habit in us, for it causes us to look away from ourselves to Christ, who has been and continues to be righteous for us. *Sanctification* includes moral formation and ethical action. Being in the process of sanctification in union with Christ by the power of the Holy Spirit makes it possible for redeemed image bearers once again to know good and evil as God knows them. In this proper context and mode, however, sanctification is not the primary focus. Being with Christ is; seeing Christ is. Intimacy with and contemplation of Christ lead to moral formation and to ethical discernment and behaviour.

A quick visit to the epistle to the Hebrews will suffice to make this point! Hebrews 5 is a decisive text for defining maturity. In verse 14 the author states that "solid food is for the mature, who by constant use have trained themselves to distinguish good from evil." This seems rather counterintuitive for an epistle about the majestic high priesthood of Christ. I might have expected that the author's test of maturity would have been a capacity test: Can you define and describe the nuanced realities of the Melchizedekian high priesthood of Christ, his all-sufficient sacrifice, or the superiority of his new covenant? But no, moral discernment defines maturity. Crucial to our case, the author of Hebrews makes it clear that what builds moral maturity is indeed the "solid food." The mature meat of the high priestly ministry of Christ allows access to the presence of God. Moral discernment, grounded in moral character, cannot be found apart from that relational intimacy with God, that is, the life of prayer in participation with God in Christ. Hebrews 6 arrives at this conclusion in verses 19–20: "We have this hope as an anchor for the soul, firm and secure. It enters the inner sanctuary behind the curtain, where our forerunner, Jesus, has entered on our behalf. He has become a high priest forever, in the order of Melchizedek." Feeding on the strong meat that makes for moral robustness and the ability to discern is a reversal of what was lost in Eden. In the epistle of Hebrews this means becoming one with the last Adam—and being in a new humanity in Christ in chapter 2. *Vocation* is restored to humanity in the last Adam, the vocation of caring for creation, of acting with justice toward creation and humanity. God intends his image-bearing humans, once they are restored to union with him, to know what is right and what is wrong, to administer the justice and the shalom that are his character, to be joined with him in his mission to bring to the world the reconciliation he accomplished in Christ, and to bring both justification and justice to persons and nations and the creation. The mission of humanity in participation with the missional triune God involves the cultural mandate, the Great Commandment, and the Great Commission, enabling converts to journey toward becoming fully human, toward living justly, that is, toward sanctification, including moral formation, ethical judgments, and ethical behaviour. Theological ethics is indeed possible for the church in the theology and praxis of participation with God. Given that the church is the new humanity and the harbinger of the whole redeemed humanity—that is, given that the identity of the church in union with the missional God is missional, its orientation ought to be outward, not just inward and upward.

Theological Ethics of the Missional God

The outward orientation of the church has been expressed also by Alan Torrance as he considers whether ethics done by the church should be heard in the public square, which will be the main focus of chapter 9. Torrance in fact goes beyond Hauerwas's approach, which proposes that the church is the ethical community formed in virtue by gospel narratives in a way that does not obviously lead to influence in the saeculum. Torrance speaks of the body of Christ imaging the nature of the persons of the Trinity and, as such, having "its *hypostasis* in a radically inclusive *ekstasis* towards the secular world."[51] That is, it is a community, a deep community, a community that takes its character from the communion of the Holy Trinity. The point is that if the church truly does reflect the Trinity, it will be a community whose influence spills over into the society around it, just as the triune God, who lacked nothing in all eternity, created the cosmos as an outflow of his infinite divine love and has now redeemed that creation by that same love.

In favour of Torrance over Hauerwas, thus, the church cannot just be a community of deep theological, spiritual, liturgical, catechetical, and moral formation and show no awareness of or intentional influence on the world of humanity and creation. The Hauerwasian approach can lead toward the critique that it is remnant theology. John Flett raises this concern with respect to "communion ecclesiologies."[52] Flett is anxious

---

51. Torrance, "On Deriving 'Ought' from 'Is,'" 184.
52. John Flett, "*Missio Dei*: A Trinitarian Envisioning of a Non-Trinitarian Theme," *Missiology: An International Review* 37, no. 1 (January 2009): 8n25. Flett takes aim at Yoder, Hauerwas,

to maintain the correspondence between the missional life of God as an overflow or *ekstasis* of God's prior intra-Trinitarian relationships and the church's witness, which "emerges as a gestalt—a natural overflow—of internally orientated practices that build up the community into a corresponding fellowship."[53] The church will have an awareness that modeling a loving community as the sign of the new humanity and kingdom of God is essential, but that is simply *not enough* in and of itself. The church will, as a consequence of its formation, always be profoundly aware of its missional identity. It will know that the *holy* priesthood within has a representative and intercessory dimension, and it will also be aware of its *royal* priesthood toward the world and in regency with Christ over creation.

God is indeed the sending God, but he sends his Son and Spirit that he might bring humanity within the sphere of his communion. One cannot understand mission without understanding that "the *perichoresis*, or interpenetration, among the persons of the Trinity reveals that the nature of God is communion."[54] This communion is not limited within the Trinity but "overflows into an involvement with history that aims at drawing humanity and creation in general into this communion with God's very life."[55] The love within that communion spilled over in the *ekstasis* of God, in the act of creation, and in the covenant to reconcile it. Love draws humanity and creation into intimate relationship with God, in a manner that preserves the agency of humans and the ontological distinctness of the creation. Mission is a natural extension of the communal nature of the Trinity. Consequently, mission "is not primarily about the propagation or transmission of intellectual convictions, doctrines, or moral commands, but rather about the inclusion of all creation in God's overflowing, superabundant life of communion."[56] This inclusion was

---

and even Miroslav Volf, accusing the latter of focusing "mainly inside, at the inner nature of the church," while sidelining "the outside world and the church's mission to his 'peripheral vision.'" See also John G. Flett, *The Witness of God: The Trinity, Missio Dei, Karl Barth, and the Nature of Christian Community* (Grand Rapids: Eerdmans, 2010).

53. Flett, "*Missio Dei*," 7n21, which references Stanley Hauerwas, "Worship, Evangelism, Ethics: On Eliminating the 'And,'" in *A Better Hope: Resources for a Church Confronting Capitalism, Democracy, and Postmodernity* (Grand Rapids: Brazos, 2000), 155–61; and Reinhard Hütter, "The Church as 'Public': Dogma, Practices and the Holy Spirit," *Pro Ecclesia* 3, no. 3 (1994): 334–61.

54. Darrell Guder, ed., *Missional Church: A Vision for the Sending of the Church in North America* (Grand Rapids: Eerdmans, 1998), 82.

55. Stephen B. Bevans and Roger P. Schroeder, *Constants in Context: A Theology of Mission for Today*, American Society of Missiology Series (Maryknoll, NY: Orbis, 2004), 288–89.

56. Bevans and Schroeder, *Constants in Context*, 288–89.

made possible by the work of Jesus through the Holy Spirit as initiated by the Father.

The very essence of who God is as Father, Son, and Spirit in his eternal processions has been revealed by the personal missions of God. For this reason we say that God is missional. For this reason we say also that the *missio Dei* is only true because of the *missio trinitatis*. As Paul Stevens, reflecting the sentiments of Colin Gunton,[57] has succinctly stated, "Mission is God's own going forth—truly an *ekstasis* of God. He is Sender, Sent and Sending (John 17:18; cf. 16:5–16; 20:21–22)."[58] But because all believers are in union with this God, and because the church is an extension of who Christ is (his body), ecclesiology is pushed back into the doctrine of God, making inevitable the conclusion that the church is missional. Ethics is indeed theological, but this means that it is also missional, for God is the sent and sending God. Stanley Grenz sums this up aptly:

> Christians declare that the touchstone of community is the eter-
> nal triune life and God's gracious inclusion of humans in Christ
> by the Spirit, constituting them as participants in the perichoretic
> Trinitarian life. This theological-ecclesiological perspective leads
> Christians to view every social reality in accordance with its poten-
> tial for being a contribution to, prolepsis of, or signpost on the way
> toward the participation in the divine life that God desires humans
> to enjoy.[59]

---

57. Colin Gunton, *The Promise of Trinitarian Theology* (Edinburgh: T&T Clark, 1991).

58. R. Paul Stevens, *The Other Six Days: Vocation, Work, and Ministry in Biblical Perspective* (Grand Rapids: Eerdmans; Vancouver: Regent College Publishing, 1999), 194. This Sender, Sent, and Sending paradigm reflects the same pattern as Barth's construal of the Trinity as Revealer, Revelation, and Revealedness, and Augustine's Lover, Loved, and Love.

59. Stanley J. Grenz, *Renewing the Center: Evangelical Theology in a Post-Theological Era* (Grand Rapids: Baker, 2000), 324.

CHAPTER 2

Theological Ethics
Are *Trinitarian*

It is one thing to say that ethics should be theological. It is another to insist that it is specifically *Trinitarian*. It was Dutch Reformed theologian Herman Bavinck (1854–1921) who said, "Though grace is superior to nature it is not in conflict with it. The thinking mind situates the doctrine of the Trinity squarely amid the full-orbed life of nature and humanity."[1] This means that the Creator behind the moral order and the moral law must be our ultimate concern in Christian ethics. The moral order in the life of the triune God is the foundation of any moral order in creation and human persons as made in the image of God. Bavinck also presaged the Trinitarian renaissance of the late twentieth century when he said,

> A Christian's confession is not an island in the ocean but a high mountaintop from which the whole creation can be surveyed. And it is the task of Christian theologians to present clearly the connectedness of God's revelation with, and its significance for, all of life. The Christian mind remains unsatisfied until all of existence is referred back to the Triune God, and until the confession of God's Trinity functions at the center of our thought and life."[2]

Predating Bavinck in the Reformed tradition, Jonathan Edwards likewise understood that the nature of ethics was determined by the nature of God as Trinity. Edwards laid heavy emphasis on the person and work of the Spirit in his soteriology, but the Trinitarian framework of the operation of the Spirit is what determined Edwards's definition of "true virtue" and his rejection of any conception of the Christian life and of ethics in which love of God and neighbour is not primary. Edwards

---

1. Herman Bavinck, *Reformed Dogmatics*, vol. 2, *God and Creation*, ed. John Bolt, trans. John Vriend (Grand Rapids: Baker Academic, 2004), 260, 330.
2. Bavinck, *Reformed Dogmatics*, 2:330.

defines true virtue as "the mutual love and friendship which subsists eternally and necessarily between the several persons in the Godhead, or that infinitely strong propensity there is in these divine persons one to another."[3] By the indwelling of the Spirit, believers participated in the triune life of God and therefore in virtue.

This conviction will guide us as we seek moral wisdom throughout this book. The chapter on sexuality especially will reveal the importance of understanding the nature of God—as persons of irreducible identity, equal in essence and glory, in a differentiated oneness of essence and communion, the One who is Lover, Loved, and Love—in order to understand human personhood and sexuality.

Christians do not pursue ethics and engage in ethical discourse in a secular and pluralistic society on the basis of a common belief in some generic God shared by other religions. Christian theologians, if they are truly Christian, believe that the one true God is the triune God, the Father of our Lord Jesus Christ, the Son, and the Holy Spirit, who is the Spirit of the Father and of the Son. God is the one God revealed as Father in the person of the unique incarnate Son, Jesus Christ our Lord. God is Father, Son, and Holy Spirit, one in essence and communion, and three in person. Indeed, there is no God behind God's back, as Karl Barth famously said,[4] as if the real God were some Quaternity in back of the three persons. The real God is the revealed God since God is trustworthy. The immanent Trinity corresponds to the economic Trinity even if all that God is in himself has not yet been fully revealed. Only in participation with the Son, his participation in our humanity, and our participation in him by the Spirit can we be participants in the new covenant of God and live out our ethics as those being made more fully human,[5] being renewed in the image of God. Ethics is only possible because we are in Christ, objectively speaking, and because in

---

3. Jonathan Edwards, *True Virtue*, in *The Works of Jonathan Edwards*, vols. 1–26 (New Haven, CT: Yale University Press, 1977–2009), 8:557 (hereafter designated YE).

4. Karl Barth, *CD* I/1, 350–53.

5. I use the term *fully human* cautiously, for there is a nondegreed sense of what it means to be human and an image bearer. This is the foundation for the human rights of all persons, from the unborn to the elderly and disabled. When I speak of becoming *more fully* human I mean this in a degreed sense, as envisioned for the growth of the believer in Christ in a passage like 2 Cor. 3:18, which speaks of transformation from "one degree of glory to another" (NRSV). This is moral rather than ontological. All humans are human and made in the divine image, in a settled and nondegreed sense, but all humans are in need of becoming more fully human, more like Christ, the last Adam, in character, love, and holiness. The notion of image as present in all humanity as nondegreed, over against the degreed nature of that image in regenerate people as they are

regenerating us the Spirit has, subjectively speaking, opened our eyes to perceive the truth about justice and shalom so that we might be transformed. Ethical perspective is shared prophetically by the church as it overflows in love in the power of the Spirit, trusting that this witness may overcome whatever epistemological barriers exist in the hearts (rather than minds) of unbelieving or post-Christian societies—not in order that they may become "a little more moral" or with the hope of a new Christendom in mind, but simply to be faithful to the mandate to be salt and light and as a pointer toward the gospel of mercy and justice for all.

If the Christian God is really triune, and if ethics cannot be done apart from life in the Trinity, then the contemporary church's lack of Trinitarian awareness does not bode well for its theological ethics and its engagement in the public square. Lesslie Newbigin's withering critique of the church in the modern period is well worth hearing. He may have arrived at his conclusion by a narrative of Western theology that not all will agree with. However, his conclusion stands. His concerns lie chiefly with Augustine's theology of the Trinity,[6] with its perceived emphasis on oneness of essence rather than hypostatic threeness,[7] and with the influence of Aristotelian rationalism as that was baptized by Thomas Aquinas into theology.[8] Newbigin blames Aquinas for making "a sharp distinction between those things that are to be known by the use of reason, unaided by divine revelation, and those things that can be known only through faith in the divine revelation."[9] Thus, for Aquinas, the existence of God was amenable to reason, whereas the incarnation, the atonement, and the Trinity could only be discerned by faith. Newbigin insists that "what Augustine had held together Aquinas had put asunder. Faith is no longer *the* way to knowledge; it is one of two alternative ways: there are things that we can know by the use of reason, other things that we can know only by faith."[10] Newbigin grieves that the consequence of this was that "the God whose existence is proved by the use of unaided reason is not recognizable as the God who encounters us in the Bible, and

---

sanctified or deified, is expressed in the work of Christa L. McKirland, "Intersex in the Image of God," *Journal of Psychology and Theology* 44, no. 1 (Spring 2016): 99–100.

6. Lesslie Newbigin, "The Trinity as Public Truth," in *The Trinity in a Pluralistic Age*, ed. Kevin Vanhoozer (Grand Rapids: Eerdmans, 1997), 2.

7. The idea that Augustine's Trinity was different from that of the Cappadocian Fathers is now much disputed.

8. Newbigin, "Trinity as Public Truth," 3.

9. Newbigin, "Trinity as Public Truth," 3.

10. Newbigin, "Trinity as Public Truth," 4.

certainly not the Blessed Trinity,"[11] and that "the Western understanding of the word 'God' is not often that of the triune God."[12] Newbigin then suggests that the Western concept of God, when it enters the public forum, "is much more recognizable as a conflation of Aristotle's prime mover with the Allah of the Qur'an."[13] Irrespective of Newbigin's reading of theological history, he is not far off the mark in assessing the familiarity of sections of the Western church with the doctrine of the Trinity. If the Trinity was removed from the creeds and confession of the contemporary church, the church would carry on blissfully as if nothing had happened.

This is not to say that we should not engage respectfully with people of other religions. In fact, the reality that all are made in the image of the triune God and that this has a nondegreed aspect,[14] which is based on God's desire for all humanity to be saved, is the ground for treating everyone with tolerance, for dialoguing well, for validating truths in every religion, and yet for respectfully pointing to Christ as the true fulfilment of all human desires and religious pursuits.

In this chapter, we hope first to speak briefly of *what the doctrine of the Trinity is*, then to clarify *what it means to be Trinitarian* in general, and specifically with regard to ethics, and finally to examine *why Trinitarian is a fitting category for ethics*, indeed *why the category Trinitarian ethics subsumes and transcends other categories*.

THE DOCTRINE OF THE TRINITY

The Trinity is often spoken of as having two aspects. Who God is in himself, *in se*, is what may be described as the immanent Trinity. How God has revealed himself in history, as the God of creation, reconciliation, and the redemption of all things, is called the economic Trinity, or *pro nobis* (who God is *for us*). The exact relationship between these two is not always agreed on by theologians,[15] but what seems to make the

---

11. Newbigin, "Trinity as Public Truth," 4. A little unfair to Aquinas, I think!
12. Newbigin, "Trinity as Public Truth," 3.
13. Newbigin, "Trinity as Public Truth," 3.
14. McKirland, "Image of God and Intersex Persons."
15. There are at least seven positions on how these aspects of the Trinity relate. See Chung-Hyun Baik, *The Holy Trinity—God for God and God for Us: Seven Positions in the Immanent-Economic Trinity Relation in Contemporary Trinitarian Theology* (Eugene, OR: Pickwick, 2010). The correspondence view is attributed to Karl Barth.

most sense given divine revelation in the Bible is that they are in *corre-spondence* to one another. They are not to be *coalesced* (as Karl Rahner did—Rahner's rule, that the economic Trinity is the immanent Trinity and the immanent Trinity is the economic Trinity,[16] seems to ignore the distinction between unknowable and inscrutable), but they must *corre-spond* to each other, for if what has been revealed to us in the economic Trinity does not correspond with who God really is, then that revelation will have proved to be misleading and unreliable. Barth's correspondence view acknowledges that the missions of God in sending the Son and giving the Spirit correspond to the eternal processions of the Son and the Spirit. The Son, for example, is *incarnandus*, oriented toward incarnation as the eternally generated Son of the Father, before he becomes incarnate. This helps ameliorate the challenge that God changed when the Son became incarnate. The Son on earth is mutually internal to the Father just as he was in heaven. He has always been *homoousios* with the Father as the Son, and in his incarnation he became *homoousios* with humanity. His participation in the life of the Father throughout life is a *model* for the church and its persons to live in union with the Father in the Son by the Spirit for moral formation and ethical decision making and action. But it is far more than a model. As a consequence of the Son becoming one with us by the Spirit, believing persons become one with Christ by the Spirit and so *participate* in the life of God.

The Trinity is also sometimes spoken of as having developed in slightly different ways and according to different analogies in the *Western* and *Eastern* traditions of the church: the *psychological Trinity* (Western), following Augustine's analogy of the human mind, and the *social Trinity* (Eastern, sometimes called by the unhelpful name "relational Trinity"[17]). On the Eastern view, the Father is the source (*font*) of the personhood and/or the essence of the persons, logically speaking (not chronologically since all three are eternal), whilst in the *social Trinity of Athanasius* the communion of the persons is the *font* (T. F. Torrance,[18] Alan Torrance,[19]

---

16. Karl Rahner, *The Trinity* (New York: Herder and Herder, 1970), 22, 24.

17. Jason S. Sexton, general ed., and Stanley N. Gundry, series ed., *Two Views of the Doctrine of the Trinity* (Grand Rapids: Zondervan, 2014), with essays by Paul S. Fiddes, Stephen R. Holmes, Thomas H. McCall, and Paul D. Molnar.

18. Favouring the Athanasian view, T. F. Torrance comments that "while the Son is certainly *of* the Father he is not thought of as derived or caused, for he is Son *of* the Father as the Father is Father *of* the Son." T. F. Torrance, *Theology in Reconciliation: Essays towards Evangelical and Catholic Unity in East and West* (London: Geoffrey Chapman, 1975), 252–53, emphasis original.

19. Alan J. Torrance, *Persons in Communion: An Essay on Trinitarian Description and Human*

Jürgen Moltmann,[20] Miroslav Volf[21]). There is also a certain version of the social Trinity that has been grounded in social theory and politicized, but this must be differentiated from the historical social Trinity that is grounded in both Athanasian and Cappadocian thought. Miroslav Volf's *After Our Likeness* offers a defence of the historic Athanasian social Trinity over against the hierarchical view of the Trinity that characterizes both of the versions of the magisteria: the Orthodox version of the social Trinity (John Zizioulas) and the Catholic psychological version (Ratzinger).

By way of summary, the positions are as follows: the Orthodox *social* Trinity view with the *Father* as *ontological* font, the Catholic *psychological* Trinity view with the *Father* as *logical* font, and the Free Church *social* Trinity view with the eternal *communion* (*koinōnia*) as *font*, similar to Athanasius. New Testament scholars Michael Bird and Scott Harrower have sought to counter the doctrine of the eternal subordination of the Son and to affirm the equality of essence and *authority* of the persons.[22] As well as being the Orthodox position, the hierarchical structure of the Trinity in which the Father is the "One" and the Son and the Spirit are the "Many," though not popular in our time, has the weight of antiquity as the oldest position. Close examination is required, however, of what this hierarchy means. We have suggested that the Catholic view proposes a logical and not ontological hierarchy, for example. Most interestingly, the Orthodox view advocates an ontological hierarchy but also claims that essence is inseparable and indistinguishable from

Participation; with Special Reference to Volume One of Karl Bath's Church Dogmatics (Edinburgh: T&T Clark, 1996), 256.

20. Jürgen Moltmann, *The Trinity and the Kingdom of God* (Minneapolis: Fortress, 1993).

21. Miroslav Volf, *After Our Likeness: The Church as the Image of the Trinity* (Grand Rapids: Eerdmans, 1998).

22. Michael Bird and Scott Harrower, eds., *Trinity without Hierarchy: Reclaiming Nicene Orthodoxy in Evangelical Theology* (Grand Rapids: Kregel Academic, 2015). See also Rodrick Durst, *Reordering the Trinity: Six Movements of God in the New Testament* (Grand Rapids: Kregel Academic, 2015). Bird, Harrower, and their contributors have sought to expose this view as a semi-Arian heresy, upholding the Nicene affirmation that each of the persons has equal honour and equal authority. While some contributors of this volume hold complementarian and others egalitarian viewpoints, there is agreement that Trinitarian relations are not a proper basis for understanding gender roles (Kevin J. Vanhoozer, in his endorsement for Bird and Harrower, *Trinity without Hierarchy*, 2). The Eastern Orthodox tradition, which is most in touch with the Cappadocian heritage of the Trinity, must be mined before making the conclusions these authors do. The actual meaning of the Father as the *font* of the Trinity requires clarification. This is on one account a reference to personhood rather than essence. See also Matthew W. Bates, *The Birth of the Trinity: Jesus, God and the Spirit in New Testament and Early Christian Interpretations of the Old Testament* (Oxford: Oxford University Press, 2015).

personhood. In the Eastern tradition *font* is *personal* in nature rather than essential.[23] Orthodox theologian Christos Yannaras confirms that "essence . . . whether in the case of God or in the case of man, does not exist apart from the specific person who gives it subsistence. Persons hypostasize essence, they give it a hypostasis, that is, real and specific existence. Essence exists only 'in persons'; persons are the mode of existence of essence."[24] For the Orthodox, each hypostasis of God is a specific and unique existence of God. Each has the same essence, coming from the origin without origin—the Father (God)—and each is uncreated. Each specific quality that constitutes a *hypostasis* of God is nonreductionist and is not shared. In the East, the Father is definitely the eternal, infinite, and uncreated reality; Christ and the Holy Spirit are also eternal, infinite, and uncreated—not because their origin is in the preexistent *ousia* of God but because their origin is in the *hypostasis* of God, called the Father. Thus, the Father is the *font* of the Son and the Spirit by way of personhood, and talk of subordination of essence or substance fades. Subordinationism is a heresy in all traditions if by it we mean something ontological rather than functional. It seems quite clear that there are *functional* subordinations, or better, functional mutual *submissions* within the Trinity, between the Father and the Son, and between the Father and the Spirit and the Son and the Spirit (the statements of Scripture point toward the sovereignty and empowerment of the Spirit toward the Son in the virgin birth [Matt. 1:20; Luke 1:35] and in his ministry [e.g., Luke 4:1, 14] all the way to his death [Heb. 9:14], and then of the Spirit being given *from* the Father *through* the Son [e.g., Luke 24:49; John 1:33; Acts 1:4] to the church).

The association of Augustine with the Western Trinity and the Cappadocian Fathers with the two forms of the Eastern Trinity is, however, a much too facile and unfair distinction. I think it is still fair to say that Augustine's analogies as *received* in the Western tradition, and specifically the psychological analogy, perpetuated an emphasis on oneness that is still present in Western theologians who consider

---

23. Gregory of Nazianzus indicates that the cause or *aition* of divine existence is the Father, which, because he is a person, makes the Trinity "a matter of ontological freedom." John D. Zizioulas, "The Doctrine of the Holy Trinity: The Significance of the Cappadocian Contribution," in *Trinitarian Theology Today*, ed. Christoph Schwöbel (Edinburgh: T&T Clark, 1995), 44, 51.

24. Christos Yannaras, *Elements of Faith: An Introduction to Orthodox Theology* (Edinburgh: T&T Clark, 1991), 27.

themselves "classical Trinitarians."[25] This school of thought suggests that the only differentiation between the "persons" (some in this school prefer "relations") is with respect to their eternal processions. Starting epistemologically with the economic Trinity rather than beginning with philosophical constructs like strict simplicity would suggest otherwise. The revealed relationship between the Father and the Son in the Gospels is clearly between two persons of *irreducible identity* (the Father does not become incarnate and is not crucified on a cross), and yet at the same time they are persons who are coinherent, each mutually internal to the other, each in the other with respect to both essence and action (the Father is in the Son as he is sent, as he becomes human, and as he dies on the cross). The doctrine of the appropriations of the divine functions must be held in tension with another Trinitarian axiom, that the persons are undivided and indivisible. Beyond these nuances of distinction it is important to affirm the creedal expressions concerning the Trinity that are held in common by the Great Tradition as a whole. God is one with respect to essence and communion; God is three with respect to persons, even if the Western or "classical" tradition prefers to call them "persons *as* relations" as opposed to "persons in relation." In neither tradition are the "persons" (*hypostases*) *individuals*, for they are mutually internal to one another, and in neither tradition are they three gods but one God in three persons.

Throughout the tradition the articulation of the Trinity has as its grounding the belief that God is love (love first, not power first), that the eternal preexistence and covenanting and sending of the Son assures us that God has chosen to create and reconcile and redeem in a way that reveals him to be the triune God, and that as such he is *for* his creation. He is the God of the *euanggelion*, the gospel, since what he has shown himself to be in the economy of grace is who he really is in his being eternally. The historic social Trinity (based on the economic revelation of the Trinity rather than philosophical speculation) leads to affirmation of *both* the irreducible identity of the persons *and* their oneness of communion by perichoresis. Person and communion are equiprimal in the triune God. This will prove to be an important model and means of human participation in understanding anthropology and thus the Christian ethics of being and doing.

---

25. Sexton and Gundry, *Two Views of the Doctrine of the Trinity*, 25–109.

WHAT IT MEANS TO BE TRINITARIAN

Now let's answer the question, *what does it mean to be Trinitarian in general and with respect to ethics in particular?* To say that one believes in the Trinity (as all true Christians must) is not to say that one has understood how pervasive and central the Trinity is to Christian doctrine and ethics. The theological academy of today may be characterized as one in which the Trinity has been recovered for Christian dogmatics and ethics. This renaissance is due in large part to Karl Barth who in the late twentieth century rescued it from obscurity in the theology of the Enlightenment and before that from its neglect even within Reformed theology. Barth reacted to Friedrich Schleiermacher's placement of the section on the Trinity in the appendix of his major doctrinal work and corresponding reduction of all theology to ethics (removing God from ethics) by making the Trinity the prolegomena, the centre, and the architectonic of theology[26] and by insisting that in fact there is no ethics apart from theology, especially theology of the Trinity. Robert Jenson, among other theologians such as Moltmann, Pannenberg, Gunton, and the Torrances, perpetuated this recovery of the Trinity. Significantly, Jenson speaks of the Trinity as "nothing less than the comprehensive statement of the gospel's most radical claims" and "therefore not a theological puzzle but the framework within which to deal with theological puzzles."[27] So being Trinitarian is much more than adherence to a doctrine. The Trinity is the doctrine that shapes all doctrine, all thought, including moral thought and action.

There are actually five uses of the term *Trinitarian*, most helpfully outlined by John Witvliet (with some adaptation and extrapolation) in the wake of the Trinitarian renaissance,[28] which highlight what it means to be Trinitarian, all of which are relevant to what it means to be Trinitarian in one's theological ethics. Far beyond mere assent to the creed, these five uses of the term *Trinitarian* are as follows:

---

26. In rescuing the Trinity from obscurity in Friedrich Schleiermacher's *The Christian Faith in Outline*, ed. Donald Macpherson Baillie (Edinburgh: W. F. Henderson, 1922), where the Trinity is appended (62–63) and spoken of as "not of equal value to other doctrines of the faith" (62), Barth made it the architectonic of his theology. Far from being a theological afterthought, the doctrine of the Trinity has both a positive and critical function in Christian theology and in the gospel according to Barth.

27. Robert Jenson, "An Interview with Robert W. Jenson," *The Christian Century*, May 2, 2007, 32.

28. John Witvliet, "The Doctrine of the Trinity and the Theology and Practice of Christian Worship in the Reformed Tradition" (PhD diss., University of Notre Dame, 1997), 299–330.

1. *Trinitarian* denotes "a theological system based on reflection on the historical actions of Jesus of Nazareth and the Holy Spirit as recorded in scripture."[29] It implies a primacy of a historically empirical way of articulating the doctrine of the Trinity in an *a posteriori* rather than an *a priori* philosophical manner, one that moves epistemologically from the economy into the immanent, not the other way around, grounded in the assumption that who God is in himself (*in se*) must be true to who he is for us in the economy (*pro nobis*). The antonym is "speculative" or primarily "philosophical" theology.[30] I might summarize this by saying that to be Trinitarian is to be *revelationally prioritized*.

2. *Trinitarian* implies a "self-consciously comprehensive, unified, and synthetic approach to theology."[31] The antonym is to be "christomonic"[32] (the idea that Jesus, or a "what would Jesus do?" mentality, is the only consideration for ethics without reference to what new situations and the leading of the Spirit might require[33]) or to be theologically Unitarian. I expand this to say that *Trinitarian* means being comprehensive and integrative in one's approach to theology. Specifically, *comprehensive* means considering all of the divine nature and works of each person of the Trinity, that is, patriological, christological, and pneumatological, whilst *integrative* means integrating all of the divine works, given that the persons and work of the Trinity are undivided (*opera trinitatis ad extra indivisa sunt*). In sum, to be Trinitarian one must be *extensively and unitedly Trinitarian*.

3. *Trinitarian* implies espousal of "a doctrine of God which insists that God is both transcendentally and immanently a personal, acting, relational, and self-giving being."[34] The antonym is to say that God is either "deistic" (transcendence without immanence) or "pantheistic" (immanence without transcendence).[35] In sum, one might say *Trinitarian* means that God is *intensively* Trinitarian,

---

29. Witvliet, "Doctrine of the Trinity," 299.

30. Witvliet, "Doctrine of the Trinity," 296.

31. Witvliet, "Doctrine of the Trinity," 299.

32. Witvliet, "Doctrine of the Trinity," 299.

33. Luke Bretherton has dubbed this approach "Jesuology." Luke Bretherton, "Beyond the Emerging Church," in *Remembering Our Future: Explorations in Deep Church*, ed. Andrew Walker and Luke Bretherton (London: Paternoster, 2007), 37.

34. Witvliet, "Doctrine of the Trinity," 299.

35. Witvliet, "Doctrine of the Trinity," 299.

that he is love, and that as such he is both *personal and rela-tional*—he is three *persons-in-relation*. This third feature stresses the nature of God as *love* and the action of the Trinity toward his creation and humanity. He is love, the triune God of love, not a monad of unbridled power. It crucially includes the notion that he has chosen to create and reveal himself to humans as the God who is *for us*, and in fact to create humans in his image as the triune God. Though the terms cannot be used of God and his human creatures univocally, they are nevertheless by analogy subjects who are persons-in-relation, or persons in community as he is persons-in-communion. As stated already, this moves beyond mere *model*. Humans are by grace enabled to pursue becoming like God, morally speaking, only in *participation* with God as persons-in-relation. This makes participation or union with Christ (what the New Testament means by "in Christ") the way that regenerated and ecclesial persons-in-relation pursue the ethical life. It is imitation in union. Imitation of God without participa-tion in the life of God is futility and folly. In other words, moral formation and ethics happen within *theosis*, Protestant versions of which (*participation* is a preferred term for some) stress that the most important soteriological category is union with Christ and (following Calvin) that the graces of both justification and sanc-tification (and therefore moral formation and ethics), inseparable but distinguishable, flow logically from that union. This third point also makes *person* a more fundamental category in theo-logical ethics, even more so than character, which is a point we will expand on. It also makes abundantly clear that persons are not individuals, but their very beings depend on relations, being bound up with God, with their parents, with their neighbours in general. Thus ethics can never be individual; it is first ecclesial.

4. *Trinitarian* infers "a formulation of the divine-human relationship which stresses that both divine revelation as well as human faith, prayer and worship"[36] involve divine action and are ensconced in grace. That is, human response, including worship and obedience in ethics, is impossible apart from the mediating work and grace of Christ, our great high priest, and the Holy Spirit. The antonym

---

36. Witvliet, "Doctrine of the Trinity," 299.

is Pelagianism. One might sum this up by saying that *Trinitarian* means "of the gospel." That is, not only does the God of love create, reconcile, and redeem us by his divine action (as in point 3), but he even engraces us for response so that our response is enabled by participation in Christ by the Spirit. This is crucial for ethical living. God the Trinity is not just the ground for our grateful response but is the very means by which he responds for us in the person of Christ and by the Holy Spirit.

5. *Trinitarian* implies "a communitarian approach to ordering human relationships in the church and in society as a mirror or icon of divine life."[37] The antonym is *individualistic*.[38] This use overlaps with the third, but the emphasis is sorely needed, especially for ethics in the Western world where the value of individual autonomy trumps all others in medical ethics and bioethics. But if the intent is that the church should reveal the way of community over individualism, the reality on the ground is that individualism is still prevalent in the church. There is a tendency to transform the appropriate personalism of the gospel (John's Gospel demands personal response to Christ, and Paul speaks of Christ's personal dying love for him [Gal. 2:20]) and make the Christian life so individualistic that the faith professed would be barely recognizable to Jesus, the apostles, or the fathers. Some contemporary evangelicalism begins with a Jesus-and-me emphasis in conversion, neglecting the fact that even our saving faith is mediated by the church and must be accompanied by baptism, which is not just a symbol that I have died and am risen with Christ but that having been baptized into Christ I am now baptized by the Spirit into the church consisting of others who are in union with Christ. Individualism is rampant also in the church's worship, if people do in fact enter into the life of the church (the "de-churched" population continues to grow in North America, accompanied by the naive assumption that a Christian can somehow not go to church, naïve because they are the church), with a very individualistic expectation that "I should be touched" or "I should be ministered to." Or even that "God has done all this for me; now

---

37. Witvliet, "Doctrine of the Trinity," 299.
38. Witvliet, "Doctrine of the Trinity," 299.

this is what I can do in return for him." There is a widespread lack of awareness that our worship is engraced, that it is a participation in the Spirit, who translates our feeble thoughts and groanings, and that it is a participation in the worship of the Son, who as our great high priest represents us in our humanity before the throne of God. Writing about the need for the church to move from assent to invocation of the Trinity, Jason Vickers urges that "instead of conceiving of the Trinity as a network of propositions to be 'explained,'" clergy should "think of the Trinity as divine persons to be *introduced*."[39] This understanding Vickers shows to have been present in the hymns of Charles Wesley, who moved from being binitarian to Trinitarian as a result of his conversion and developed a profoundly Trinitarian understanding of worship. Vickers states that this perspective "will help reorient Christian worship," since his concern is that much Protestant worship has fallen on hard times, having devolved into various forms of self-help and therapy in which talking about ourselves replaces talking to and listening to God. Instead Vickers offers the perspective that worship is an occasion of communion with the triune God through invocation and other forms of direct address.[40] Profound formation in worship, which includes hearing the Word and freshly participating in the life of the Son in the Eucharist, is a *communal* moral formation. Flowing from the *gathered* communal life of the church and in union with Christ, the *scattered* life of the people of God, where amongst other things they bear witness to evangelical ethics, is then lived by the power of the Holy Spirit. It is from the communal life of the church that ethical perspectives may be offered. And in looking back on the long life of the church, the perspectives of the doctors and teachers and liturgy of the church triumphant may be gained. The authority of the Scriptures as properly interpreted will be final, but the longevity of moral teaching and ethical positions will not easily be overturned.

One can easily see why Cornelius Plantinga suggested that the doctrine of the Trinity is "attached with conceptual gears and pulleys to

---

39. Jason E. Vickers, *Invocation and Assent: The Making and Remaking of Trinitarian Theology* (Grand Rapids: Eerdmans, 2008), 193.

40. Vickers, *Invocation and Assent*, 196–97.

other areas of Christian interest."[41] It is conceptually related to all of Christian thought and life, and especially worship. Barth made what was peripheral to be the centre of Christian theology, a return to the Bible and to the theology of the fathers and apostles. A number of metaphors are used to describe the doctrine of the Trinity: "It is like a foundation, a grammar, a backbone, a substructure, a linchpin, a capstone, or a cornerstone of Christian theology."[42]

Therefore, we can begin to see that Trinitarian *ethics* involves the *formation* of the moral subjects, that is, persons-in-relation, in participation with Christ by the Spirit, in the communion of the church where they hear the Word expounded and encounter the living Word, and where they feed on Christ as he is made really present by the Spirit in the Eucharist and are taken up afresh into union with the ascended Christ, and where in the cut and thrust of the messiness of communal church life they are shaped and formed.[43] The moral subjects are described first and ultimately as "persons" formed to be persons-in-relation, which means persons of love, who love God and neighbour. And through their formation, character is formed, virtues are cultivated, and vices begin to be overcome. This formation of character has a christological and a pneumatological shape to it. It is christological in the sense that formation (sanctification) is always in the Epistles accomplished in active union with Christ in his death (mortification of the vices) and resurrection (vivification of the graces or virtues). It also has a pneumatological shape or empowerment, in that participation in Christ is enabled by the Spirit. Paul says, for example, in Romans 8:13, "If *by the Spirit* you put to death the misdeeds of the body, you will live" (emphasis added). And in Galatians 5:22–23, Paul outlines the graces as particularly the "*fruit of the Spirit*," love being the first virtue that includes all the others. But Trinitarian ethics also involves *ethical decision making and action.* Human *persons* are agents (though only as persons-in-communion with God in Christ and by the Spirit). They encounter ethical situations, almost always new, and as they do so they pray to the Father *above* for wisdom and discernment of the moral order; they seek to hear the

---

41. Cornelius Plantinga, "The Threeness/Oneness Problem of the Trinity," *Calvin Theological Journal* 23 (1988): 37–53 (37).

42. Witvliet, "Doctrine of the Trinity," 300.

43. See L. Gregory Jones, *Transformed Judgment: Toward a Trinitarian Account of the Moral Life* (Eugene, OR: Wipf & Stock, 2008).

Word of Christ, including the moral law, that comes to them from *outside* of themselves, the Word as properly interpreted, which includes its interpretation in the tradition by the church; they listen for the promptings and guidance of the Holy Spirit *within*; and they consult with the church and the community *around* them, including people with expertise pertinent to the situation they are encountering.

Implicit in this is that their character and virtues may prepare them for making good ethical decisions, but first it must be emphasized that this character and those virtues have no existence apart from participation with Christ and his virtues, and second, there will still be a need for dependence on the Word and the Spirit in the moment, no matter how well developed the character. It is as human *persons* dependent on divine persons that moral action is carried out. They will be persons *with* character, but the larger category is necessary to describe Trinitarian ethics, for no human person can have confidence in their own character when called upon to make complex ethical decisions in an imperfect world, which in the "now but not yet" of the kingdom of God is an imperfect exercise requiring forgiveness again and again.

WHY *TRINITARIAN* IS A FITTING CATEGORY FOR ETHICS

Finally, we want to try to answer the question, *why is* Trinitarian *a fitting category for ethics, and indeed the best category for Christian ethics, surpassing but including deontological, utilitarian, and virtue ethics?* Most crucially, this is so because of the inseparable intertwining of the Trinity and the gospel. As we have stated, the gospel includes ethics once it is properly ensconced within an understanding of participation. As we have stressed in the theological section, and will see again in the biblical section, there cannot be such a thing as legitimate ethics apart from the gospel of God's unconditional love for humanity and the expression of that love in the history of Jesus Christ (the *ordo historia*), which then by the Spirit through faith becomes the history of those who believe (*ordo salutis*). *Trinitarian* means that an ontology of love is at the centre of the universe and that God is *for* humanity and creation. We are not left alone in the moral quest. Trinitarian ethics thus implies grace-filled ethics, ethics in the context and ethos of the gospel. Specifically, it expresses the triune God as the norm, the ground, and the power of ethics, as has been outlined already by Geoffrey Bromiley[44] and Dennis Hollinger.[45]

Hollinger speaks of a "Christian worldview foundation" for ethics as being ultimately rooted necessarily in the nature and actions of the triune God. He speaks first of the *nature* of the triune God as the foundation of ethics and thus as the ground and paradigm for Christian ethics, and second of the *actions* or works of God within the biblical story as the basis for a Christian worldview for ethics: creation, fall, the redemption of humanity and creation, and the consummation of creation. The actions of God within the eschatological framework of God's work in the world will be discussed in chapter 4. The consideration of both the nature and the acts of God is important, first because God's being and acts, or being in act, are indivisible, and second because contemporary theology has a tendency to focus on the *horizontal* dimension of God's work in the world as recorded in the biblical story to the neglect of the *vertical* reality of who the revealed God actually is. In the field of theological ethics, narrative ethics is popular. The power of the biblical narrative and individual biblical stories to form character and virtues is implicit in this viewpoint. Trinitarian ethics includes this, but it also insists that the nature and actions of the triune God come first and actually inhabit and empower the stories. Furthermore, narrative is not the only genre of the Bible. The encounter with the triune God happens also through didactic, poetic, and indeed all other genres of Scripture.

There are, in fact, *three* elements that shape a worldview, or better, to be more Augustinian, a "heartview" (only a heartview is compatible with virtue): the narrative component, a rational component, and a ritual component.[46] The narrative component "embodies the stories we tell to make sense of reality,"[47] and for the Christian this would be the biblical stories and the overarching biblical narrative of creation, fall, redemption, and consummation. The rational component is also necessary—as a point expressed with regard to the "vertical" or doctrinal component

---

44. Geoffrey Bromiley, "Ethics and Dogmatics," in *International Standard Biblical Encyclopedia*, vol. 2 (San Francisco: Harper and Row, 1987), 186–90.

45. Dennis P. Hollinger, *Choosing the Good: Christian Ethics in a Complex World* (Grand Rapids: Baker Academic, 2002), 64–68.

46. Hollinger, *Choosing the Good*, 63. See James K. A. Smith, *Desiring the Kingdom: Worship, Worldview, and Cultural Formation* (Grand Rapids: Baker Academic, 2009). Smith does not propose a dichotomy in which we need to choose between the mind and the heart, but he does acknowledge the priority of affectivity in our knowing and in our formation.

47. Hollinger, *Choosing the Good*, 63.

that Christian ethics requires. This is the analytic formulation of beliefs based on the Scriptures and includes the doctrines of the nature and actions of God, the person and work of Christ, the nature of the church and the kingdom of God, and so on. It is vital because it shows the interrelationships of the ideas in the biblical story and their connection to the moral life.[48] The ritual component acknowledges that we are embodied and communal people and that the symbols and rituals of our gathered life reenact our view of reality in light of God's nature and creational and redemptive actions. We focus now on the second component of worldview, ethics, as formed first and foremost by the triune God.

God as the Ground of Ethics

With respect to the nature of the triune God as the *ground* of ethics, there are two dimensions: the *character* of the triune God as holy love, who in his majestic, moral, and aesthetic holiness defines "the good," and the *covenant love* of God, which is unconditional love expressed in Christ that precedes any command of God. Before God gives any commandments, he first declares that he is the God of the covenant and redemptive actions of Israel. The Ten Commandments are, in one sense, a "get to," not a "have to." At the heart of the gospel as revealed in its fulness in the New Testament and its commands is the covenant love of God, which has in Christ already provided righteousness for us, implanting it by the Spirit within us.

The tone of the New Testament Epistles is shaped by the telling of the gospel: to tell us that in Christ God is for us, to tell us who we are in Christ, and only to give ethical commands in light of this participation in the life of God. In other words, the indicatives of the gospel always precede the imperatives of the gospel. Take Paul's letter to the Ephesians, for example. Chapters 1–3 are doctrinal or kerygmatic, whilst the contents of chapters 4–6 are paraenetic or ethical. The proclamation in praise language of the first three chapters is expressed largely by indicatives; the exhortations that follow are in the form of imperatives or hortatory subjunctives (though both indicatives and imperatives are often in the form of participles). So Ephesians seems, at first glance, to reflect that pattern—God's love for us in Christ, God's election of us in Christ, our identity in Christ, and our ecclesial calling in Christ

---

48. Hollinger, *Choosing the Good*, 63.

in chapters 1–3, followed by the paraenetic section in chapters 4–6 (orientated around five "walking" commands). Markus Barth suggested that the connection between our identity in Christ's identity and the paraenesis is much more intricate.[49] He thought that imposing too solid a structure on a very "hymnodic and prayer-filled letter" does an injustice to the literature that is this epistle.[50] Even more serious is the notion that some might gain from such a division that indicatives and imperatives can be widely separated. The notion that God in Christ by the Spirit has done *this* for you and now it's up to you to do *that* for him is far removed from a true understanding of the gospel.[51] It is not that what he did is gospel and now what we do is law. Rather, all is gospel, and the fulfilment of *torah* is gospel also. *It is that God in Christ by the Spirit continues to act, and we act in participation in him as persons-in-communion with him and in community and so fulfil the moral law and bring hope to the world.* Thus Barth offers another way to see the structure of Ephesians. He considers 1:3–14, which takes the form of benedictory praise of the triune God in the community of his people, as an introductory overture to the whole letter. But this prologue makes it clear that the whole creation is under God's action and that all things are being subjected to Christ and therefore subjected to his people, whose redemption and incorporation into Christ signal the restoration of the cosmos. His redemptive work by which he forms the church in his Son is with a view to restoring his creation work. The Trinitarian structure of that overture in 1:3–14 is evident. There are three stanzas in this great Trinitarian overture, each of which ends with a similar phrase of praise to the grace and the glory of God. The reconciling, redemptive act of God is *from the Father* who elects and blesses with every spiritual blessing in the heavenlies in Christ and *to the Father* who makes us holy and blameless for his presence (vv. 3–6); it is *in the Son* who redeems and lavishes wisdom and understanding and reigns (vv. 6b–12); and it is *by the Spirit* in whom we are sealed and whom we are given as a deposit guaranteeing our inheritance (vv. 13–14). And there is a christological phrase that is common to all the parts: "*in Christ.*" Barth maintains that this opening ecstatic, Trinitarianly structured overture in verses 3–14

---

49. Markus Barth, *Ephesians: Introduction, Translation, and Commentary on Chapters 1–3*, Anchor Bible (New York: Doubleday, 1974), 29.

50. Barth, *Ephesians*, 54.

51. Barth, *Ephesians*, 53.

reverberates and is worked out throughout the book. "All that the epistle has to say about faith and life (dogmatics and ethics) is wrapped up (and not in appearance only) in the form of prayer."[52] God as the ground of ethics enables participation in his life and love.

God as the Norm for Ethics

The second aspect of the nature of God that Hollinger refers to as an expression of the Trinitarian nature of ethics is that God is the *norm* for Christian ethics. Paul speaks of being imitators of God (1 Thess. 1:6), which of course would be an impossible reach were it not that God is first the ground of ethics. God is the norm for ethics in a three-fold sense. The first relates to the *attributes* of God. The triune being of God models perfect love and perfect holiness and calls us to love because he has first loved us (Ex. 20:1–2; 1 John 4:10) and to be holy because he is holy (Lev. 11:44–45; 19:2; 1 Peter 1:16). Love is a crucial dynamic in Christian ethics as demonstrated by the summing up of the Ten Commandments into the Great Commandment to love God and neighbour. More will be said on this in the following chapter. Holiness is inseparable from love, however, for if God's love was not holy it might be characterized by favouritism, and if holiness did not contain love, it might be capricious and unreasonably wrathful.[53] Second, there is a particular aspect of the *being* of God that is his Trinitarian personhood-in-perichoretic-communion that we image as human beings made in the *imago Dei*, which in light of the New Testament we know to be the *imago trinitatis*. Trinitarian ethics entails what it means for human beings to *be* and specifically to be *persons* and as such to be *persons-in-communion* or *persons-in-relation*.

This notion that the triune God is the norm for Christian being and doing has specifically to do with who Christ is as the true human, the man for all humanity, the *eschatos* Adam. This moves humans in Christ to want to know what it means to be truly human, a criterion that has weight in many aspects of ethics. It also clarifies what it means for humans to be image bearers. This in turn addresses the issue of

---

52. Barth, *Ephesians*, 29.

53. Augustus H. Strong, *Systematic Theology*, vol. 1, *The Doctrine of God*, ed. Anthony Vyl (Woodstock, ON: Devoted, 2017), 199; and 2:121. Augustus Strong thought of holiness as the chief attribute of God that subsumed love. Certainly it is hard to separate these two fundamental attributes of God. Love is presented as that which seems to define the nature of God in 1 John 4:8 ("God *is* love"), and the triune nature of God seems to confirm love as the very essence of God.

vocation—human vocation, ecclesial or particularly Christian vocation, and personal vocation. These will be considered in chapter 4.

God as the Power for Ethics

The third aspect of the nature of God that Hollinger refers to as an expression of the Trinitarian nature of ethics is that God is the *power* for Christian ethics, a power that enables both the being *and* the doing of the human person-in-relation. God's *grace* as empowerment is first that which moved the Son to become one with humanity, to recapitulate humanity as the last Adam, to live a holy life for us, to accomplish atonement for our moral failures, and to rise again from the dead to reaffirm creation and the moral order (O'Donovan). God's participation in humanity in Christ is empowerment, therefore, but then by the Spirit people of faith are conjoined to the humanity of Christ so that they are in Christ. This is what Hollinger calls God's *presence* as empowerment, the participation of humanity in God by the Spirit. The same Spirit who gave birth to the humanity of Christ, who empowered Christ through-out his life, and who enabled Christ's offering up of himself to God (Heb. 9:15) is the Spirit who grafts us into Christ so that not only are we in Christ, but Christ is in us (Col. 1:27: "To them God has chosen to make known among the Gentiles the glorious riches of this mystery, which is *Christ in you*, the hope of glory" [emphasis added]). This is the Christ in whom "all the fullness of the Deity lives in bodily form." In this Christ we "have been brought to fullness." And that same Christ who indwells us by the Spirit is referred to in the same epistle as "the head over every power and authority" (Col. 2:9–10) and the one "in whom are hidden all the treasures of wisdom and knowledge" (Col. 2:3). Ethical living is possible only because of this indwelling of Christ by the Spirit.

This does not remove the need for work on behalf of the human agents in participation, delightful though participation in Christ is. In Galatians, Paul's heart cry for the people of God is that Christ might actually be formed in them: "My dear children, for whom I am again in the pains of childbirth until Christ is formed in you" (Gal. 4:19). Of course, the Spirit is required for the work by which Christ is actually *formed* in us, ordering our desires, but Paul implies that this is something the Galatians play a role in. In Philippians 2, Paul establishes a concept that may be termed *asymmetric concursus*, which means that God's work and human work are compatible and complementary, not conflicted.

Paul states, "Therefore, my dear friends, as you have always obeyed—not only in my presence, but now much more in my absence—continue to *work out your salvation* with fear and trembling, for it is *God who works in you* to will and to act in order to fulfill his good purpose" (Phil. 2:12–13, emphasis added). God works and we work, and in his working we work, and in our working he works. This is the very essence of participation. Significantly, this passage follows an exhortation (2:1–4) of the virtue of humility that is reinforced by the great christological hymn on the mind of Christ (2:5–11). The exhortation to imitate is sandwiched between assertions that imitation is enabled only by participation. Before the exhortation, Paul says, "Therefore if you have any encouragement from being *united with Christ*, if any comfort from his love, if any *common sharing in the Spirit*" (2:1–2, emphasis added). After the exhortation he speaks of this concursus arrangement by which our working is in God's working (2:12–13). This is classic Trinitarian ethics in which the persons of the Trinity work together (here the Son and the Spirit) perichoretically to empower human persons in Christ, including their human actions in character development. The christological dimension is emphasized again by Paul in Colossians 2:6–7: "So then, just as you received Christ Jesus as Lord, continue to live your lives in him, rooted and built up in him, strengthened in the faith as you were taught, and overflowing with thankfulness." The pneumatic element is stressed greatly in Galatians 5 and Ephesians 5. And in Romans 8:9–11, Paul refers to the work of the Son and the Spirit together in sanctification in a way that is true to their coinherent nature and working:

> You, however, are not in the realm of the flesh but are in the realm of the Spirit, if indeed the Spirit of God lives in you. And if anyone does not have the Spirit of Christ, they do not belong to Christ. But if Christ is in you, then even though your body is subject to death because of sin, the Spirit gives life because of righteousness. And if the Spirit of him who raised Jesus from the dead is living in you, he who raised Christ from the dead will also give life to your mortal bodies because of his Spirit who lives in you.

In this post-Pentecost and pre-*parousia* era of the narrative of God's grace, the Holy Spirit makes the presence of the Son real to us because as the God-man in a human body the Son is seated at the right hand of the Father. The Son is in the Spirit, and thus the indwelling presence of the Spirit mediates the indwelling presence of the Son to us. Evangelical theologian Carl Henry honours the Spirit aptly in this comment in his *Christian Personal Ethics*:

> The Spirit is the dynamic principle of Christian ethics, the personal agency whereby God powerfully enters human life and delivers . . . from enslavement to Satan, sin, death, and law. . . . It was the Holy Spirit alone who had transformed the inescapable and distressing "I ought" which philosophical ethics was compelled to acknowledge and the tormenting "thou shalt" which Hebrew religion adduced as its complement into the "I will" of New Testament ethical dedication and zeal.[54]

Ethics as Trinitarianly empowered is thus very much evangelical. Four corollaries related to this empowerment are relevant for the ethical quest: (1) ethics outside of this cradle becomes legal and endemically sinful, as already suggested, whereas ethics in this participational reality is gospel; (2) ethics within this context still requires human effort even if it is effort "in His effort," and this suggests that there are ecclesial and personal practices or rituals that are critical in the ethical life; (3) we must have realistic expectations regarding what may and may not be accomplished in the now-but-not-yet phase of the kingdom. There is a spectrum of opinion about how much a person may be transformed and how moral a Christian can be in this age. This theme will emerge in chapter 4, but suffice it to say that the New Testament does not promise perfectionism, nor can it be used to promote other forms of triumphalism that may suggest there can be a time in life when we graduate beyond the struggle for holiness. On the other end of the spectrum, mere suppression of inner sinfulness is not consistent with the tenor of the New Testament. Rather, *"growth* in grace" is a real possibility for those who are active in practices that are a means of grace for participation with Christ in his death (mortification, disciplines of abstinence) and resurrection (disciplines of engagement[55]).

---

54. Carl Henry, *Christian Personal Ethics* (Grand Rapids: Baker, 1977), 437–38.
55. Classifying disciplines or practices into "disciplines of abstinence" (fasting, silence, solitude, chastity, secrecy, etc.) and "disciplines of engagement" (worship, hearing the Word, participating in the Lord's Supper, community, prayer, confession, fellowship, service, etc.) is Dallas Willard's

The Most Fitting Category

Having asserted that *Trinitarian* is an appropriate and sufficiently broad category for ethics, it remains to show that it is *the most fitting category* for Christian ethics. Why, for instance, is *theological* ethics or *biblical* ethics not sufficient? Certainly the assertion that theological ethics are theological is true in the most obvious sense, that what God says about any particular issue is what we must as Christian people be concerned with. The difficulty is that *theological* ethics could, as noted earlier in this chapter, simply be the ethics of a generic god. The truth is that to be truly theological in the Christian sense is to be christological and pneumatological and therefore Trinitarian. The term *theological ethics* could also be interpreted as implying (rightly) that the authority in ethics is the Holy Scriptures, which orthodox Christians believe to be the inspired written Word of God and are the final source of authority in all matters of faith and *practice* for the community of faith. This statement does not, however, resolve all theological issues. The Scriptures are only authoritative as properly interpreted by Christians *enabled by the Spirit*, and the matter of interpretation, though accessible to all believers, sometimes requires great skill and therefore dependence on the Spirit-dependent scholarly community of the church, past and present. Even when what may be called the normal interpretation of Scripture has been applied to a text or texts, that is, grammatical, historical, rhetorical interpretation, there may be unresolved tensions regarding ethical issues. Texts can be in seeming conflict with each other. What's more, many of the ethical issues we face today were not heard of in biblical times. In vitro fertilization, stem cell usage, iPhone usage, Twitter manners, creation and deployment of nuclear weapons, among many other things, were not possibilities in biblical times. So how do we apply what we discern to be applicable biblical propositions regarding issues that the Bible does not address? In other words, even when ethics is "biblical," we need the work of the Spirit. It is not that *theological* and *biblical* ethics are not good titles. My point is simply that *theological* requires the greater gospel specificity and dynamic power that *Trinitarian* carries, and *biblical* can only work under the broader category of Trinitarian ethics.

---

helpful way of making sure spiritual disciplines or practices are practised in the crucible of grace and in participation with Christ and his saving history. See Dallas Willard, *The Spirit of the Disciplines* (New York: HarperCollins, 1991), 156–92.

One of the greatest challenges in the field of ethics, or the "moral field," is its situational nature. That is, the reality that we cannot know the answer in advance of the situations we encounter, as almost every encounter in which we are called upon to make ethical decisions is unique (and not to be confused with the situation ethics of Joseph Fletcher, for whom "love" was the only rule, and who excised the moral content out of love: "It can't be wrong when it feels so right," or "How can love ever be wrong?"). Ethical decision making in a fallen world is somewhat messy, though not as messy as some might think. It requires that the moral subject be in communion with the persons and work of the holy Trinity—yes, attentive to Scripture, and yes, aware of all theological truth, but in need always of the dynamic enabling of the Spirit to be in participation with the Son and oriented toward the Father, who gives wisdom liberally to all (James 1:5).

An Inclusive Category

Having vouched for *Trinitarian* over *theological* or *biblical* ethics, the question arises as to why *Trinitarian* surpasses yet includes the three traditional categories used for ethics. The first is the *deontological* approach to ethics: a command- or rule-based ethic. In philosophical ethics, this was championed by Immanuel Kant, with his belief in the categorical imperatives. It is implicitly expressed in the expositions of the Decalogue as the basis for Christian ethics by Martin Luther, John Calvin, and other Protestant Reformers (although there is much more to Reformed ethics than deontology, which includes virtue ethics and Trinitarian ethics), it is prominent in at least one strand of Catholic moralist ethics, and it was promoted in recent times within evangelicalism by Norman Geisler.[56] In this approach there is a categorization of rules into a hierarchy (principles, rules . . .). Even the Decalogue is categorized to resolve conflicts between how particular commandments may command a person. Thus if Corrie ten Boom, who harboured Jewish people in her house during World War II, was faced with Nazi soldiers at the door asking her at gunpoint whether she was harbouring Jewish people, she could lie in good conscience and say no. Lying is permitted when a worse offence is prevented, murder in this case. The murder

---

56. See Norman L. Geisler, *Christian Ethics: Contemporary Issues and Options*, 2nd ed. (Grand Rapids: Baker Academic, 2010).

commandment, being the sixth commandment, takes precedence over the false witness commandment, the eighth. When this is extrapolated to other commandments, insurmountable difficulties arise, however. The value of the Ten Commandments is undisputed in the Christian theological heritage, but they must be interpreted within the broader Trinitarian nature and acts of God and their gospel context.

The alternative to Kantianism is the *utilitarian* theory of ethics, that is, the invocation of means and ends. Frustration with the divine command and utilitarian theories, and even proportionalism, which lies between them (rule utilitarianism, for example, says a principle may be neglected if there is a proportionate reason that overrides it; a "lesser of two evils" approach), has led to the development (some would say the recovery) of *virtue* or *character* ethics, sometimes also called *narrative* ethics in the sense that the narratives of a community shape the virtues and character of its members. A primary influence in the renaissance of this now-flourishing field in anglophone philosophy since the 1970s and then in Christian ethics has been Aristotle. At the risk of oversimplification, the principal idea here is that the cultivation of character more or less assures the correct ethical action in the moment of decision. Aristotle argues precisely in book 2 of *Nicomachean Ethics* that the person who possesses character excellence does the right thing, at the right time, and in the right way. The four cardinal Aristotelian virtues are prudence, temperance, courage, and justice, though thoughtful Christian virtue ethicists would be careful to insist that the supernatural virtue of charity obtained in participation in the life of God is the source of all the virtues.[57] The telos for Aristotle was living well and *eudaimonia*, a Greek word meaning well-being, happiness, or human flourishing.[58]

Despite the recent surge of interest in virtue ethics within academic evangelical theology, there are a number of reasons why I think it is inadequate as a theological ethic that is distinctively Christian. A fully Trinitarian ethic is offered here, one that does not rule out divine command or the employment of utilitarian and proportionalistic approaches, and that definitely incorporates virtue ethics[59] but transcends them all.

---

57. Fergus Kerr makes this point with reference to the manner in which Thomas Aquinas borrows but commandeers Aristotle in this regard. Fergus Kerr, "Doctrine of God and Theological Ethics according to Thomas Aquinas," in *The Doctrine of God and Theological Ethics*, ed. Alan J. Torrance and Michael Banner (London: T&T Clark, 2006), 77.

58. Aristotle, *Nichomachean Ethics*, trans. T. H. Irwin (Indianapolis: Hackett, 1999), book 2, xv.

59. Jonathan R. Wilson, *Gospel Virtues: Practicing Faith, Hope, and Love in Uncertain Times*

It transcends character ethics because the category of *person,* derived by way of analogy from Trinitarian and specifically christological personhood, is larger and more fundamental than character (how this works itself out into the place of personhood and personhood in ecclesial community will be worked out in chapters 7 and 8). Character belongs within personhood and not the other way around. It transcends virtue ethics also because participation of the Christian in the virtues of God cannot happen apart from ecclesial and personal participation in the life of God, in Christ, and by the Spirit.[60] It transcends the other ethical theories because it more intentionally and repletely grounds ethics within theology and the gospel. As has been contended, Trinitarian ethics makes God the ground, the norm, and the power of Christian ethics. Ethics apart from relationship with God is the primal sin of humanity, as Bonhoeffer warned. Stated positively, the ethical life flows from participation in Christ, who has died and now lives for us and in us by the Spirit. It flows from life together in the ecclesial community, its practices of Word, sacrament, and discipline enabling us to live into the story that shapes us. Ethics flows from life in the Spirit, who incorporates us and empowers our formation by imparting love and all the virtues, the spiritual dynamic for the moral ethic. It flows from and to the Father, who with the Son and the Holy Spirit is the source of love, holiness, and justice.

An Epistemological Category

Even with respect to the critical consideration in ethics of epistemology—how we know what we know and what we need to know in ethical deliberation—a Trinitarian ethic means knowing within the Trinitarian hermeneutical circle. We know as knowledge comes *from* the Father, *in* Christ incarnationally and objectively, and *by* the Holy Spirit subjectively. The certainty of knowing by pure reason has been debunked in postmodernity, even in science where critical realism is more acceptable than logical positivism. The concern of postmodernity

---

(Eugene, OR: Wipf & Stock, 2004), illustrates the pursuit of particularly *Christian* virtues, and he does so within a participatory framework.

60. Fergus Kerr writes a very compelling case that the exposition of "virtue ethics" in Thomas Aquinas in the *Summa* is grounded in a theology of participation and contemplation of the divine beatitude. It is "participation in the divine bliss" for which humans were created, and it is in this that they are able to be formed to be virtuous. Kerr, "Doctrine of God and Theological Ethics according to Thomas Aquinas," 82–83.

is with hermeneutics: How is reason skewed by context and presuppositions? All truth seems relative in light of the impossibility of eliminating the thinker's subjectivity. All that is left for postmodernity are disjointed stories. They do not need to make sense in light of a metanarrative, which is found to be oppressive. However, the obsession with story betrays an actual hunger for a big story in which all the little ones may find their place. The Trinitarian story has two things to offer a postmodern person. The first is a big story, which is not oppressive, for it comes from a triune God defined by love, not arbitrary power, a God who in Jesus gave himself for us on a cross, a God who in the Spirit does not coerce but woos persons to God, often using imperfect humans to do so. The second is an incarnational, pneumatological, Trinitarian hermeneutic, which provides a way through the maze of subjectivity. If our subjectivity can actually be that of God—that is, the Holy Spirit, who has guided the community of the saints of the past and continues to do so in the present—then we offer some basis for assurance about doctrinal and ethical truth. It will always be a critically realistic, humble, faith-seeking-understanding posture. In the book *Incarnational Humanism*,[61] Jens Zimmermann argues that modernity silenced the Word of God precisely through the processes of secularization (Kant and Schleiermacher) that severed hermeneutics from its explicitly theological underpinnings. Zimmermann suggests that credit for the reconstruction of an adequate philosophical hermeneutics must go to Gadamer and Levinas, the former for his brilliant articulation of the hermeneutical process and the latter for "regrounding" hermeneutics ontologically and transcendentally on ethics. Left on its own, however, the trajectory of Gadamer and Levinas results in the radical hermeneutics of Derrida and Caputo, which either deconstructs finitude endlessly (bereft of transcendental norms) or leaves us ignorant of both self and other (as the self can never really know the transcendent other). What is needed, Zimmermann proposes, is an understanding of the "self-other" relationship that not only preserves the distinction between self and other but also articulates the differences in relational and ethical terms. The "answer" lies also in Zimmermann's incarnational-Trinitarian theory, which proposes a personalist and intersubjectivist ontology, ethics, and hermeneutics in

---

61. Jens Zimmermann, *Incarnational Humanism: A Philosophy of Culture for the Church in the World*, Strategic Initiatives in Evangelical Theology (Downers Grove, IL: IVP Academic, 2012).

dialogue with Dietrich Bonhoeffer. Such an incarnational-Trinitarian model is explicitly theological, epistemologically communal, and directively ethical. Yet the result is also a theological aesthetics (here, in dialogue with von Balthasar) that recovers the beautiful in both ethical and incarnational terms (against the iconoclastic tradition of Reformation thought), even as the beautiful both reveals and conceals the gloriousness of God. The Trinitarian epithet for ethics becomes even more apt in light of these hermeneutical considerations offered by Zimmermann and in light of the fact that beauty as a characteristic of virtue and ethical life stems directly from the God who, as Edwards described him, *is* beauty. Beauty is not an attribute we ascribe to God. Rather, it arises in and is defined in God, who is three persons in perfect harmony, the supreme harmony of all.[62]

The Trinity viewed as differentiated (persons of irreducible identity) implies that there are distinctly patriological, christological, and pneumatic emphases in Trinitarian moral formation and ethics. *Trinitarian* also means recognizing the Trinity as being one in essence and communion (coinherence) and that the undivided and perichoretic nature of the Trinity has implications for moral formation and ethics as being communal and ecclesial. *Trinitarian,* as already noted, is a way of saying that the concept and reality of irreducible human persons is derived from the concept and reality of irreducible persons within the Holy Trinity, not in a univocal way but by way of analogy and by means of the bridging of the divine-human person of Christ. This has two consequences for human persons: (1) they are persons of irreducible identity, and therefore there is a personal nature to ethics, but (2) they are by definition "persons-in-relation" and as such communal and specifically ecclesial. Human persons are neither collectivist nor atomistic. They are communal and personal. We will therefore introduce these Trinitarian aspects of personhood and community and develop them in subsequent chapters.

---

62. See Jonathan Edwards, *Religious Affections,* YE 2:238, for just one example. As Gerald McDermott claims, Edwards's aesthetic vision "distinguishes him as probably the foremost of Christian theologians who relate God and beauty." Gerald McDermott, review of *The Sermons of Jonathan Edwards: A Reader,* ed. Wilson H. Kimnach, Kenneth P. Minkema, and Douglas A. Sweeney, American Religious Experience, December 1999, http://are.as.wvu.edu/mcderm .htm. Robert Jenson sums up his own important study of Edwards (*America's Theologian*) in this fashion: "As we have had occasion to note in almost every chapter, the very template of his vision is that God as Triunity is 'the supreme Harmony of all.' . . . Indeed, he did not merely maintain trinitarianism; he renewed it." Robert Jenson, *America's Theologian: A Recommendation of Jonathan Edwards* (New York: Oxford University Press, 1988), 91.

The Trinitarian caption is the most comprehensive, evangelical, personal, communal, and participation-based model, one that includes virtue ethics but clarifies its source in union with Christ and offers the category of personhood as larger than character though inclusive of it.

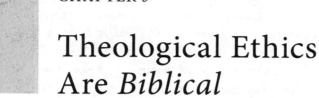

CHAPTER 3

Theological Ethics
Are *Biblical*

If ethics is theological and Trinitarian, where does this leave the role of the Bible in ethics? As an evangelical theologian committed to the teaching of the Bible about itself, that it is the God-breathed and final authority on all matters of faith and practice, I believe the answer is pretty clear. The Scriptures that made Timothy "wise for salvation through faith in Christ Jesus" (2 Tim. 3:15) are affirmed as having their origin in God and as designated for the doctrine and practice of the church: "All Scripture is God-breathed and is useful for teaching, rebuking, correcting and training in righteousness, so that the servant of God may be thoroughly equipped for every good work" (2 Tim. 3:16–17). One could say the Scriptures are the church's authoritative source for theology ("teaching," or "doctrine," KJV) and ethics ("rebuking, correcting and training in righteousness, so that the servant of God may be thoroughly equipped for every good work").

THE CRUCIAL PLACE OF HOLY SCRIPTURE IN CHRISTIAN THEOLOGY AND ETHICS

All of the magisteria in the great tradition of the Christian church, Catholic, Orthodox, and Protestant, profess that the Holy Scriptures are the final authority in all matters of doctrine and ethics. They may differ in the nuanced ways they see the relationship between the church and the Scriptures and on who may interpret them competently, but at the end of the day it is the question of what the Holy Scriptures teach that is definitive and determinative for dogmatics and ethics in all the traditions. As a Protestant theologian, I adhere to the creeds as a distillation of the essentials of Christian theology, but with Karl Barth, I believe that although they are an important authority for the church, they are to be considered at a level (of authority) below that of Scripture.

If Scripture is *norma normans*, the norming norm or guiding principle for determining biblical truth, the creeds are *norma normata*, the thing normed or guided by the norming norm.[1] One might add that the scholarly work of the great theologians, or "doctors," of the church throughout the ages stands also in the same relationship to the Scriptures and the creeds. Tradition, as it is sometimes called, has a subservient but real role in how we interpret the Scriptures. *Sola Scriptura* is not the same as *nuda Scriptura*. The first allows for the person studying Scripture to be informed by the community of scholarship that is deep and wide: deep in that it goes back throughout the history of the church to hear the community of scholars who inform our study, and wide because it must consider the scholarship that is being done in the countries and cultures across the world. *Nuda scriptura* is the idea that I can study my Bible on my own, "just the Holy Spirit and me," and hope to interpret it without any reference to church community, past and present. One sometimes hears this last approach professed with pride amongst some evangelical Christians. It is the equivalent in salvation theology of professing it is just "Jesus and me" when in fact our faith is mediated by the church past and present. There is a valid personal aspect to our saving encounter with Christ, one that evangelicals treasure, but it must be accompanied by an awareness that most often we meet Jesus as he is presented to us by the church and by Christians we know. We cannot meet Jesus without being bonded to everyone else who has met Jesus. This is signified by baptism into Christ and therefore into the church. Similarly for reading the Bible, we are given grace to understand it adequately for salvation as persons, but we cannot grow in our interpreting it outside of the church community.

It is important to say as a theologian that I respect the distinction that is made between biblical studies and theology. The guilds have their own rightful existence in the academy. However, I equally affirm that there can be no separation of these guilds.[2] They are in an iterative relationship

---

1. Karl Barth, *CD* I/1, 112–17. Barth's affirmation of the personal revelation of God in the Son as primary regrettably led him to fail to affirm Scripture *as* revelation; instead, Barth sees Scripture as a witness to revelation. His high view of preaching (if it was exegetical and enabled by the Spirit) as the word of the human preacher becoming the word of God is to be commended.

2. Princeton Reformed theologian B. B. Warfield made an impassioned plea toward biblical scholars in this regard: "It is hoped that the time will come when no commentary will be considered complete until the capstone is placed upon its fabric by closing chapters gathering up into systematized exhibits, the unsystematized results of the continuous exegesis of the text in the

that does go both ways. First, exegesis of the text, as arrived at by the hard work that is involved in historical, grammatical, rhetorical (genre), and contextual interpretation (immediate and wider canonical context), leads to statements about the text that cannot help but be theological! Fear of ontotheological statements may be understandable, but the product of exegesis is unavoidably theological. But second, knowledge of the essentials of Christian theology as has been present in the church before the canon was complete, from New Testament times ("the faith that was once for all entrusted to God's holy people," Jude 3), through the patristic era (the rule of faith), and on into the postcanon era as expressed in the creeds, has guided the exegetes or biblical scholars. In particular, the gospel of the triune God of grace as revealed in Christ has been the church exegete's interpreter. Theology and biblical studies belong to each other.[3]

Thus the Scriptures are crucial for the moral formation of the Christian, our "training in righteousness" as Paul puts it. And they are crucial also for moral and ethical discernment and for guidance in ethical living. Biblical assertions cannot be taken for granted in contemporary evangelical church culture, where the enculturation of the church has led many within it to be guided by cultural narratives of individualism and "rights" of all kinds—the right to sex outside of marriage between a man and a woman, the right to take my own life when I choose, the right to gun ownership, and so on. To be sure, awareness of contemporary culture is crucial if we are to avoid indiscriminate enculturation. In biblical interpretation, awareness of the culture within which biblical texts are embedded is also important, as are the steps to transposing their meaning appropriately for today. But this can be done. However, the assertions that follow from the biblical text when properly interpreted cannot be taken for granted in evangelical scholarship where revisionism of texts related especially to matters of sexual ethics has led some prominent leaders within evangelicalism to move from nonaffirming to affirming stances on homosexual marriage. The hermeneutics of inclusion have trumped the hermeneutics of discipleship, which are grounded in the

---

spheres of history, ethics, theology, and the like." B. B. Warfield, *Studies in Theology* (Edinburgh: Banner of Truth, 1988), 65. There is no such thing as exegesis without theology and vice versa.

3. B. B. Warfield is noted for his perspective that systematic theology is built from biblical theology, which in turn is built on exegesis of the biblical text. See B. B. Warfield, "The Idea of Systematic Theology," *Presbyterian and Reformed Review* 7, no. 26 (1896): 243–71.

consistent witness of Holy Scripture in the Old and New Testaments and in the witness of the scholars of the church from the church fathers to the present.

SCRIPTURE AND MORAL FORMATION

What internal evidence do we have that the Scriptures are intended to form people morally with respect to both character and action? It does seem to me necessary to affirm both character and action, given what we have said in the previous chapter about *persons* being a larger category than *character*. The nature of the image of God as it is conveyed in the beginning of the biblical narrative, specifically that it is not just ontological and relational but also *functional*, is evidence of this holistic nature of what God wished to image in us and requires of us.

Both the Old and the New Testaments contain many direct statements about the role of the Scriptures in moral formation and action. Just a few will suffice to make the point (consideration of the great ethical centre of the Old Testament, and indeed the New Testament, in Exodus 20 is developed below). The Psalms, which form part of the Old Testament but became also the inheritance of the New Testament people (Eph. 5:19), speak of this sanctifying role of the Word repeatedly. Psalm 119, which has the word for the Word or the Scriptures (using a variety of terms like *law, words, statutes, commands, precepts*) in almost every one of its 176 verses, is a tribute to the transformative power of the Word of God. By way of example, the psalmist says in verse 2, "Blessed are those who keep his statutes and seek him with all their heart." The lifestyle actions are grounded first in a heart that has been formed and transformed to seek God; seeking God with a transformed heart does not mean that the psalmist is separated from obedience to his moral commands. There is no doubt about the source of moral formation for the young person being tutored by this psalmist:

> How can a young person stay on the path of purity?
>   By living according to your word.
> I *seek you with all my heart*;
>   do not let me stray from your commands.
> I have *hidden your word in my heart*
>   that I might not sin against you. (vv. 9–11, emphasis added)

Another instance of this, this time related to *doing* good, is found in verse 168: "I obey your precepts and your statutes, for all my ways are known to you." It is observable that, as in this verse, the context for obedience is always covenant relationship with God, not legal motivation. In another section (vv. 127–28), the psalmist states,

> Because I love your commands
> > more than gold, more than pure gold,
> and because I consider all your precepts right,
> > I hate every wrong path.

That the psalmist has undergone heart transformation, which has changed his affections and stoked his love for the Word of God, is a crucial piece of the puzzle. The psalmist's deep spirituality points to a great continuity between the people of God in the Old and New Testaments. Both are to have the written Word of God before them for moral formation and ethical action, for being good and doing good. The whole Psalter actually opens on this note. The avoidance of immoral and unethical counsel, sinful ways, and mockery is enabled by a "delight in the law of the LORD," upon which he "meditates day and night" and in so doing reflects shalom, the flourishing ("like a tree planted by streams of water, which yields its fruit in season and whose leaf does not wither") that characterizes those who follow *torah* and its Giver (Psalm 1:1–3).

In the New Testament, similarly, Paul equates the "fulness of the Holy Spirit" (see Eph. 5:18), the spiritual dynamic for the moral ethic of the gospel, with the "word of Christ," appealing to believers to let it "dwell among [them] richly" (Col. 3:16, which is followed by commands of an ethical nature that are almost identical to those in Eph. 5:18–6:4). The author of Hebrews similarly expresses the value of the Word of God for moral formation and especially for making ethical judgments: "For the word of God is alive and active. Sharper than any double-edged sword, it penetrates even to dividing soul and spirit, joints and marrow; it judges the thoughts and attitudes of the heart. Nothing in all creation is hidden from God's sight. Everything is uncovered and laid bare before the eyes of him to whom we must give account" (Heb. 4:12–13).

If the church is to develop morally formed Christians, and if it is to wisely address the great moral crises of our time, it must preach and teach the Word of God extensively. It must do so in an expository fashion that enables the words of the preacher to become the words of God and so enable frequent encounters with the living Word. It must, through preaching and personal pastoral care, seek to make disciples who are avid Bible readers.

GUIDELINES FOR INTERPRETING SCRIPTURE FOR ETHICS

But what are the guidelines needed in *interpreting* biblical ethical material properly? It is evident from observation of the biblical narrative and the content of Scripture in both Testaments that *torah*, the revelation of God's law centred in the Ten Commandments, is the primary foundation and form of biblical ethical material. Attention must be paid, of course, to the nature of the God who gave this revelation and the unconditional nature of the covenant framework and ethos within which this ethical material is first given and then expounded in the rest of Scripture. The theological and Trinitarian nature of ethics, which is the witness of the whole biblical narrative (as expressed in the previous chapters), must be carried with us as we seek wisdom for interpreting biblical ethical material. That is, the theological, gospel, covenantal nature of *torah* must be stressed. Its nature as a reflection of the moral order of the creation must also be stressed. The burden of the book of Proverbs is to speak of a moral order related to a created order and of a wisdom that is not mere intellectual acumen, but moral acumen. Wise people are people who are skilled in living, who live rightly and justly in relationship. They are people who do so by going with the grain of the creation and not against it. *Torah* is gift, the very expression of God's moral order, the grain of the universe.[4] It is not bondage but the only way to be free. It must be stressed that *torah* lived in this way is a source of the shalom, or flourishing, intended for humans made in the image of God. So even the old covenant is given in gospel tones. Then,

---

4. This is not to advocate for some form of New Age or "mother earth" pantheism or any natural theology that is not informed and qualified by God's revelation of himself in the history of Israel and most lucidly in the Word himself, Jesus Christ. See Stanley Hauerwas, *With the Grain of the Universe: The Church's Witness and Natural Theology* (Grand Rapids: Brazos, 2001), which is a sustained argument that natural theology is only intelligible when it is considered as one branch of a christological, Trinitarian revelation of the being of God. It is thus a vindication of Barth's viewpoint that the most important voice to a postrationalist, postmodern world is the church's witness to the revelation of God in Jesus Christ through its gathered life.

as to content, we must pay attention to transcovenantal continuities and discontinuities to ascertain what was particular to Israel as a community and what transcends it.

Torah as Transcovenantal Core of Biblical Ethics

First, the statement that *torah* is the substantial core of biblical ethical material needs to be justified. It is important to clarify what we mean and what we do not mean when we say *torah*. To reiterate, *torah* can never be isolated from crucial Old Testament concepts of covenant and human persons made in the image of God. At the core of Judaism is the concept of covenant, which in turn subsumes the totality of the relationship of Yahweh with the whole created order. Alan Torrance has outlined three key elements to the essential grammar of that covenant of God with his people and the creation:

1. "the divine covenant is unilaterally established by God with humanity (it is not a mutual, bilateral arrangement);
2. it is unconditional and thus unconditioned by considerations of human worth—it is free;
3. this prior, unconditional and unconditioned covenant commitment in the part of Yahweh carries equally unconditioned obligations—the apodictic obligations summarized in the 'ten words' of the *Torah*."[5]

For these reasons, Karl Barth, following the apostle Paul, emphatically insisted that the "*indicatives of grace precede and sustain the imperatives of law.*"[6] To get this the wrong way around would be to conceive of the "relationship between God and humanity as *contractual* rather than *covenantal.*"[7] It has often been noted that before any words of *ought* are given by God in the Ten Commandments, he speaks a gospel, covenantal word of *is*: "I am the LORD your God, who brought you out of Egypt, out of the land of slavery." And then and only then, "You shall have no other gods before me," and so on (Ex. 20:2–3). The response of the people of God to his unconditional, covenant faithfulness is to "co-respond by

---

5. Alan Torrance, "On Deriving 'Ought' from 'Is,'" in *The Doctrine of God and Theological Ethics*, ed. Alan J. Torrance and Michael Banner (London: T&T Clark, 2006), 172.
6. Torrance, "On Deriving 'Ought' from 'Is,'" 172, emphasis original.
7. Torrance, "On Deriving 'Ought' from 'Is,'" 172, emphasis original.

'imaging,' by reflecting, God's faithfulness to her."[8] This is an important aspect of the fundamentally relational and covenantal meaning of the *imago Dei*. The part of the people was to be "unconditionally faithful to God and to each other,"[9] to their spouses, and to their neighbours. In other words, in response to God's covenant love, they love.

For this reason, New Testament scholar E. P. Sanders suggested that when Jesus uttered the Great Commandment, he was expounding, not contradicting, the heart of Judaism.[10] Another New Testament scholar, Richard Hays, is in sympathy with this. Hays states, for example, that the world according to Matthew's Gospel is "a world stabilized and given meaning by the authoritative presence of Jesus Christ," and that in that world "the Father of Jesus Christ is the same God who gave the Torah through Moses; even though Jesus has brought a new interpretative perspective on the Torah, it remains abidingly active. Thus the moral order of God's dealing with the world remains stable and continuous."[11] What is that new interpretative perspective? Jesus on the one hand is simply repeating the *shema* of Deuteronomy 6:5 in giving the "love God" command, and he joins it to what was already in Leviticus 19:18, "You shall love your neighbor as yourself." However, Hays points out that Matthew's addition to Mark's rendering of Jesus's pronouncement, "On these two commandments hang all the law and the prophets" (Matt. 22:40), introduces a subtle but important claim. Hays explains that the double love commandment is not just the greatest of the Torah's commands, but that it has become "a hermeneutical filter—virtually synonymous with Hosea 6:6—that governs the community's entire construal of the Law."[12] He concludes that Matthew's moral vision is that "those who are trained for the kingdom of God are trained to evaluate all norms, even the norms of the Law itself, in terms of the criteria of love and mercy."[13] Just how new to the New Testament this is, is debatable. Jesus seems to be radicalizing and reviving what God had instituted, as he does in the Sermon on the Mount, where he repeatedly says, "You have heard it said, but I say . . ." Jesus does not delete the

---

8. Torrance, "On Deriving 'Ought' from 'Is,'" 172.

9. Torrance, "On Deriving 'Ought' from 'Is,'" 172.

10. Torrance, "On Deriving 'Ought' from 'Is,'" 173.

11. Richard Hays, *The Moral Vision of the New Testament: A Contemporary Introduction to New Testament Ethics* (Edinburgh: T&T Clark, 1997), 109.

12. Hays, *Moral Vision of the New Testament*, 109.

13. Hays, *Moral Vision of the New Testament*, 109.

Ten Commandments for the new-covenant era, but he reinforces them, taking them back to their original deep meaning. Certainly, if all the law hangs on this double love commandment, we may conclude safely that the Ten Commandments are simply being summarized by Jesus under the headings "Loving God" and "Loving neighbour" in response to the love of God and, as the New Testament more fully reveals, *in participation with God.*

Evidence from the Image of God and Torah

Yet even the concept of participation in the life of God is present in the Old Testament from the start. Torrance maintains that the "underlying conceptuality of covenant communion is in fact the key to interpreting the telos of creation," which is the concept of the image of God. The purpose of the creation of men and women was that they might live in communion with God and thereby participate in God's relationship with creation (the functional aspect of the *imago Dei*). The image was neither to be usurped nor replicated,[14] says Torrance. Rather, "they were to be co-responding participants and 'image' God's faithfulness," and as such to be dwelling with God "in koinonial correspondence to God's faithfulness towards his creatures."[15] In sum, the concepts of covenant, *imago Dei*, and *torah* are "intrinsically interrelated in the Hexateuch [the first six books of the Bible] and interpret each other by articulating a theology of koinonial participation."[16] We may conclude from this, as Torrance does, that (1) the *imago Dei* does not entail "some internal, individualistically conceived ethical or epistemic capacity,"[17] an assumption that is elsewhere called "the epistemic immanence of ethical criteria"[18] (an assumption that will be tested later in discussion with the Thomistic *analogia entis* concept that undergirds natural law ethics of creation assumptions[19]), but is rather concerned with "being

---

14. Torrance, "On Deriving 'Ought' from 'Is,'" 173.
15. Torrance, "On Deriving 'Ought' from 'Is,'" 173.
16. Torrance, "On Deriving 'Ought' from 'Is,'" 173.
17. Torrance, "On Deriving 'Ought' from 'Is,'" 173.
18. Torrance, "On Deriving 'Ought' from 'Is,'" 177.
19. The appeal to nature is evident in a teaching guide released by the Vatican on June 10, 2019, called "Male and Female He Created Them." It affirms the binary nature of human sexuality and standard biblical positions on matters of human sexuality and transgenderism. It addresses trends in society as having generated an "educational crisis," indicating that the current debate can *"annihilate the concept of nature"* (emphasis added) and "destabilise the family institution." See "Vatican Issues Guidance Questioning Modern Gender Identity," BBC News, https://www.bbc .com/news/world-europe-48584892. One is grateful for the Roman Catholic Church's consistent

created as human beings to correspond to—to reflect/image—the unconditional faithfulness of the covenant-God";[20] (2) the covenant of God with humanity is "emphatically non-contractual," meaning that it is grounded in Yahweh's unconditional and unconditioned covenant to be faithful to his creation and is co-responded to with "an equally unconditional or apodeictic obligation";[21] (3) the concept of law as *torah* is not to be confused with Stoic or Latin readings of *lex* that might easily "open the door to contractual renderings of God's orientation toward humanity grounded in an essentially legislative will," an error that Torrance believes to have been made by Scholasticism of both the Catholic medieval kind and that of sixteenth- and seventeenth-century Reformed theology; and (4) the "grammar of the categories of covenant (*bᵉrît*), covenant faithfulness (*hesed*) and *torah* are fundamentally *filial* (and not *legal*) in character," and "any legislative function requires to be interpreted in this [koinonial and participative] context."[22]

Covenant, creation, and the image of God are similarly integrated in the witness of the early church, as reflected in the New Testament, as we have already noted. *Imago Dei* becomes embodied in the person of Christ, as the fulfilment of what was eternally God's covenantal and creational plan (Col. 1:15). As such, Jesus the incarnate Son lives as the elect suffering servant of God who fulfils *torah* to the full for humanity. He does so in a context in which he reveals himself to be the one who institutes (Luke 22:20) and mediates the new covenant (as interpreted by the author of Hebrews in Heb. 8:3–13) and the new creation (2 Cor. 5:17; Gal. 6:15). As the *eschatos* Adam and the "priest of creation," Jesus inverts "the dynamics associated with the old Adam"[23] and the old creation. In contrast with the first Adam, who lifted himself up in pride to know good and evil apart from communion with God, the last Adam did not consider equality with God something to be grasped but humbled himself so as to embody the imaging of God and his covenantal commitment. The "koinonial character" of this is revealed "in the identification of the New Creation with the Body of Christ," the

---

ethical stances, even if one might prefer an evangelical rather than a natural law approach in the public square.

20. Torrance, "On Deriving 'Ought' from 'Is,'" 173.
21. Torrance, "On Deriving 'Ought' from 'Is,'" 173.
22. Torrance, "On Deriving 'Ought' from 'Is,'" 173.
23. Torrance, "On Deriving 'Ought' from 'Is,'" 174.

church.[24] The church is spoken of as the new humanity (Eph. 2:15), and its character is one of participative communion with the image of the invisible God (being "in Christ"). This is a communion in which *torah* has already been fulfiled for us in Christ, yet it is one in which by the Spirit we are empowered to fulfil: "For what the law was powerless to do because it was weakened by the flesh, God did by sending his own Son in the likeness of sinful flesh to be a sin offering. And so he condemned sin in the flesh, in order that the righteous requirement of the law might be fully met in us, who do not live according to the flesh but according to the Spirit" (Rom. 8:3–4).

We may conclude, therefore, that there is legitimacy to a theological ethic centred on the image of God as fulfilled in Jesus Christ *and* a theological ethic that has a place for *torah*—and indeed one that states that these are inseparable.

Evidence from the Nature of Torah

However, when we say that *torah* is all-important and transcovenantal, it is important to recognize the concepts that undergird and surround, indeed are endemic to, *torah*. It is preceded and immersed in the gospel of the unconditional covenant of God to humanity. It is that which persons made in the image of God fulfil as co-responders to and with God. And it will be important to make the distinctions that the New Testament makes: that we are not justified by the works of the law, that law is not the primary ethos of Christian life, yet that it has a normative role in Christian life and ethics. One cannot hope to make ethical judgments apart from what the commandments say and their interpretation across the Testaments. The practice of expounding the Ten Commandments in the life of the church was modelled in the Reformation tradition, perhaps most notably by John Calvin, who did so employing the literary tool called synecdoche (the part stands for the whole).[25] This means that if the commandment is stated in the negative, its positive corollary must be true, and vice versa. The positive of the first commandment, "You shall have no other gods" (Ex. 20:3), is expressed in Deuteronomy 6:5 as "Love the LORD your God with all your heart and with all your soul and with all your strength," which Jesus

---

24. Torrance, "On Deriving 'Ought' from 'Is,'" 174.
25. See John Calvin, *Institutes of The Christian Religion*, trans. H. Beveridge (Grand Rapids: Eerdmans, 1995), 2.8.9, pp. 169–70.

repeats (Matt. 22:37), and similarly, "Fear the LORD your God, serve him only" (Deut. 6:13), which Jesus reaffirms in his triumph over the devil's temptation (Matt. 4:10). The fourth commandment, regarding the sabbath, which is stated in the positive, implies a theology and ethic of work and workaholism. The seventh commandment, "You shall not commit adultery," becomes "Love your spouse faithfully and fully give yourself to her/him." And so on. Calvin taught the commandments in both negative and positive modes and as they appear in both the Old and New Testaments. He did so undergirded by what he believed to be the three legitimate uses of the law (a civil use for the state, a convicting use for the sinner, and a normative use for the Christian, as outlined in more detail below), which included its normative function in Christian ethics. Calvin understood what we have been saying about the unconditional, covenantal, gospel context in which this is true (even if some of his followers did not). This practice of expounding both the negative and positive forms of the commandments signals another rationale for the continuity between the covenants with respect to the *torah* as ethical material.

One approach to theological ethics is to treat each commandment as an area code that can encompass every area of ethics, but it must be clear that this can only function in light of what has been said about the ethos of these ethical considerations. That is, *torah* as expression of the unconditional covenant of God to be for humanity and creation, *torah* as fulfilment of image bearing, a co-responding hearing and obedience in participation with the one who is the image of the invisible God and who has made us his body and the new humanity.

Evidence from the New Covenant

A further evidence of its transcovenantal and substantial importance is that the law plays a significant role in how the *new covenant* is voiced in both testaments. In Jeremiah 31, when the new covenant is anticipated, the law is not abrogated or dispelled from God's dealings with his people. It remains. It is, however, internalized. The covenant, which has as its core God's unconditional expression of belonging to his people and they to him ("I will be their God, and they will be my people," Jer. 31:33—a *filial* reality is its foundation) and their intimate knowing of the Lord (v. 34), and which has as its forensic basis a statement of God's forgiveness of his people (v. 34, forensic justification, one might say), does not neglect the law and its role in forming and guiding God's people: "'This is the covenant I will make with the people of Israel after that time,' declares the LORD. 'I will put my law in their minds and write it on their hearts'" (v. 33, sanctification including ethics, one might say). In Ezekiel we learn that the internalization of the *torah* is the work of the Holy Spirit: "I will give you a new heart and put a new spirit in you; I will remove from you your heart of stone and give you a heart of flesh. And I will put my Spirit in you and move you to follow my decrees and be careful to keep my laws" (Ezek. 36:26–27). Notice that the work of the Holy Spirit is not contrary to the law understood in this covenantal way. He is the empowering that brings about both formation around *torah* and the following of its decrees in practical living. Hebrews 8 is where we find the fulfilment of the new covenant instanced and expounded for the New Testament people of God, who are the people of the one priest of the covenant—a priesthood of believers, yes, but first a priesthood in the one great high priesthood of Christ, who has borne the penalty of the broken law by his life and death for us, and who lives to empower us for holy living that includes, as a minimum, observing the shalom-giving law of God.

A significant theme of Hebrews is that Christ is the mediator of the new covenant and that he does so as both the supreme priest and the sacrifice of that covenant. As high priest he offers the sacrifice that enables God to forgive his people *and* enables God's people to become holy: "For by one sacrifice he has made perfect forever those who are being made holy" (Heb. 10:14). As high priest he is the one God-man in whom humanity becomes human again; he is the one Human who took humanity into himself and cleansed it, the last (*eschatos*) Adam (Heb. 2). He is the one who ever lives to make intercession for us (Heb. 7:25) so that "on the basis of the power of an indestructible life" (Heb. 7:16) he is "the guarantor of a better covenant" (Heb. 7:22).

In sum, we may say that a transcovenantal validity of *torah* is grounded in these texts from the Old and New Testaments. There is a graphic picture of this in the Jewish feasts of Yahweh outlined in Leviticus 23. Passover anticipated the redemption enacted by the Passover lamb (1 Cor. 5:7). The Feast of Firstfruits, which marked the beginning of the harvesting of the barley crop three days later, is fulfilled in the resurrection of Jesus (1 Cor. 15:20, 23). But on the day of Pentecost, fifty days from the first Sunday of Passover, two loaves were made from the harvest, perhaps anticipating the birth of the church that consisted of both Jews and gentiles. On Pentecost Sunday the church celebrates the climax of redemption, which is the indwelling of the third person of the Trinity. It also celebrates the beginning of a new and intimate relationship between Christ and his people, the church, made up of every nation. It celebrates becoming the expression of Christ on earth to bring revelation to the world as the story of Acts 2 confirms. If Christ became incarnate to bring revelation and redemption, then we, in a derived and secondary sense, become his body to bring revelation and redemption for him whilst he is in heaven. There is, in fact, another set of Jewish traditions behind the Feast of Pentecost that accentuate this aspect of its application. This tradition arose in the intertestamental period or what is referred to as later Judaism. They made a chronological deduction from Exodus 19:1 that Pentecost was the anniversary of the giving of the law at Sinai. God gave the law to Moses in the third month after the Exodus. Pentecost was therefore considered by the Jewish people the "birthday" of Judaism. Both the giving of the law and the notion that this marked the birth of Israel find an interesting parallelism with the notion that on the Day of Pentecost in Acts 2 the church was birthed because the Spirit was given. The relevance of this parallelism becomes apparent when we apply the rubric of "covenant." Under the old covenant, the law was given in writing on two tablets of stone, and this marked the birth of the old covenant people of Israel on the first Pentecost after the first Passover. If Christ's sacrifice on the cross fulfilled the type of the first Passover, it is not improbable that the Day of Pentecost following Jesus's death should fulfil the symbolism of the first Pentecost, and this is the critical point—to fulfil the new covenant and apply it to the hearts of the new covenant people necessitated the coming of the Holy Spirit. Why? If the law was now to be written on hearts rather than stone tablets, the Spirit would need to indwell and renew and write that law there. And this is exactly what the Old Testament Scriptures on the new covenant anticipated, as we have seen.

Evidence from the Decalogue in Its Transcovenantal Usage

More evidence of the transcovenantal validity of *torah* for the people of God is that the Ten Commandments are repeated in the New Testament and expounded as ethical material. A revered professor of Christian ethics at Regent College, Klaus Bockmuehl, has gone as far as to say that there is no new ethical material in the New Testament. He saw basic Christian ethics as an exposition of the Decalogue in both Testaments in the way of Calvin.[26] It is true that the New Testament reveals more about the gospel grounding for ethics given that it is post-Christ rather than pre-Christ. It also reflects the democratizing of life in the Spirit for all of God's people in the New Testament church, not just special prophets, priests, and kings, as in the Old Testament, and the permanent rather than transient nature of the indwelling and empowering of the Spirit. The New Testament also hints at the fact that keeping the law definitely does not save people, and that it is a secondary, almost natural consequence of being in Christ and walking in the Spirit. Thus, for example, when Paul in Galatians 5:22–23 completes his list of the fruit of the Spirit, he does so with an odd phrase: "Against such things there is no law." It is as if to say, when you live in intimate relationship with Christ by the Spirit, these graces will be formed in you, and you will have found that you have kept the law without trying or making the law your aim. Law keeping is not the *gestalt* or ultimate aim of Christian life; life in the Spirit is. But the latter will include the former as a bare minimum. Paul explains in the following verses that Christian life has as its focus participation with Christ in death and resurrection, life lived in an intimate keeping in step with the Spirit: "Those who belong to Jesus Christ have crucified the flesh with its passions and desires. Since we live by the Spirit, let us keep in step with the Spirit" (Gal. 5:24–25). Nevertheless, Christian antinomianism is not permitted by Paul. Christians do keep the law. One could say they "get to" keep the law.

True Christian ethics is the freedom of a life ensconced in Christ, in the gospel of union with Christ by the Spirit, in the gospel of the love of God, who is for humanity in covenant faithfulness. It is a "being in Christ" in response to the Word of Christ that creates and forms us and that speaks to us in every situation. It is to live in love as loved by God, and it is to live out the love of God by love to God and neighbour in community. This understanding of the theology in theological ethics is what makes ethics a thing of freedom, not bondage. A freedom *from . . .* the weightiness of a life of "I should" in which the law or expectations of

---

26. With affection and humour, students called the course Bockmuehl taught on the Decalogue the "Six Commandments" because he almost never finished all ten in the term.

others hang over us. A freedom from sins and vices that are the product of our fleshly orientation and that may be the result of brokenness from what has been done to us by broken people in our lives. And a freedom *for* . . . for life, for shalom, for flourishing, for virtues to be formed in us in union with Christ and by the Spirit's grace and power. Freedom for ethical discernment and just judgments that are not made from some kind of "Bible rule book of ethical answers" that is the result of casuistry (a compilation of precedents based on multiple cases in the past). There is a *torah* but not a Talmud in Christian ethics. Rather, we have freedom for being and acting in the following way, which sums up our approach to theological ethics: to engage boldly in prayerful consideration of each fresh situation as it comes to us in its uniqueness; to do so as a *person* in union with the wise and personal triune God, a person growing in *character*; as such to seek to hear the Word of God from *outside of ourselves* (all that Scripture in both testaments, properly interpreted, has to say to the issue); to do so in conscious dependence upon the Holy Spirit *inside of ourselves*; to do so in consultation with other persons of wisdom in the past in the whole Christian tradition (where precedence may indeed be helpful) and in the present (people of wisdom and knowledge in fields that are relevant to the ethical case); and to entrust ourselves to the grace of a merciful God, staying conscious of the fact that we may still make mistakes in a fallen world in which the kingdom has come but has not yet fully.

Evidence from the Transcovenantal Primacy of Love

Further evidence for continuity between the Testaments, which guides our interpretation of the ethical material of the Bible, is the theme of *love*. Jesus reaffirms the commandments when he is asked, "Teacher, which is the greatest commandment in the Law?" (Matt. 22:36). His response is well known: "'Love the Lord your God with all your heart and with all your soul and with all your mind.' This is the first and greatest commandment. And the second is like it: 'Love your neighbor as yourself.' All the Law and the Prophets hang on these two commandments" (Matt. 22:37–40). Beyond the significance of these words for uniting the revelation of God to humanity and for uniting the people of God under both covenants, this summary of the commandments into the two love commandments has powerful theological, spiritual, and ethical import.

Their convicting nature is obvious—for who can keep this law? This was one of the reasons in addition to passages like Galatians 3:24–25 ("So the law was our guardian ["schoolmaster," KJV] until Christ came that we might be justified by faith. Now that this faith has come, we are no longer under a guardian") and Romans 7:7, 12 ("Is the law sinful? Certainly not! . . . For I would not have known what coveting really was if the law had not said, 'You shall not covet.' . . . The law is holy, and the commandment is holy, righteous and good") that the Reformers spoke of the "use" of the law for this era as the convicting use (*usus elenchticus*). The other two uses of the law that Philip Melanchthon[27] outlined were the civil use (*usus civilus*), based on passages like 1 Timothy 1:8–11 ("We know that the law is good if one uses it properly. We also know that the law is made not for the righteous but for lawbreakers and rebels, the ungodly and sinful, the unholy and irreligious, for those who kill their fathers or mothers, for murderers, for the sexually immoral, for those practicing homosexuality, for slave traders and liars and perjurers—and for whatever else is contrary to the sound doctrine that conforms to the gospel concerning the glory of the blessed God, which he entrusted to me") and Romans 2:14–15 ("Indeed, when Gentiles, who do not have the law, do by nature things required by the law, they are a law for themselves, even though they do not have the law. They show that the requirements of the law are written on their hearts, their consciences also bearing witness, and their thoughts sometimes accusing them and at other times even defending them") and the teaching use (*usus normativus*). This normative use assumed that the Ten Commandments as summarized in the twofold Great Commandment and were thus the norm for Christian ethics. This was based on passages like Romans 13:8–10 ("Let no debt remain outstanding, except the continuing debt to love one another, for whoever loves others has fulfilled the law. The commandments, 'You shall not commit adultery,' 'You shall not murder,' 'You shall not steal,' 'You shall not covet,' and whatever other command there may be, are summed up in this one command: 'Love your neighbor as yourself.' Love does no harm to a neighbor. Therefore love is the fulfillment of the law") and Romans 8:4 ("in order that the righteous requirements of the law might be fully met in us, who do not

---

27. Philip Melanchthon, *Loci Communes rerum theologicarum seu hypotyposes theologicae* (versions from 1521, 1535, 1555), in *Melanchthon on Christian Doctrine*, trans. and ed. Clyde L. Manschreck (Oxford: Oxford University Press, 1965).

live according to the flesh but according to the Spirit"). This summing up of the commandments by Paul into the Great Commandment (see also Gal. 5:14), at least the second half of it, as well as the assumption that one cannot separate them, gives evidence that there is indeed no new ethical material in the New Testament. Ensconced by participation in Christ and motivated by the grace of God, we are empowered by the Spirit to live out the commands in both their negative and positive forms. As Bockmuehl has written, "The Ten Commandments, shorn of their curse and condemnation, return to the regenerate believer as ethical instruction, lights by which to steer the life of sanctification."[28]

THE PRIMACY OF LOVE . . . THAT HAS ETHICAL CONTENT

A primary presupposition of our approach to theological ethics, therefore, will be the primacy of love, but without diminishing the importance of the moral law, the Decalogue, as expounded in Old and New Testaments and as unified by Jesus himself in the "love commandment" (love God and neighbour). As Oliver O'Donovan has stated, "Love is the principle which confers unifying order both upon the moral field and upon the character of the moral subject. It is the fulfilment of the moral law on the one hand, and the form of the virtues on the other."[29] That love commandment is, as we shall affirm, the summary of the moral law, not a priority over the moral law (as in situational theology).

This assertion challenges a cherished value of our times, upending the oft-heard question: How can love ever be wrong? If two people respect each other, and if they want to express their love in sexual ways outside of the covenant of marriage between a man and a woman, how can this love be wrong? The problem with this reasoning is that it contains the assumption that there is no moral content to love, that love and morality are in opposition to one another, and that prohibitions placed on sexual expression cannot possibly be loving. If there is no moral content to love as Jesus suggested by summarizing the commandments with two love commands (which are really united), then how can limits be applied to

---

28. Klaus Bockmuehl, *The Christian Way of Living: An Ethics of the Ten Commandments* (Vancouver: Regent College Publishing, 1994), 22.
29. Oliver O'Donovan, *Resurrection and Moral Order: An Outline for Evangelical Ethics* (Grand Rapids: Eerdmans, 1986), 226.

love's expression? What makes pedophilia wrong then? What criteria do we use for saying adultery is wrong if two people say they fell in love and it just feels right? There is no love without morality; indeed, love is both the means and the telos of the moral life. To say it another way, love cannot be separated from holiness.

With respect to the great commandment to love God and neighbour, it is important to stress that these are not two loves but one. There is a duality, but it is a *duality-in-unity*. The *duality* arises necessarily because the second love command is toward persons who are created and therefore are not God. Creation is not the self-differentiation of God (pantheism) but the making of a world *ex nihilo*. Love of neighbour is thus love of something that is not God, and this love is to be kept distinct from love of God. The love-of-neighbour stream of the one love command, although distinct, is inseparable from the first stream.

In what sense is the love for God and man a *unity*? Love of neighbour originates in and has its end in love of God. Love of neighbour has no meaning were it not for God and love of him. The common origin of myself and my neighbour is in God. The common end of myself and my neighbour, according to the gospel, is the high calling and destiny of fellowship with God. Were these assertions not true, love of neighbour would not have any ontological grounding. It would collapse into one of two possible corruptions: the tyrannizing of fellow man or the enslavement of the self to fellow man. As O'Donovan so clearly affirms, "Take away love for God, and the ontological parity which makes true neighbour-love possible is upset; one human being takes the place of God and confers value or significance upon the other."[30] "True neighbourliness," says O'Donovan, "requires the recognition of the supreme good simply in order that we may see the neighbour for what he is. But that means that our pursuit of the neighbour's welfare has to take seriously the thought that he, like ourselves, is a being whose end is in God." Thus, to love one's neighbor without considering their relation to God "would be an exercise in fantasy."[31] O'Donovan goes on to speak of Saint Augustine's statement that our first duty to our neighbour was to "seize him for God," which, properly understood, sheds light on the meaning that the first aspect of the love command gives to the second.

---

30. O'Donovan, *Resurrection and Moral Order*, 229.
31. O'Donovan, *Resurrection and Moral Order*, 229.

Augustine did not mean that all acts of love should have the motive of a religious goal in a manipulative way, such as evangelizing without concern for the whole personhood and well-being of my neighbour. He meant that we should love our neighbour, recognizing their calling and destiny to be in fellowship with God and with a view to furthering that destiny. O'Donovan suggests that we must be wary, on the one hand, of evangelistic zeal that ignores all aspects of the neighbour's being and, on the other hand, give consideration to the possibility that repudiation of evangelism that is fashionable in some ecclesiastical circles may in fact reveal a refusal to take the neighbour's vocation seriously.

Neighbouring is the verb with which Jesus upends the question "Who is my neighbour?" summarizing the second half of the Decalogue, indicating that *torah* has moral content and that shalom is the consequence of its pursuit. But this love commandment can only be fulfilled in the context of love for God, who has in Christ become our neighbour, which in turn is motivated only by reception of the love *of* God. This keeps the ethical life in the place of communion, of contemplation, of worship. The love of neighbour is steeped in the love of God who is also the holy God as revealed in the Holy Scriptures, not as we might wish him to be. Theological ethics must not miss being theological, and therefore it cannot miss the biblical nature of ethics. Ethics must involve serious study of the witness of the whole Word of God, under the tutelage of the covenant God we love, led by the Spirit who breathed the Scriptures into being, who employed real humans with all their idiosyncrasies yet said what he wished to say. This involves careful hermeneutics, as we have noted.

With respect to the Old Testament, which was fully affirmed and followed by Jesus and the apostles as the Word of God and as authoritative in ethical matters, Old Testament scholar Iain Provan offers some wise guidelines on how it is to be read. To affirm its *status* as the Word of God is one thing, but *interpretation* of it still requires care, as Provan affirms.[32] First, he suggests that one cannot quote Old Testament laws "unless you understand what these laws are for and what they are not for, and what it is that laws have to do with ethics in the first place."[33] He points out that "law and ethics are not the same thing" in either modern

---

32. Iain Provan, "St. John's Twinning Process: The Old Testament and Sexuality/Homosexuality," in *Anglican Church of Canada Discussion of Homosexuality 1* (2003), 2.
33. Provan, "St. John's Twinning Process," 2.

or ancient times. By way of example, he comments that "generosity is widely considered to be ethically good, but you can't be prosecuted for being mean."[34]

According to Provan, the Old Testament laws must be understood within their creational purpose and therefore their eschatological telos:

> What Jesus is saying here (Matt. 19:4–9) is that the law of Moses *must be understood in the context of God's creation purpose.* God's creation purpose is that people who get married should stay married, and not become divorced. The fact that the law of Moses allows divorce under certain circumstances does not make divorce good. It simply makes it legal, which is a very different thing. From a biblical point of view, then, quoting a law on this or that topic (divorce or anything else), by itself, is not going to get you very far one way or the other. We need to understand first of all *what God's creation purpose is*, and *where God is heading with creation*, if I can put it that way. Only then shall we understand what to do with individual laws, and indeed individual texts.[35]

Related to this, rather than quoting texts out of context and focusing on what God is against, Provan suggests that another important principle is to seek to ascertain "what God is *for* in creation," and thereby to make sense of "the various prohibitions concerning what he is against." Only in this manner can we subvert the impression that prohibitions are "arbitrary and unfair limitations of our human freedom."[36] These principles will become relevant in a later chapter as the issue of homosexuality is discussed.

Proper interpretation also involves distinctions that must be made between genres of law that guide us in discovering transcovenantal ethical decision making. The first distinction to be made is that between moral law and ceremonial law. Paul and the author of Hebrews are clear that having been fulfilled in the person and work of Christ, ceremonial laws such as those relating to sacrifices and the Aaronic priesthood no longer apply (Rom. 10:4; Heb. 7:12, 9–10). Moral law as a category is not restricted just to the Decalogue as it is found in Exodus 20 and

---

34. Provan, "St. John's Twinning Process," 2.
35. Provan, "St. John's Twinning Process," 3, emphasis added.
36. Provan, "St. John's Twinning Process," 3, emphasis added.

Deuteronomy 5. It extends to expositions of those commandments in Exodus 21–23, Leviticus 18–20, and Deuteronomy, much of which is devoted to exhortation around the first three commandments. Leviticus 18 expands the implications of the seventh commandment, highlighting all categories of sexual relations that are forbidden. The penalties for infractions were related to the theocratic nature of Israel as a kingdom under God, but the egregious nature of these violations was thereby made evident. The command regarding homosexual relations is unequivocal (Lev. 18:22), and it is listed alongside child sacrifice and bestiality as particularly detestable. An important evaluation of the ongoing validity of Old Testament commands is whether they are upheld in the New Testament, and despite revisionistic attempts to suggest that Romans 1 and 1 Corinthians 6 are not about homosexual relations, these passages do indeed confirm what the Old Testament affirms. This anticipates a much broader-ranging discussion of this issue in chapter 8.

THE ETHICAL MATERIAL OF THE NEW TESTAMENT

The ethical material of the *New Testament* centers on the concept of love *to* God in response to the love *of* God, revealed in the giving of the Son, and the concept of love to neighbour, as expressed in the second table of the Ten Commandments, enabled by the Spirit. We may summarize this under the following points:

1. The paraenetic material of the New Testament is always expressed in light of the gospel, even if it does so in various creative genres. For example, Jesus uses parables like the Good Samaritan to illustrate both the gospel love of God and the neighbourly ethic of love.[37] Paul most often comes to moral imperatives by first describing gospel indicatives and identity and then carrying the indicatives over into the imperatives. Romans and Colossians are structured in this way. Philippians, by contrast, mixes the tones with powerful indicatives and descriptions of Christ being enclosed within the paraenetic passages (e.g., 2:1–11, where the christological hymn flows from but injects the force of the command for humility).

---

37. In the parable of the unjust judge in Luke 18:1–8, it is interesting to observe that Jesus implies that the widow's seeking of justice ("Grant me justice against my adversary," v. 3) is the concern of his heart and the kingdom of God.

Peter, James, and John also follow this more Hebraic pattern of the indicatives being contained within the flow related to imperatives of the gospel. For example, John, in his concentration on love for God and love between the members of the family of God, keeps referencing the love of God in many different ways. In 1 John 4:7, when in hortatory tone he says, "Dear friends, let us love one another," he immediately gives power to the command with the indicative, "for love comes from God," and then by way of reinforcement, he moves to the incarnation as a proof of divine love: "This is how God showed his love among us: He sent his one and only Son into the world that we might live through him" (4:9; the example of Christ's condescension, that is, *his participation in our humanity*, motivates us, and the life we live in him, *our participation in him*, empowers us), and then to the cross as the climax of divine love: "This is love: not that we loved God, but that he loved us and sent his Son as an atoning sacrifice for our sins" (4:10). He returns to the hortatory mood with "Dear friends, since God so loved us, we also ought to love one another" (4:11).

2. The "love your neighbour" half of the Great Commandment is spelled out to be a reference to the second table of the Ten Commandments (Gal. 5:13–14), and the paraenetic material of the Epistles references all of these commandments (e.g., Eph. 4:25–28). One helpful example is what Paul exhorts in Ephesians 4:28, "Anyone who has been stealing must steal no longer, but must work, doing something useful with their own hands, that they may have something to share with those in need." The eighth commandment, "You shall not steal," is obviously in mind. In fact, Paul brings the positive and negative versions of this commandment together. This is moral formation in its essence, what Bockmuehl calls the "transformation from parasite to provider."[38] Bockmuehl sees here a threefold sequence of reform: desist from thieving, adopt the positive alternative (i.e., work), and implement the positive outcome, which is included in this commandment as "give to the poor" (i.e., generosity). "So the New Testament replaces theft with thrift and greed with giving. Instead of covetousness, charity."[39]

---

38. Bockmuehl, *Christian Way of Living*, 114.
39. Bockmuehl, *Christian Way of Living*, 114.

3. This is, however, not the primary focus; rather, it is a given for those who are in Christ and live in the Spirit. Knowing Christ more and more intimately (Phil. 3:8) and participating in his death and resurrection (Phil. 3:10) by contemplation (2 Cor. 3:18) and in communion with his people (Acts 2:41–47); participating in priestly worship and prayer in the one priesthood of Christ (Rom. 12:1–2; Heb. 4:12–16; 8:1–2; 10:19–25); imitating the character of Christ in union with Christ (Phil. 2:1–11) under the influence of the Holy Spirit (Eph. 5:18; Gal. 5:13–23); and engaging in acts of witness and justice and compassion empowered by the Spirit (Acts 2:42–47; 4:32–37; Gal. 6:2)—all these priorities will guarantee that *torah* is being kept even when the telos of being like Christ as persons-in-communion is higher. In other words, the ethical life is a byproduct of the life of participation in Christ in fellowship with his church.

4. The "good" of the Old Testament—like justice for the poor and the widow—is assumed as a commanded pursuit in the New Testament. What is required of the people of God in Micah (6:8, "He has shown you, O mortal, *what is good*. And what does the LORD require of you? To act justly and to love mercy and to walk humbly with your God" [emphasis added]) is in an identical way required of the new community of the people of God. For example, the widows are cared for, and measures are taken to ensure this when they are neglected (Acts 6:1–7), and the poor Jerusalem saints are provided for at Paul's apostolic appeal and his own hands (2 Cor. 8–9, a passage in which Paul appeals based partially on the "equality" of the people of God). The generosity of God and the christological example of Christ are appealed to as primary motivation and empowerment for generous giving, and justice is the result. The concern for justice begins from within the church community, but it emanates to the world at large, as Paul indicates: "Therefore, as we have opportunity, *let us do good to all people*, especially to those who belong to the family of believers" (Gal. 6:10, emphasis added). The rationale is that we cannot be a source of justice or compassion to the world with integrity if we are neglecting the nearest neighbour in our own church. This inside-out generosity reflects the direction of the church's witness and its sharing of justice and ethics in the public square. The church

is God's community of justice and compassion, but as we have seen, it is the community of God in *ekstasis*. It is highly unlikely that the ethics of the church community will be received in the public square if the compassion and generosity of the church are not seen there!

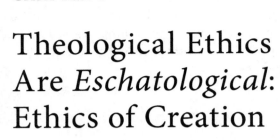

CHAPTER 4

Theological Ethics Are *Eschatological*: Ethics of Creation

Whereas in chapter 2 the importance of the *being* of God as triune for theological ethics was emphasized, here in chapter 4 the relevance of the *acts* of God, creation, redemption, and consummation, as well as their outcomes, comes into focus. Crucial to the understanding of God's work in the world is the understanding that the kingdom of God has already come.[1] The first advent of the Son into the world signalled the inbreaking of the kingdom into the world, and the giving of the Spirit to the church made the church the sign, servant, and messenger of the kingdom. Eschatology is thus first what may be called *realized* eschatology. We live in the so-called "in-between" time in which the kingdom has come, but not yet fully. We are incorporated by the Spirit into the church and empowered by the Spirit for holiness, ethics, mission. We are profoundly aware that in the "now but not yet" there is struggle and imperfection in the church and in Christians. There is the possibility of growth, *not* perfection (overrealized eschatology) and *not* despairing antinomianism (underrealized eschatology). Our ethical decisions are made with awareness that we often must "make the best of it."[2] *Future* eschatology has to do with the second coming of Christ when we will be perfected, a hope that motivates us. As we think about ethics in an eschatological way, it will be helpful to do so in synchronicity with God's acts in the world.

---

1. Jesus pronounced the kingdom and his presence constituted it (Matt. 3:2), and the apostles preached and lived into it in Acts (Acts 8:12; 20:25). The "last days" begin with the advent of Jesus and the outpouring of the Spirit (Acts 2:17; Heb. 1:2).
2. For a realistic approach in this vein, see John G. Stackhouse Jr., *Making the Best of It: Following Christ in the Real World* (New York: Oxford University Press, 2011).

CREATION

Being eschatological means that theological ethics take place within the history of God's work with the world, from creation, through the fall, through the redemption of creation and humanity, through the consummation of creation, and to the resurrection of human beings. The continuance of creation throughout the history of the triune God's work in the world signals God's commitment to his creation, and this is an important guiding factor in many areas of ethics, including what it means to be human and the mandate to care for creation, which was given by God to humanity. This mandate, called the *cultural mandate*, remains for all time. Redemption and consummation are *of* creation. They are not the redemption and consummation of humans *out of* creation. God's creation is fundamentally "good," as Genesis 1 is at pains to stress, and so God perseveres with it right on into its redeemed form in the new creation.

Creation was good, but it was not *complete*. Genesis 1 must always be thought of as both historical *and* eschatological. It anticipates the rest of the biblical story. It could not be complete until the One who recapitulated the first Adam, Jesus, the last Adam, had redeemed it from its oppressed state as a result of the fall—that is, until he reconciled it (Col. 1:20) and assumed his place at the head of creation as the "firstborn over all creation" (Col. 1:15), the One who reigns over creation in the way intended for the first Adam. Christ and new humanity in him have fulfilled and will fulfil what was always God's *first* thought for his creation and its leadership under his image bearers. Specifically, one might say, his first thought was to see creation under the One who is "the image of the invisible God" (Col. 1:15). This fits well with the idea of recapitulation in Irenaeus and the idea espoused by Jonathan Edwards that God's first thoughts are his last revealed as they move toward the revelation of his own glory.[3]

Christ brings about new creation under the new covenant. Thus creation is vitally important not only for what it tells us about God but also because humanity cannot understand itself apart from its createdness,

---

3. This is an indirect quote that reflects a number of statements in Jonathan Edwards, "A Dissertation concerning the End for Which God Created the World," YE 8.

its image-bearing nature, and its need for Christ, the true human for humanity. The commitment of God to creation and his trusting it to image-bearing humans suggest also the importance of all of God's creation, including animals and plants.

We begin with creation, therefore, and its givenness. Creation is "spoken, given, designed"[4] by the Creator, ordered toward him, and aesthetically beautiful. His human creatures are called to live with the grain of that creation. The vertical ordering of the creation toward God has a corresponding "internal horizontal ordering among its parts."[5] Humans find their true meaning within the givenness of creation, its form and order and beauty, including its moral order and spiritual goodness. "Our very capacity to act within the world," says Hollinger, "comes because God has acted with form and order."[6] Whilst they are part of the wider creation (suggesting we must not be anthropocentric), humans are chosen to be the regents of God, colabouring and even cocreating with God. Even prior to the fall, the first humans do so in participation with God, with a derived authority that enables them to name and to tame and to feed animals as stewards of God's good creation. This is only possible because humans are made specifically in the image of God. They *are that*, and this accounts for the sheer wonder of the human being with remarkable intellectual powers and volition and affective sensibility and moral consciousness. But they are *only that* and no more, godlike but not God, and not able to be what they are apart from God. John Calvin interestingly expresses the view that even before the fall, the first humans needed to participate in the preincarnate Christ because there was a metaphysical distance between God and humans before there was a moral distance. The distinction of being like God but not God is a guide for the activity and limits of creational ethics that constitutes one guide in ethical deliberation in bioethics and medical ethics, for example. Furthermore, it is important to stress that one's view of the image of God in humanity must be properly *anthropological* in that humans are given privilege and capacities usually greater than other animals. However, it is important to stress that one's view must not be

---

4. Dennis P. Hollinger, *Choosing the Good: Christian Ethics in a Complex World* (Grand Rapids: Baker Academic, 2002), 73.

5. Oliver O'Donovan, *Resurrection and Moral Order: An Outline for Evangelical Ethics* (Grand Rapids: Eerdmans, 1986), 31.

6. Hollinger, *Choosing the Good*, 73.

anthropocentric. Human regency over the world is as creatures among other creatures whom humans name and care for. These animals have dignity and value also, and this forms the basis of the ethics of how we treat animals on our planet. David Clough's work *On Animals* develops this point very ably.[7]

But what exactly does the image of God mean, and with what ethical repercussions?

Created in the Image of God

Much ink has been spilled in the Christian tradition on what the image of God in humans actually means. There are three main clusters of interpretation,[8] as derived from the Genesis text in the wider context of biblical revelation: these entail the ideas of relationality (the relational view), reason (the substantial or structural view), and rule/reign, which includes being coworkers with God in his ongoing reign over creation (the functional view). The reason for this variety of opinion within the scholarly tradition relates to the brevity of the Genesis reference and the paucity of references to the term elsewhere. Jeremy Kidwell, in reviewing this tradition, has commented wisely that "appreciation for the polyvalence of the doctrine allows for a composite meaning."[9] Even so, most theologians have opted for the elevation of one of these viewpoints as primary, even if polyvalence is evident. Stanley Grenz offers a slightly different classification involving the structural view, the relational view, and the dynamic view. The structural approach "understands the image of God primarily as an anthropological concept. Being a formal structure of the human person, the divine image is something we 'possess,' and it includes the properties which constitute us as human beings."[10] This view focuses on ontological realities, whereas Grenz thought of the relational view as that which is concerned with functionality and a personal definition of the *imago*. The third model, the "dynamic view,

---

7. David Clough, *On Animals*, vol. 1, *Systematic Theology* (London: T&T Clark, 2014); Clough, *On Animals*, vol. 2, *Theological Ethics* (London: T&T Clark, 2018)

8. There were other viewpoints also, such as that of John Cassian (c. AD 360–c. AD 435), who insisted that "all the leaders of the churches were unanimous in teaching that the image and likeness of God should be understood not in an earthly, literal sense but spiritually." *The Conferences of John Cassian*, 10.3, http://www.documentacatholicaomnia.eu/03d/0360-0435,_Cassianus, _The_Conferences_Of_John_Cassian,_EN.pdf, 174.

9. Jeremy Kidwell, "Elucidating the Image of God: An Analysis of the *Imago Dei* in the Work of Colin E. Gunton and John Zizioulas" (MA thesis, Regent College, 2009), 42.

10. Stanley Grenz, *Theology for the Community of God* (Grand Rapids: Eerdmans, 2000), 169.

is an eschatological one: the image of God is neither the present structures of the human person nor the idyllic past relation to God lost by Adam but restored in Christ. Instead . . . the divine image is the goal or destiny that God intends for his creatures."[11] Kidwell adds, "In this way, [Grenz] connotes a teleological orientation for the *imago* which also often incorporates the redemptive work of Christ, describing the *imago* in the light of this."[12] Grenz exposes the tendency within modern discourse toward univocal interpretations of the *imago* and the related tendency to read premodern interpreters as defending one particular interpretation. Recognizing the validity of Grenz's classification, I prefer to speak of the structural (ontological[13]), the functional (ruling, vocational), and the relational, and to see all three as finding christological fulfilment and eschatological fulfilment for the new humanity in Christ.

It is very important from an ethical perspective to recognize within these and other classifications that there is within Scripture and theological anthropology both a universal *nondegreed* aspect to the image and a *degreed* one. In Genesis 9:6, for example, even after the fall, humans are spoken of by God as made in his image, and therefore their lives are sacrosanct and not to be taken by another human. By contrast, Paul in 2 Corinthians 3:18 speaks about the image of God being restored to the believer from one degree of glory to another by contemplation in the power of the Spirit of freedom. The first conviction, then, is that *all* human persons from the moment of implantation until death, irrespective of the *degree* of their intelligence quota, vocational "success," state of employment, or integrity of sexual anatomy,[14] are made in the

---

11. Grenz, *Theology for the Community of God*, 173.

12. Kidwell, "Elucidating the Image of God," 22–23.

13. I recognize that this is a confusing term in the literature of the *imago Dei*, and I will use *structural* most frequently. For example, the term *person* as employed from early Christian metaphysics implies ontologically relational. The ontological battle with the accompanying loss of metaphysics in contemporary ethics is described in Alasdair C. MacIntyre, *After Virtue: A Study in Moral Theory* (Notre Dame, IN: University of Notre Dame Press, 2007); and Charles Taylor, *Sources of the Self: The Making of the Modern Identity* (Cambridge, MA: Harvard University Press, 1989).

14. There is controversy in the tradition on whether the matter of anatomical sex (*gender* is a social construct; thus the term is avoided here) is intrinsic to the image of God or extrinsic to it. On both views, the nondegreed core of the image is the relatedness to God of all irrespective of the degree of brokenness. For further discussion, see Ray S. Anderson, "Bonding without Bondage," in *On Being Family: A Social Theology of the Family*, by Ray S. Anderson and Dennis B. Guernsey (Eugene, OR: Wipf & Stock, 1981), 85–104; and Christa L. McKirland, "The Image of God and Intersex Persons," paper presented at the Logos Institute, St. Mary's College, University of St. Andrews, October 12, 2016.

nondegreed image of God, and must be treated with dignity and granted basic human rights.[15] It will also reflect the conviction that the fall marred but did not destroy the image. Sin defaced but did not erase it (Gen. 9:6). Christians and non-Christians are made in his image. This matter is at the core of its meaning, which is *relatedness* to the Creator. All human beings, having been created by God, are in relatedness to him, which is not the same as being in *relationship* with him. A further conviction is that *Christ* is, in an ultimate and representative sense, *the* image of the invisible God, the last Adam, *the* Man who as the full image represents all humanity and reigns with the new humanity united to him, bringing in a new creation.

Another way to say this is that at the level of God's design, all human persons are intended to be restored to the fulness of the image of God in Christ (1 Tim. 2:4). In this sense too, all human persons are in a nondegreed manner in the image of God, related to the matter of God's intended telos for them. They are all human and therefore are recipients of dignity and human rights. However, as human persons come into union with the living Christ by faith, they begin a journey toward the fulness of what was intended for them, by degree—from one degree of glory to another (2 Cor. 3:18), which is the same as to say, toward being *fully* human. The scope of their recovery journey will include the use of cognitive and emotive faculties toward the development of shalom in their relationships and shalom with the creation, and a sense of significance in vocation related to the cultural mandate and participation in bringing in the new creation. For those who do not enter that redeeming union, relatedness remains, but not relationship—that is, humanness remains, but it is something short of being fully human as God intended. Matters of structure, such as degree of intelligence, remain independent of being Christian or not. What is forfeited is a sense of the ultimate significance of work and an orientation toward God and creation that provides a worshipful posture and a meaningful affect.

The basis for the nondegreed category can be eschatological, as is expressed by Christa McKirland, who sees humanity in light of its

---

15. "Rights" is in quotation marks to signal a certain ambivalence toward "rights" language signalled by Oliver O'Donovan, "The Language of Rights and Conceptual History," in *Journal of Religious Ethics* 37 (2009): 193–207, related to the power connotations of the word. He suggests that Nicholas Wolterstorff's "attempt to find the implicit recognition of rights in the Scriptures depends very heavily on what he takes to be implied rather than on what is stated, and at best can establish a *pre-history* of rights-language" (193).

desired end.[16] Similarly, it can be on the basis of God's desire and design for all humanity (1 Tim. 2:4), one that accords with Barth's christological view of election, or it may simply fall under Grenz's category as a structural reality related to being human.

Having established this, it is helpful to look at the three aspects of a polyvalent view of the image for further insight that will have ethical implications.

Imago as Structural

The *structural* or ontological view refers to cerebral, self-reflexive, emotional, and volitional capacities, to freedom and creativity, all of which are part of the human person. This relates mostly to the God-given capacities of the human mind, although even bodily features such as the fact that humans walk uprightly have been mentioned in the tradition. Given modern insights into the interrelatedness of the body and the mind, theologians today must speak of the mind-body unity. Furthermore, despite the highly disputed nature of the relationship between the brain and the mind, that is, between consciousness and the human brain, theologians today must speak of consciousness as an aspect of the image of God.[17] In the Western theological tradition, the structural has been centred on the human capacity for self-reflection and self-love. This tradition has been influenced by Augustine's conception of the Trinity according to which there is a psychological analogy in which the Son is the Father's beatific self-reflection and vice versa, and the Spirit is the self-love or mutual love of the Father for the Son and vice versa. This analogy already assumes a structural view of the image centred in mirroring the reason, affections, and will of the triune God. A primary concern of the structural view has been the distinguishing of humans from the rest of the animal creation. This entails the extent of our consciousness, our capacity for abstract reasoning, and so on.

I once observed a Canada goose at Harrison Lake in British Columbia, Canada, standing and appearing to look out at the same amazing vista I was contemplating. I was looking at the vista with worshipful wonder . . .

---

16. This is the idea that the intended telos in God's mind is the full Christlikeness of all human persons.

17. Does the brain *emit, transmit,* or *permit* human consciousness? The materialist position is not prevalent even among secular philosophers. See the work of philosopher Philip A. Goff, *Consciousness and Fundamental Reality* (Oxford: Oxford University Press, 2017), and psychiatrist Ian McGilchrist, who is currently writing in this important area.

the blueness of this large lake silhouetted by snowcapped mountains and then the blueness of a different variety in the sky. As I looked at this goose, I had to smile. It looked like it was taking in the scenery too. In truth, I suspect it was looking for its next meal. This is not to deny that higher animals have some form of intellect, emotion, and will. Rather, it is a question of degree. Indeed, nature itself is depicted in Scripture, at least metaphorically, as having some intellect, will, and emotion, for it both groans and travails for the state of its human "rulers" and the presence of sin in the world, and it rejoices in anticipation of the revelation of the sons of God. However, it is clear that animals and nature do not possess the self-reflective and ruling capacity of humans. In this sense, humans are the crowning glory of creation, being in the image of God in a way that animals are not. If the heavens declare the glory of God, so do humans "fully alive" reflect the glory of God.

One important aspect of the structural nature of the *imago* is the givenness of the fact that humans are human like God, but they are *not* God. As "like God," they have the capacity to be creative like the creative God who has made a contingent and magnificently beautiful creation with galaxies and animal and plant species adapted to their environments. As "not God," however, they are given limits—the limit of being human but not superhuman, the limit of being creative yet not playing God with their own lives and the lives of their fellow image-bearing humans. The givenness of being human, not God and not beyond human, informs an important ethic in the controversy of transhumanism, for example. God does not intend for human brains to be bypassed or "improved" by the addition of electronic devices. It seems evident that the call to be human and embodied and located is already threatened by the addiction to the iPhone, which in some way attaches to us as an extension, functions in place of the brain, and gives us a total accessibility that was not intended for human persons. It is already a manifestation of the desire to be transhuman. Further, this basic relationship of being godlike but not God can guide us in the ethics of the scientific and medical community's treatment of human life from conception (or implantation) to the vulnerability of old age.

An important corollary of the image of God as structural is that in its created givenness we find the key to understanding anthropology, which in turn has an ethical bearing. It was freely admitted by Karl Barth that many forms of anthropological understanding, derived from sociology, psychology, biology, existential philosophy, naturalism, and evolutionary science, hold some significance, for "in their limits they may well be accurate and important."[18] They all describe humanity in its uniqueness, based on the unique methodological features of each field of study. These descriptions can be helpful, useful, and accurate, but they cannot fully describe humanity, Barth insisted, for they are "all bracketed, and no decisive enlightenment about man is to be expected from within these brackets, but only from a source outside. This source is God."[19] True humanity cannot be understood apart from God. To remove the Creator from the definition of humanity is to remove humanity's foundation. Barth suggests that if "we think of man in isolation from and independence of God, we are no longer thinking about real man."[20] For Barth, humanity exists because of the election of God and only in relationship with God. Outside of this relationship humanity ceases to be human. The significance of this relationship means that it "is not peripheral but central, not incidental but essential to that which makes him a real man, himself."[21] Evolutionary understandings of humanity that pay particular attention to humanity's environment are no doubt helpful in understanding humanity. But, as Barth states, "if man does not know himself already, long before his attention is directed to these phenomena, he will be blind even though he sees. In face and in spite of these phenomena he will always look on the wrong side. He will always think with the animal and the rest of creation generally."[22] The dignity of what a human being is lies at the core of Christian ethical dialogue on issues such as human rights (properly conceived), the rights of the unborn human, even what it means to be human in relation to the proper use of social media, and so on.

Imago as Functional: Rule That Is Participative, Caring Stewardship

The functional aspect builds on the structural aspect, or the capacity of the human image bearer for the creativity, self-reflection, and order that are involved in work. The structural aspect is what enables the work and the evaluation of goodness of the work. The functional aspect is

---

18. Barth, *CD* III/2, 122.
19. Barth, *CD* III/2, 122.
20. Barth, *CD* III/2, 123.
21. Barth, *CD* III/2, 123.
22. Barth, *CD* III/2, 90.

also very much dependent on the relational aspect. In relationship with God, there is joy in carrying out the work and shalom that develops in its outcomes. In relationship, in participation with God, work was intended to bring glory to God and joy and a sense of significance to the worker, and to result in the flourishing of the fellow human and the creation. It is instructive that an integral part of human being is human doing, just as the being and act of God cannot be separated.

The functional component of the image of God is evident from the fact that immediately when the first humans are pronounced as image bearers, they receive the command of God to act in ways that reflect God. Genesis 1:26 has an implicit causal relationship that qualifies the statement of God's creation of human beings in his image: "Then God said, 'Let us make mankind in our image, in our likeness, so that they may rule over the fish in the sea and the birds in the sky, over the livestock and all the wild animals, and over all the creatures that move along the ground.'" Part of the givenness of creation, therefore, is *work* as God worked (the human is *homo faber*, the person as doer or maker), to tend the garden and care for the earth, and to *live in families* even as God is a social God. However, the creation act that forms humans in relation to their Creator precedes and therefore qualifies the ruling function, as does the emphasis on the inherent relationality of humans as gendered (v. 27). With God and with each other as male and female in unconflicted complementarity, and with sensitivity and care for creation as created by God, humans were mandated to manage it as stewards (Gen. 1:27–31).

This command of God, the cultural mandate, includes the creation order of work. It is made even more explicit in Genesis 2, which emphasizes creation care: "The LORD God took the man and put him in the Garden of Eden to work it and take care of it" (v. 15). Work is sometimes spoken of as if it were a consequence of the fall, but it is in fact a gift given in creation, passed from the Creator to the created image bearers. It is somewhat tragic that many Christian have no theology for what they spend most of their life doing. A theology and therefore an ethics of work are very important, first because the command of God within the cultural mandate describes what being in the image of God means.

An important conclusion one may draw from the functional aspect of the image of God is that human *doing* is important for human *being*, that doing cannot be separated from being, and that being is not sufficient on its own. Undue emphasis on being, one that neglects doing, is actually a modern form of gnosticism. One of the reasons unemployment and firings hurt so much is that a crucial piece of the human makeup that reflects our triune Creator is the ability to work. In underemphasizing doing, we undermine the pain of the unemployed persons who feel the lack of part of their identity as a human being: the opportunity to work. Of course, there are workaholics who make an idol of work and who work to mask feelings of insecurity and inadequacy. God has made us to work, and he has also urged us to keep sabbath to relativize work and self-sufficiency as idols. God worked in Genesis 1, and then he passed the baton to his image bearers for the completion of his work.

Work is spoken of in the New Testament as that which enables humans to meet their financial needs (1 Thess. 4:11–12); to meet the needs of others ("Anyone who has been stealing must steal no longer, but must work, doing something useful with their own hands, *that they may have something to share with those in need,*" Eph. 4:28 [emphasis added]); to do so in a way that is conducive to the care and continuation and consummation of creation, not its destruction (as is evident from the context of Genesis 1 and 2, as well as passages like Romans 8:19–21); and to do so with an orientation toward the Lord with a view to reflecting his glory (Col. 3:23). Paul even speaks of his work as an apostle as coworking with God (1 Cor. 3:9; 2 Cor. 6:1). As with all the actions of redeemed image bearers, they work in participation with God.

A theology of work shapes ethics at work. Consider the following fourfold model: (1) Work brings fulfilment to the individual, according to each one's vocation. (2) Work provides for the needs of the community and especially the poor. (3) Work continues God's creation toward its completion, though the *creatio continua* (continuing creative activity) is not of the same order as God's *creatio ex nihilo*. (4) Work is carried out in participation with God and with a primary orientation toward God for his glory. One might call this a Trinitarian theology of work, not because one might associate the various functions with particular persons of the Trinity, but because it reflects both the irreducible identity of persons and the ensconcement of persons in community, and because it envisages work as participation in the work of the triune God who is both Creator and Redeemer of creation.

Much has been made in recent biblical/theological scholarship of the importance of *history* in the outworking of the gospel. Thus the gospel narrative, according to a Kuyperian way of speaking, follows the events of creation, fall, redemption or reconciliation, and consummation. Along with this has come an emphasis on valuing *creation* and keeping creation and redemption of humanity and the cosmos together. The gospel is not a gospel of evacuation. The gospel entails a doctrine of creation in which *creation matters*. It matters because it is the product of God's creating action; it matters because it has been pronounced good by the Divine Creator; it matters because it has been entered in the incarnation of the Son and because Christ has reaffirmed creation by his resurrection. The *creatio ex nihilo* and the *creatio continua* have led through the advent of the Christ of creation to the *creatio ex vetere* (transformation of the old creation) in which humanity in Christ, the last Adam, can participate. The Christian faith, in light of God's estimation of and purpose for creation, should foster the pursuit of science with the care of creation in mind. Furthermore, the cultural mandate by which God passed the baton of creating to his image bearers positively urges the Christian to seek restoration and redemption to become more fully human *according to particular vocations*. The Protestant Reformers strongly emphasized the doctrine of vocation, which stressed first that *all* persons, not just pastors, are called. R. Paul Stevens speaks of a sense of calling that overcomes aimless consumerism and "gives our lives direction and purpose because our Creator summons us into a personal relationship with God and into a wonderful purpose that will outlast the world."[23]

A full Christian doctrine of vocation says that every Christian is called because God calls them, that they are called *first* to be human, in accordance with the cultural mandate, to be in community and to work in accordance with their abilities; *second* to be Christian, to conversion, to worship, to Christlikeness of character, and to be obedient to all of the commands of God in the Scriptures; and *third*, to be persons who are uniquely gifted and called into particular vocations. Swiss theologian Klaus Bockmuehl called this arrangement of the doctrine of vocation the wedding cake of vocation. Western obsession with particular individual calling is overcome by living faithfully and obediently into the larger layers of the wedding cake. Bockmuehl associated the three persons of the Trinity with each level of calling, associating the Father with the human mandate, the Son with the Christian vocation, and the Holy

---

23. R. Paul Stevens, *Doing God's Business: Meaning and Motivation for the Marketplace* (Grand Rapids: Eerdmans, 2006), 20.

Spirit with the equipping and guiding that take us into our personal vocations.[24] It is really important to consider also the mutual overlap of each of these layers grounded in the doctrine of the indivisible nature of the works of the Trinity. Overemphasis on God as Creator and Father of all easily leads to a secularized notion of vocation in which the finality and uniqueness of Christ and evangelistic urgency lead to conceiving of marketplace influence as a mere "comfortable chaplaincy to secular, pluralistic societies and workplaces."[25] An obsession with the Spirit without reference to the christological layer can lead to antinomianism, to a deep frustration about work as if it is a waste of time, or to a view of work as a means to an evangelistic end, whereas neglect of the Spirit robs the worker of a sense of "the Spirit's intimate and intrusive involvement in our life and work in creation,"[26] and so on. The coinherence of the three levels, reflective of the coinherence of the persons of the Trinity, along with a good doctrine of creation, will go a long way in ridding the church of dualisms with respect to work: the dualism between faith and reason, the dualism between Sunday and Monday, the dualism of clergy and laity, the dualism that separates the Great Commission from the Great Commandment and the cultural mandate,[27] the dualism that separates evangelism and justice and creation care. Creation and its reaffirmation in the incarnation spell death to all such dualisms.

The following definition may sum up the notion of calling: it is "the truth that God calls us to himself so decisively that everything we are, . . . do, . . . and have is invested with a special devotion, dynamism, and direction lived out as a response to his summons and service."[28] Personal vocations include being scientists committed to understanding creation; priests of creation, giving creation a voice; artists who in their painting and sculpting take their cue from the God of triune beauty, who has created a beautiful world; musicians who in their particular

---

24. This has been referred to and employed also by Paul Stevens in his excellent work on calling. R. Paul Stevens, *The Other Six Days: Vocation, Work, and Ministry in Biblical Perspective* (Grand Rapids: Eerdmans; Vancouver: Regent College Publishing, 1999), 73–74.

25. Gordon Preece, "Vocation in Historical-Theological Perspective," Theology of Work Project, https://www.theologyofwork.org/auxiliary-pages/vocation-depth-article.

26. Preece, "Vocation in Historical-Theological Perspective."

27. The nature of the ruling function of the human in the *imago* is, as we have said, qualified by submissive relationship with God and it is guided and informed by the cultural mandate, which in turn moves humans toward a state of shalom. This is the first great commission ever given to humanity.

28. Os Guinness, *The Call* (Nashville: Word, 1998), 4.

emanating sounds reflect the "Supreme Harmony of All." It is perhaps easier to imagine that theologians might be image-bearing, priestly persons in their vocation. T. F. Torrance spoke of theology as being "our communion with God the Father through Christ and in the Spirit," which in fact "shares in the inner Trinitarian consubstantial or *homoousial* communion of the Father, Son and Holy Spirit," and within this communion and polarity "Christian theology becomes what essentially is and ought always to be, *logike latreia*, rational worship of God."[29] But given that, as Torrance saw it, science is coinherent within theology and contributes to an encyclopedic theology, he had no difficulty in saying that, correspondingly, and in accordance with science's peculiar subject matter and techniques and levels, scientists too can become participants in the rational priestly worship of God and of his Son, by whom and through whom all things are made and in whom all priestliness is recapitulated, through the work of the Holy Spirit.

The importance of work is thus very evident and this sharpens the need for a carefully thought out ethics of work in society that will be for the good of both the individual and the society, bringing shalom and the glory of God.

The command of God also included the order of *community and family*. This particular givenness is grounded also in the givenness of the binary of male and female in Genesis 1. Great care is required in interpreting what these givens actually are. Not all human persons marry, and indeed our Saviour, Jesus, did not. Marriage, though it is itself a sacrament of the nature of God, does not add image-bearing status! Single persons are equally in the image of God, as is evidenced by the greatest and prototypical human, Jesus. Genesis 1, as already noted, says nothing about marriage. It implies that all humans whether single or married are made in the image of God and that their sexuality is a significant part of that image. This must, of course, be carried over into chapter 2 and the marriage context. The givenness of creation, the grain of the universe, is marriage as a God-given institution in which a man and a woman enter into lasting covenant, and re-create and procreate so that a certain type of family is formed. We go against the grain when we propose alternative types of marriage.

---

29. T. F. Torrance, "Theological Realism," in *The Philosophical Frontiers of Christian Theology: Essays Presented to D. M. Mackinnon*, ed. Donald MacKenzie MacKinnon, Brian Hebblethwaite, and Stewart R. Sutherland (Cambridge: Cambridge University Press, 1982), 193.

But familying, to use the verb form, is not restricted to those families that are formed by marriage, or what we call "nuclear" families. The will of God and the givenness of creation are that *all* humans live in *community* and not as isolated individuals. Genesis 1 allows for familying of a more flexible kind, which includes single-parent families, families of friends, missional communities, and so on. Ray Anderson argued that from its inception as the penultimate contingent relation to God, family has to do with the fulfilment of the core social paradigm and therefore is a larger concept than the nuclear family.[30] In the era of the new covenant, the family of God—the church—becomes the primary community of the Christian, though not to the exclusion of human families. The family of the church, one might say the family of "grace," includes and mutually nourishes and equips the natural biological family, one might say the family of "nature," as passages like Ephesians 6:1–3 and Colossians 3:18–21 allow. Grace does not destroy nature but restores it.

Imago as Relationality of Persons

The *imago* is relational in the sense that it is established by the initiative of God and in covenantal relationship with him, and in the sense that relationality that is within the Godhead is also embedded in the first humans ("male and female he created them," Gen. 1:27). We may assume that the personal freedom and the relational communion of humanity echo loudly the coinherent relationship of the three divine persons-in-communion of the Trinity, as illustrated through the primary relational category that defines the image of God. The relational dimension is presented well by Helmut Thielicke, though he may do so at the expense of the structural:

> We have to see the nature of God, not in his attributes [*Eigenschaften*], but in his outward relations [*Aussenschaften*], in what he does with us, in his relation to us, in his being "Emmanuel" [God with us]. The image of God in man is to be similarly defined. *It is not a constituent capacity inherent in man but a relational entity*, namely, man's ruling function vis-a-vis the other creatures.[31]

---

30. See Ray S. Anderson, *Something Old, Something New: Marriage and Family Ministry in a Postmodern World* (Eugene, OR: Wipf & Stock, 2007), 168–70.

31. Helmut Thielicke, *Theological Ethics*, vol. 1, *Foundations*, trans. William H. Lazareth (Philadelphia: Fortress, 1966), 157, emphasis added.

As helpful as Kidwell's comments above are (with respect to a composite meaning gleaned from the polyvalence of the doctrine), the christological aspect of this doctrine of the image of God cannot be neglected as a unifying theme, for without removing any of the aspects mentioned, it makes them all possible. As suggested in Irenaeus, the image is recapitulated in Jesus, who, by his representative actions from incarnation to resurrection and ascension, makes possible the restoration of the *imago*. The resurrection of Christ was the first day of the new creation, and as noted by Oliver O'Donovan, the resurrection reaffirms creation,[32] which involves the moral order of creation. I would add that with this resurrection came the restoration of the image of God in humanity in the form especially of the new community of humanity in Christ, who cannot *but* bear the image of the Trinity given they are in union with the incarnate Son and in communion with the triune God. Persons, as a communion, the church, are the image or icon of the Trinity (a well-known concept in at least the Orthodox church). But in addition, when humans are regenerated and restored into relationship and not mere relatedness to God, the vocational purpose of God for humanity becomes possible again. Human persons in relationship with God also fulfil the cultural mandate for earth-keeping (which includes science) in ways that are constructive, intellectually and in actuality, for the good of the creation.

Given that God as revealed in the Old Testament is profoundly covenantal and relational, and that the triune being of Yahweh as revealed fully in the New Testament is confirmed to be essentially relational, so, inevitably, human beings made in the image of this revealed God may expect to image him by being in relationship with God and other human beings and creation and therefore to be essentially relational beings, persons-in-relation. The first man and woman were made "facing God," if you like, and they are immediately spoken of as facing each other in gendered relationship with one another ("male and female he created them" is explicatory of the phrase "image of God"). At an ontological level, this means that by the very act of being created by God, humans are *ipso facto* related to God as creature to Creator and in relatedness to their fellow human. In other words, the foundation of the prototypical human self is "the internalized response of the significant other," first the divine "Other" and then the significant human "other."

---

32. O'Donovan, *Resurrection and Moral Order*, 14.

Prior to the fall, this ontology corresponded with an actual relational intimacy between God and Adam and Eve, between Adam and Eve themselves, and between Adam and Eve and creation. Furthermore, in that a stated purpose of the creation of humans is expressed as ruling on behalf of God in creation, the *imago Dei* seems to mean that humans were made with the capacity for relationship with God so that the reigning over his creation is done in communion with him as his coworkers, and of course this did necessitate the use of reason. Thus the relational viewpoint, when recapitulated in light of Christology and the Trinity, takes precedence over and is foundational to the structural and functional aspects of the *imago*.

One could press the relational Trinitarian analogy as Barth did by suggesting that the gendered nature of the humans reflected a "common identity and equality-with-differentiation" that is reflective of the ontological reality of God in three persons who are one in their equality and essence as God and yet differentiated as persons of irreducible identity. In this new entity of image-bearing humanity, each was equal to the other, each was equally in the image, and each together was the image, and yet each was not like the other, being differentiated with respect to embodied sex.

Certainly sexual identity is a core concept of the *imago*. The words of Genesis 1:27, "male and female he created them," seem very closely tied to the primary indicative statement, "*So God created mankind in his own image, in the image of God he created them*," and this has justified the notion of sex as *intrinsic* to the image and of the inclusion of sexuality within personhood. Sex is the only ontological descriptor that legitimately differentiates otherwise identical and equally human persons. Others have preferred the view that sex is *extrinsic* and not definitive of human personhood, seeking to assure intersex persons, for example, that they are fully validated as image bearers. The intrinsic and defining aspect of the image has, on this account, been the telos of all human persons in the eschaton as persons like Christ, *the* image in whom all participate by grace. The intrinsic view does not in and of itself preclude the embrace of all persons as image bearers. It allows for the fall in which *all* are broken and insists that all are image bearers even if the anatomical sex is unclear.

In favour of the intrinsic view, not only is the phrase "male and female he created them" mentioned in Genesis 1:27, but this diversity within unity seems to be invoked to explicate, at least in part, what being in the image of God means. Thus, in keeping with this text, E. F. Rogers reflects Barth's interpretation of it, which is to say that along with men, "women are *constitutive* of the image of God" and that women are, with men, "integral to the co-humanity consummated in the neighbour-love of Jesus."[33] The place of gender, or our preferred term, *sexedness*, in the image of God is important—indeed, ontological. Rogers fears that taking the concept of "male and female" as evidence of cohumanity in a Barthian manner does, however, threaten to compromise the perfect humanity of Jesus, who was, after all, single and male. But this is to misunderstand both Barth and Genesis 1. This passage says nothing about marriage, which is not introduced until Genesis 2. The point being made in the *imago* passage in Genesis 1 is that, irrespective of marital status, we image God in our very sexedness. In being male or female, we are a sacrament of a God who, as the full scope of revelation shows, is a differentiated unity of persons who are equal in essence, one in communion, and differentiated with respect to function within both the economic and immanent Trinity. Jesus, as the perfect Man, does not need to be married to be in the image of God. He needs to be male and in relation to females as a male. The essential definition of *sex* is not the act. Rather, it is a gift of God, something contemplative, designed to drive us out of ourselves toward the divine and human other, in a manner appropriate to our particular sex, whether male or female. It may be defined as "other-orienting energy. Sexuality is the energy for relationships that compels us to seek connections with others."[34]

Marriage, at its best, is an image of Christ offering himself for the church (Eph. 5:25–27). Friendship, at its best, is the laying down of one's life for the other (John 15:13). Sexedness, therefore, though it is a crucial aspect of the irreducible identity of persons and undeniably an important aspect of human identity, is not the *most* crucial aspect, which is being human as persons—and that essentially as personhood in community. We are human persons first and gendered human persons second. As human persons we discover community in the church as an ecclesial hypostasis, and this keeps gender in its rightful proportion.

---

33. Eugene F. Rogers Jr., "Supplementing Barth on Jews and Gender: Identifying God by Anagogy and the Spirit," *Modern Theology* 14, no. 1 (January 1998): 43–81. Rogers affirms Barth's innovations generally, but he critiques, unfairly I think, Barth's comments on Jesus (CD III/1, 308).

34. Clinical pastoral education training material cited in Bonnie Bucher, "Personal Response to 'Betrayal of Trust,'" Pastoral Ethics APPL 630, Regent College, 2008.

The most fundamental meaning of the image of God, the one that governs the structural and functional dimensions, then, is that of rela-tionality. Relationality may be understood in two related senses. The first is that God's gracious and covenantal relation to humanity is what stamps the image upon us. It is being in relation to God, the relational God, that constitutes the image. The second is that by stamping his image upon us by entering into relationship with us, God created humanity as relational. That is, he created us to model him, to be intrinsically rela-tional persons who image him as Trinity, as persons-in-relation. Another way to express these two aspects of relationality is first to say that the primal foundation of the human self is the knowledge of God, that is, it is participational. This is the capacity given by God to humanity to be in relationship with him ("in the image of God created he them") in an intimate and covenantal way. T. F. Torrance notes that *God* is the primary actor when it comes to human beings bearing his image: "It is, fundamentally, God who does the beholding of the image. He images Himself in man."[35] Secondly, as a result of this, by God's grace, each person is a model of God, as a person-in-relation. That is, each human person is both personal and relational, able to be in relationship to God, and then in relationship with the fellow human in a manner that reflects equality and otherness ("male and female he created them"). Implicitly they are also in relationship with creation, as God's representatives in the temple of his creation. *Imago Dei*—or in light of revelation, *imago trinitatis*—is the communal nature of persons who are mutually loving and self-giving, persons-in-relation with God, each other, and creation. We are therefore an analogy of the relational and personal God. Thus we are remarkably unique persons, and at the same time, we are persons who are profoundly interpersonal. Though we cannot be completely mutually internal to one another, we are interdependent. We know a measure of mutual interpenetration. We are able to interanimate one another.

The term *person* is as important as the term *relation* in this relational view of the *imago*. The gravitas of the concept and meaning of the term *person* may be measured by the comment of Joseph Ratzinger, who, upon narrating the history of the term *hypostasis* or *persona* through its chal-lenging theological journey in which it bore the weight of the theological battles toward establishing the doctrine of the hypostatic union and the

---

35. T. F. Torrance, *Calvin's Doctrine of Man* (Grand Rapids: Eerdmans, 1957), 42.

Trinity, stated that ultimately the "passage from individual to person contains the whole span of the transition from antiquity to Christianity, from Platonism to faith."[36] The ontological reality that God is three interpenetrated persons, persons of irreducible identity yet persons in a mutuality of communion, means that the ontology of image-bearing human persons is that we are by analogy persons-in-relation.

Our self-understanding (epistemology) ought thus to be that we are neither atomistic individuals nor a collective of nondescript persons. We are genuine persons of unique and irreducible identity with unique DNA and relational history, and yet we are persons who cannot be persons apart from community, from the moment of conception onward. The biblical and Christian tradition validates the nature and dignity of each human person and requires personal response to God in salvation and worship. But equally, these traditions recognize the communal nature and orientation of the human person. From a biblical perspective, *communal* means first and foremost being communal in the ecclesial community in Christ. Given that all humanity is image-bearing, it is likewise communal. We might expect that, within the literature of anthropology and sociology and psychology, there might be theories that postulate a consonant view of the nature of the human person as a social self, or as an "interpersonal self," which is indeed the case.[37] Understanding who God is and therefore who we are, in the spirit of Calvin's concept of double knowledge, is crucial to an awareness of what human beings are.

The coinherent reality of the Trinity has served to define healthy human relationships between pastor and counselee. For example, David Cunningham's language of polyphony describes the coinherence of oneness and threeness within the Trinity as "simultaneous, non-excluding difference: that is, more than one note is played at a time, and none of these notes is so dominant that it renders another mute."[38] Thus, as opposed to a zero-sum game, Cunningham makes the observation that "a theological perspective informed by polyphony would challenge any view that claims that any two contrastive categories must necessarily work against each other."[39] Building on this and the relational ontology of

---

36. Ratzinger, *Introduction to Christianity*, 2nd ed. (San Francisco: Ignatius, 1990), 160.
37. See the works of John Bowlby, e.g., *The Making and Breaking of Affectional Bonds* (London: Tavistock, 1979).
38. David S. Cunningham, *These Three Are One: The Practice of Trinitarian Theology* (Oxford: Blackwell, 1998), 128.
39. Cunningham, *These Three Are One*, 131.

Colin Gunton, Neil Pembroke states that the "fundamental polyphonic categories are unity and difference."[40] He extrapolates this to refer to the "nearness and differentiation" in a pastoral relationship (which might equally be extended to all healthy relationships).

All in all, if the relational nature of human persons is a reality, the assertion "You are nothing but a pack of neurons"[41] is patently reductionistic. If genes may be selfish in general, and this has been contested, then what constitutes the fulness of a human person fully alive is a person who loves and who loves sacrificially.

Validating the concepts of both personhood and community in the notion of the human as *imago Dei*, as well as never separating them, is crucial to the imaging of a God in whom persons and communion are equiprimal. The relational reality of the *imago* is of course perfectly realized in the man Christ Jesus (2 Cor. 4:4; Col. 1:15; Heb. 1:3) who lives in complete fellowship with his Father throughout his life, who is filled without measure by the Spirit, and who has been aptly described as the "Man for others."[42] The specifically communal dimension of the *imago* in humans also finds its fulfilment in Christ in that Christ as the *imago* includes his people in union with him (1 Cor. 15:22; Heb. 2:9–15). This is the concept of the collective Christ, in which the church is the bride and he the Bridegroom. This does not negate the personal nature and function of the human person, but it does inform the communal nature of the person profoundly.

Relationality is key for understanding the nature of humans made in the image of God, and that becomes unsurprising when the fulness of the revelation of God as Trinity is unfolded in *Scripture*. This rooting of our understanding of human persons in the doctrine of the persons of the Trinity, which has been revealed historically to us in the coming of the Son and the giving of the Spirit, is a reversal of the deistic or atheistic disjunction between God and the world and specifically between the knowledge of God and our self-knowledge. It arises from observation of the mutual engagement of the divine persons in the economy of salvation. Wolf Krotke agrees, observing that the question of

---

40. Neil Pembroke, "Space in the Trinity and Pastoral Care," *Journal of Pastoral Care and Counselling* 65, no. 2 (2011): 3.2.

41. This is how DNA scientist Francis Crick imagined Lewis Carroll's Alice might have said it in *The Astonishing Hypothesis: The Scientific Search for the Soul* (New York: Touchstone, 1994), 3.

42. The way in which both Dietrich Bonhoeffer and Karl Barth often refer to Jesus.

God is unavoidable in the discussion about what it means to be human, suggesting that theological anthropology should not, by using language incomprehensible outside of the theological guild, "gamble away a significant opportunity . . . to explain . . . that precisely when human existence is at issue at least the *question of God* is unavoidable."[43]

One must of course argue from carefully interpreted biblical texts about what human persons are. But in addition, a specific focus on the nature of the Genesis text itself also gives favour to the relational and communal view as predominant and determinative. The relational view fits well also with the literary genre of Genesis 1, which is poetic, highly stylized, and in form (but not content) comparable to other ancient Near Eastern accounts of creation. "It would be very odd if Genesis 1 were not to be understood along the lines of cosmic palace-temple building," notes biblical scholar Rikk Watts, given "the rather widespread Ancient Near Eastern notion linking creation, defeat-of-chaos, and temple-building, and the thorough-going architectural imagery which characterizes the biblical conceptualizing of creation."[44] Within this concept of creation, the notion of humanity as the image of Elohim as vice-regent in his temple has a natural place:

> After all, what is the last thing placed inside the deity's house, if not his image? . . . Thus, both Israel (Exod 4:22) and her king (Ps 2:8) are called to be God's son in the sense of being faithful bearers of his image, that is, to reflect his character and act as his vice-regents as they live in his palace-temple. . . . From this perspective, Genesis 1 is a "poetic" account in which Yahweh, Israel's god, is proclaimed the builder of creation, his palace-temple.[45]

According to this view, the *imago* bearers are such only as a consequence of their relatedness to *Elohim*. When the New Testament unfolds Christ as the *imago* and the church in Christ, the corporate nature of the *imago* is realized. Christ and his church together form the new humanity as the image of God. The Pauline (Eph. 2) and Petrine (1 Peter 2) use

---

43. Wolf Krötke, "The Humanity of the Human Person in Karl Barth's Anthropology," in *The Cambridge Companion to Karl Barth*, ed. John Webster (Cambridge: Cambridge University Press, 2000), 159.

44. Rikk E. Watts, "Making Sense of Genesis 1," American Science Affiliation: Science in Christian Perspective (2002), https://www.asa3.org/ASA/topics/Bible-Science/6-02Watts.html.

45. Watts, "Making Sense of Genesis 1."

of temple metaphors, which see a church in which Christ is the head of the body, the chief cornerstone of the living stones, or the high priest of the holy priesthood, speaks to the corporate nature of the image of God. The Johannine use in Revelation indicates that in the age to come, the temple, which is the church in this age, expands or, better yet, merges to incorporate all of the renewed creation. Watts hints at this in his discussion of the significance of John's description of the New Jerusalem as coming down out of the heavens to earth (Rev. 21), and he points to the absence of any temple in the city (Rev. 21:22):

> In other words, the climax of the new creation is not the abandonment of the earth, but instead the coming of Yahweh himself to the earth to dwell among us. Here, then, is the climax of Genesis 1's six-fold affirmation of the goodness of creation with its progression in both sets of days from heaven to earth. The final goal is not the destruction of creation, but rather the unification of heaven and earth such that the renewed earth itself now becomes Yahweh's very throne room.[46]

This perspective brings together the missional dimensions of the *imago Dei* very nicely. The cultural mandate, which is the first missional command of God to his human representatives or coregents, is often neglected within the concept of the church's mission. The formation of the new humanity in Christ has as its telos the ultimate renewal of all creation, as passages like Colossians 1 and Romans 8 confirm. Those in this age who are by grace brought into the new humanity in Christ cannot dismiss the importance of the cultural mandate and all it has to say about earth-keeping, the status of work, and the pursuit of the arts and sciences within this creational-temple view. The new humanity will both model this creational living and offer perspective to the world as its dispersed members engage in all aspects of the life of the world. This new humanity will also never forget its telos—the restoration of creation when the church is complete and fully redeemed—and it will therefore be motivated by this eschatological hope in its mission to all of humanity. It will by its very essence be an open community, drawing others into its communion constantly.

---

46. Watts, "Making Sense of Genesis 1."

The foundational aspect of the *imago Dei* that humans are persons-in-relation has profound consequences for how we view personhood. The relational view leans on the fulness of the revelation of the God of Genesis 1, as expressed in Scripture and particularly in the two greatest revelational events of the biblical story: the comings of the Son and the Spirit. Thus the relational view means that just as God is three persons-in-relation, not three individuals, so too are we persons-in-relation, not individuals.[47] We are persons with irreducible identity and dignity, yet we are persons defined by the Other, that is, by our Creator, human significant others, and ever-widening community. This upends the notion of Western individualism that has dominated Western culture for centuries and that has influenced the Western Christian church. Like the triune God, we are defined by "otherness within sameness," that is, otherness within essential equality, and we are defined by otherness within a complementary communion. Both the wonder of the irreducible identity of the triune persons and their conjoined essence and communion are to be praised and valued. Similarly, humans share in the communion of other humans and of God, but we have irreducible identity that is the basis for appropriate individuation yet not individualism.

How may we characterize the irreducible identity of a human person? There appear to be three dimensions to this: *unique personal embodiment or physicality (DNA), personality as shaped by genetics and relational experience* (I recognize I am glossing over a fair bit of complexity here), and an identity and otherness defined by *sexedness (gender)*. This means that males and females together reflect the image of God both in that they have essential equality as humans in God's eyes and in that they exhibit otherness and distinctiveness within this equality of essence. The distinctness of gender and not the blurring of genders, that is, the complementarity of the genders, is crucial to human being. Gender in its distinctness and in its complementarity does not completely define human beings, yet it does run deep in its defining of our identity as persons made in the image of God.

Bringing discussion of the image of God to a close, we observe that it is a notable feature of the interpretation of the *imago Dei* by premodern theologians such as Augustine and Calvin, that they tended not to advocate for singular categories in light of the paucity of biblical reference to

---

47. This analogy is justified in light of the human person of Christ.

the concept. Rather, they were comfortable with a composite meaning, even if one category may have been more dominant than another. In sum, all three aspects of a polyvalent approach are valid, but the structural and functional take their cue from and act as subsets of the relational and are dependent for their optimal functionality or imaging upon the relational. Thus the ruling or functional aspect is a consequence of the command of God, with whom the human being is in gracious relation, to care for nonhuman creation.[48] In other words, the idea here is that relatedness-relationship drives function and affects structural capacity to some extent.

---

48. This approach is consonant with the views of Colin Gunton, John Zizioulas, and Miroslav Volf, whose work has been well summarized in this regard by Steve Bachmann, "Enigma Variations: The *'Imago Dei'* as the Basis for Personhood with Special Reference to C. E. Gunton, M. Volf and J. D. Zizioulas" (PhD diss., Brunel University, 2002), 232.

CHAPTER 5

Theological Ethics Are *Eschatological*: Ethics of Reconciliation

The narrative of the reign of God on earth is a story of creation. It is also the story of the fall by which humanity is estranged from God and profoundly affected by sin in every aspect of its being. It is also the eternally anticipated story of the loving reconciliation and redemption of humanity by means of the advent of the last Adam, Jesus, the one Human for all humanity. By his incarnation, vicarious life, death, resurrection, and ascension, he recapitulated humanity, atoning for its guilt and triumphing over the power of sin and death that held it captive. From the Father, and through the Son, the Spirit was sent to effect the regeneration and empower the sanctification (including ethics) of reconciled humans. Ethics is always understood within the realism of what the fall has done to humanity, what reconciliation has accomplished for it, and what measures of transformation are possible by the Spirit's power in the "now but not yet." Ethics is also understood in anticipation of the consummation of redemption, a prospect that woos us from the future into all that we long for by way of communion with Christ and transformation of character and behaviour. In the unfolding drama of the reconciliation and redemption of humanity and creation, we begin with consideration of the effects of the fall.

THE FALL

The second part of the biblical story concerns a humanity characterized by sin and sins. The account of human nature is crucial to how one views any system of ethics, or moral character, thinking, and action. There is some disagreement in the tradition as to the nature and extent of the damage that was done to humanity by its fall into sin. The Eastern tradition, following Irenaeus, has tended to say that the fall was evidence of immaturity rather than rebellion. A distinction is sometimes made between the words *image* and *likeness* in Genesis 1:26, with the understanding that by the fall the image was not lost, but the likeness to God was lost and is recoverable by deification. Though it is not now uniformly held within Orthodoxy,[1] a typical critique of the West from this tradition is that Augustine's "exaggeratedly negative teaching on original sin and its consequences for human freedom and spiritual capacity" is "unsupported by Patristic consensus,"[2] and this Augustinian theology compromises "the spiritual goal of man, his theosis."[3] Following Augustine, the Western tradition, especially the Protestant wing, has understood the fall to be much more serious, characterized by alienation from God, from the human other, and from the self. The human apart from Christ is spiritually dead, and sin has distorted every aspect of human thinking and feeling and doing. Even within the Reformed view, however—which rightly insists that as a result of the fall, the heart is disoriented, the will is bent, the thinking is deluded, and the character has become self-seeking[4]—these distortions do not mean the negation of created givens, which are still givens. Every human person is not as bad as they possibly can be. They have a total inability to save themselves, but they still have the givenness of a rational mind (though their hearts suppress spiritual truth) and may have healthy emotions and even morals that may sometimes outshine those in a Christian community. As Albert Wolters has said, sin has the "character of caricature, . . . a distorted image that nevertheless embodies certain recognizable features," and "what something in fallen creation 'still is' points to the enduring goodness of creation."[5] The human being is a messy combination of *dignity* coming from having been made in the image of God and *misery* stemming from the sin that entered by the fall. Any philosophy that plays up the dignity evokes human pride, and those who emphasize

---

1. Fr. Georges Florovsky, for example, has expressed a more pervasive view of sin in *Collected Works of Georges Florovsky*, vol. 3, *Creation and Redemption* (Belmont, MA: Nordland, 1976), 91.

2. Victor Klimenko, "The Orthodox Teaching on Personal Salvation," http://orthochristian.com/46465.html, 1.

3. Michael Pomazansky, *Orthodox Dogmatic Theology: A Concise Exposition* (Platina, CA: Saint Herman of Alaska Brotherhood, 1984), 165.

4. Dennis P. Hollinger, *Choosing the Good: Christian Ethics in a Complex World* (Grand Rapids: Baker Academic, 2002), 75.

5. Albert M. Wolters, *Creation Regained: Biblical Basics for a Reformational Worldview* (Grand Rapids: Eerdmans, 1985), 48.

the misery create despair. As seventeenth-century French philosopher and mathematician Blaise Pascal asserted, only Christianity could "cure these two vices . . . according to the simplicity of the gospel."[6]

The biblical account of the fall elucidates its nature as it relates to the three aspects of the image of God discussed in the previous chapter. It especially vindicates the notion that the relational aspect is primary. Related to this relationality issue was a fundamental exocentricity and with that an "obligated responsiveness" of humans to God and to each other. This has been fouled up by the fall and a consequent fundamental egocentricity is the result, even though there remains that sense of obligated responsiveness.

What is signalled first in the Genesis account is a loss of relationship, which in turn affects the functional aspect and specifically the two main orders of creation spoken of above radically: work and sexuality/familying. There is trouble at work and tension at home. Structure and especially reason are affected. The unregenerate human retains some moral knowledge, ontologically speaking, which is related to the still extant moral order in the universe, but the knowledge is always somewhat distorted. Exactly how the unregenerate have this knowledge and how much they know are debated in the tradition. This debate is particularly relevant to whether Christian ethics should be presented in the public square and, if so, how it should be presented.

The Effect of the Fall on the Relational *Imago*

The first effect of the fall that is highlighted in Genesis 3 is the alienated distancing *between God and the prototypical humans* because they sought autonomy (3:5). Noticeably, God comes walking to them as is his usual custom, but this time they "hid themselves from the presence of the LORD God" (3:8 NRSV), and the very first question in the Bible is, remarkably, "Where are you?" Fear and shame in the divine presence arise for the first time in human existence. The desire to know goodness over against God and the givens of creation now prevails. The primary distortion of the human knowledge is that of the knowledge of God. From now on, the sense of transcendence that remains in humanity is distorted to form idols, false gods (ancient and modern) made in their own image, which can never satisfy or save. Reconciliation is the only

---

6. Blaise Pascal, *The Pensées*, trans. W. F. Trotter (New York: Random House, 1941), 7.435.

hope for alienated people. The second alienation in Genesis 3 is that *between human and human.* There is a succession of blame by Adam and Eve (3:12), and what was once partnership with mutual submission becomes competition and conflict (3:16). The given distinctions between male and female give way to mutual "domination, inverted desires, power plays and manipulation,"[7] to say nothing of abuse and violence, which erupt in chapter 4. The relational virtues of love are distorted into lust, control struggles, and manipulation of the other to meet our own psychological needs. But third, alienation *of the self to itself* becomes apparent in the story (3:7). The two sew fig leaves to cover their nakedness in shame and guilt. They "do not really know themselves, flee no less from self than from God, and try to make this unknown self the centre in place of God."[8] The self that they desired autonomy for is now unknown to them, for they cannot know themselves apart from knowing God. And self-deception is also evident in the dialogue between God and the two, which is initiated by the second significant question of the Bible: "What is this you have done?" (3:13). The self-deception in the deflections of both Adam and Eve betrays an inability to give truthful accounts of reality, what is really real. Dennis Hollinger comments, "Personal narrative triumphs over a metanarrative that is grounded in God, the truth and truthful one. It is through self-deception that fallen humanity with all its education and sophistication is able to do evil and not wince." Human beings can be "intellectually brilliant and artistically sensible and at the same time morally bankrupt."[9] He cites George Steiner, who said, "A human being can play Bach in the evening, and play him well, and read him with insight, and proceed in the morning to do his job at Auschwitz."[10] There is evidence, fourth, of an alienation *between humanity and the creation* in Genesis 3, metaphorically characterized by a cursed ground and thorns and thistles growing from it (3:17–19). Whilst the givenness of inanimate creation, the plant and animal world, and then human beings as stewards of all continues, the once harmonious relationship between those elements is damaged. Humanity is now over against the creation rather than loving, stewarding

---

7. Hollinger, *Choosing the Good*, 77.

8. Geoffrey Bromiley, "Sin," in *International Standard Biblical Encyclopedia*, vol. 3 (Grand Rapids: Eerdmans, 1982), 521.

9. Hollinger, *Choosing the Good*, 77.

10. George Steiner, *Extra-Territorial: Papers on Literature and the Language of Revolution* (New York: Atheneum, 1971), 36.

rulers within it. They will from this point on frequently abuse and even rape the creation. The givenness of creation will survive this and find reconciliation in the last Adam, and one day creation will be released from its bondage to decay (Rom. 8:20–21). In the meantime, those who are redeemed are to recover their roles as people of loving care for the creation in ways that affect their homes and work. Ecology is an important ethical issue for true Christians.

In sum, ethics will always be done in a context of global fallenness and deep personal fallenness, relationally speaking and consequently in the realm of character and behaviour. Ethics will often have to take into account the proclivities of humans for sin, including policies and procedures in the church and in all levels of government. Extremes of utopianism and complete disdain for the dignity of humans will need to be avoided.

The Effect of the Fall on the Functional *Imago*

The relational alienation in turn affects the functional aspect of the *imago* and specifically the two main orders of creation: work and sexuality/familying. Work, a given of the Creator, designed to bring appropriate self-fulfilment, becomes an arena in which great vocational ambivalence can occur, which often comes from broken upbringings in which there has been a lack of parental acceptance and affirmation or excessive demandingness. On the other hand, work can become an obsession, even an idol, through which self-acceptance is gained or childhood poverty is overcome. The egotistic nature of self-made billionaires is evidence enough. The power struggles at work in almost every company or school give further evidence of fallenness. Conflict between union and management is unavoidable as a result of the self-deception of managers or workers or union members. The pain of unemployment also plagues humanity, especially in Majority World countries. Ethics at work are almost always necessary, including and maybe especially in the church, which is a community of saints and at the same time a community of sinners.

The effects of sin and brokenness on sexuality, relationships, and marriage are legion. This is a larger discussion that we will defer until the chapter on sexuality. Both the created and the fallen components of human sexuality are vital to our understanding of sexual ethics, as is indeed the redemption of these areas now and in the future.

The Effect of the Fall on the Structural *Imago*

There is both a personal and a corporate or structural component to human beings as fallen image bearers. A biblical worldview incorporates the notion of structural sin. This does not compromise either personal worth or personal responsibility. Rather, it acknowledges our being as persons-in-relation and invokes even greater responsibility to act in the church and then in the public square on behalf of justice. The Bible is strewn with expressed concern for justice and for the rights and care of the poor, especially the Old Testament, which is the heritage of the New, which has its own fair share of exhortations in this regard. The New Testament references the "powers" (referred to as rulers [*archai*] or powers [*exousia*] or principles [*stoicheia*]), which are interpreted by New Testament scholars to refer not just to demonic powers at work in society but also to forces within the structures of society. These are to be prayed against and confronted by the Christian church in appropriate ways. A Christian worldview is, in a word, deeply aware of the pervasive nature of sin in persons and in structures and in the *world*, as New Testament authors refer to it. And in this case, *world* does not mean the earth or people; it means the ideas and ideologies of the age in its secularity and independence of God, revealing distorted values, thinking, and culture. The call of these authors is to be distinctive and not enculturated, to be separate from such values whilst not separated from the people of the world whom God loves and whom we are to seek to bring to Christ (Rom. 12:1–2; 1 Cor. 5:9–10; 1 John 2:15–17).

There is a need for caution in this call for prayer and protest against the powers and for avoiding the world in the right way. This relates to the tendency we have to neglect the realities that humanity is both fallen and made in the image of God ("mixed"), that there is goodness in humanity and in culture, and that there are social concerns for shalom that non-Christian image bearers may share, in which the Christian can participate. We must celebrate the good, the true, and the beautiful, which exist in societies because of the created givenness of humanity in all its sheer wonder (and deep contradictions). That means we can enjoy Bach (and Mozart) and all good music of every genre; we can delight in scientific discovery, for it has brought us many benefits—electric light, ovens, antibiotics, heart medication, surgical techniques . . . and so on.

Circling back to the *personal* structural component of the *imago*, we may summarize the structural effects of alienation and sin on humans as the endemic propensity to sin, to seek a knowledge of good and evil independent of God, to distort legitimate urges, to succumb to self-deception, and with this to forgo self-knowledge. The givenness of the capacities of the brain remained, but the heart prevented the saving knowledge of God. There was a continuance of relatedness to God as humans even when relationship was gone, and a continuance of the moral order and the capacity of humans at least ontologically to be aware of the moral law. The particular ordering of relationship and *reason* as definitive of the image of God has been the source of great controversy, in particular between the Catholic and Protestant traditions.

In what sense are we to understand the analogy between God and humanity expressed in the *image of God* concept, in light of both the metaphysical gap between deity and humanity and the sinfulness of humanity? Creation is presupposed in the doctrine of the incarnation. In turn, historically speaking, the doctrine of the incarnation precipitated the doctrine of creation *ex nihilo* (creation is distinct from the essence of God and thus could not have been made out of his being; thus, of necessity, it must have been created out of nothing) in that it allows a distinction between God and creation in the act of God's creation whilst insisting that the infinite and transcendent God can be immanent to creation without compromising his divine essence. The imaging or the analogy between God and humanity must therefore come by way of the incarnation of Christ. How are we to understand the *being* of creation, and of humanity, that is not univocal, and how do humans know God? The incarnational answer just offered is, in sum, the distinctively Protestant one, sometimes called the analogy of faith or relations or *adventus*. In Catholic theology, this question was answered by the notion of analogy and, in particular, the *analogia entis* or analogy of being. Affirmed at the Fourth Lateran Council (AD 1215), it was then developed notably by Polish Jesuit Erich Przywara. In essence, this concept affirms an ontological correspondence between God and humanity that results in the noetic capacity of all human persons to know God. It is a consequence of the person and work of Christ as *Logos* who grants reason (*logos*) to all human beings, who can in fact reason their way to God. These two components of the *analogia entis*, the ontic and the noetic, have, within the Thomist and Catholic tradition, been located in the created state in the image of God. Thus our ontic correspondence to God in this original created state involved a noetic correspondence understood as reason, which remained intact after the fall. Humans are therefore considered to be free to think metaphysically from their creaturely state to God.

In Protestant theology, the analogy is stressed to be one of faith (*fidei*) or faithfulness or relations (*relationis*) rather than of being. To be more precise, however, it is not that an analogy of being is denied but rather that the *source* of the analogy of being is different in the Protestant heritage. This tradition has considered the fall to be more radical and has considered the analogy between God and humanity to be expressed in Christ alone, the one Human for all humanity, in whom true correspondence exists between God and humanity, and through whom believing humanity recovers the analogy. The real basis of analogy is Christ *the* human, not the old humanity, which is fallen and would find its fulfilment in Christ, the unfallen last Adam.

Thus, in contrast with the *analogia entis* school of thought, the Protestant Barth-Jüngel-Spencer tradition looks to Christ first.[11] The *entis* school of thought emphasizes *reason* as the core meaning of the image of God (*imago Dei*) in humanity in a manner that is abstracted from the *imago Christi*, Jesus Christ, the *eschatos* Adam, the prototypical man for humanity, who is the image of the invisible God, and who in grace confers this upon all in the believing covenantal community of faith.

It is easy to see then why another term for *analogia fidei* is *analogia relationis*. The latter term came originally from Bonhoeffer, though it was Barth who developed it. The nexus of the relations of the person of Christ as the Son of God within the Trinity and his relationship as man with all humanity for Barth expresses the appropriate analogy between God and humanity by this technical term, the analogy of relations (*analogia relationis*). As Barth states, it "follows that the person who corresponds to, and reflects, the being of God bears the stamp of God's own dynamic character. Each human person then is destined to be in relation: to be I and Thou. I implies Thou, and Thou refers back to I. I and Thou are not coincidental or incidental but essentially proper to the concept of 'man.'"[12] The *analogia relationis* is a critical concept in Barth's anthropology and a major contribution to human thought. This was the notion that when speaking of human persons we must speak

---

11. Archie J. Spencer, *The Analogy of Faith: The Quest for God's Speakability* (Downers Grove, IL: IVP Academic, 2015).

12. Karl Barth, *CD* III/2, 248.

of relations, not merely of being. Another way of saying this is that he viewed the correspondence between the humanity and deity of Christ as analogous to a correspondence between human love and divine love.

As Barth scholar Bruce McCormack has noted, Barth understandably reacted to the *analogia entis* once some of his theological colleagues embraced nationalist ideologies on the basis of this kind of understanding of human capacity.[13] Barth's corrective actually preceded this. The *analogia entis* was understood "as a given, created continuity between the being of God and the being of the creature, by virtue of which the creature could understand herself as 'open upward,' that is, as containing within herself an abiding revelation that made the knowledge of God a human possibility."[14] Barth as a Reformed theologian was against such a notion, and as McCormack has suggested, he could have used the language of *entis* as *corrected* by the *analogia fidei*.[15] McCormack emphasizes the important reality that the *analogia fidei* has ontological implications. He states that in light of the stress Barth places on the Creator "in his relation" to the creature, this "means that the true *analogia entis* must be understood to be the consequence of a dynamic relation of God to the creature, a relation that is never simply a given (a *datum*) but is always, in every moment, to be given (a *dandum*)."[16] As hinted by McCormack, the *basis* for the analogy is what is at stake. Barth insisted on the close relationship between God's creation and his covenant, and in this understanding, the analogy between God and humanity (and creation), between image (and the trace) is a gift, not a given. As Barth himself avowed, the knowledge of God is not in "Platonic fashion . . . a reminiscence, as Ancient Beauty."[17] Here Barth is critiquing Augustine's description of conversion as if it were the recalling of a memory from an innate knowledge of God. Even though creation is a gift of grace, which is a rebuttal offered by the *entis* tradition, the analogy is not innate but is based on relationship initiated by God in his gracious covenant relations, and specifically the incarnation. "There is," as Barth says, "no original endowment in the human creature, but only . . . a second marvel of God's love, as the inconceivable, undeserved, divine bestowal on his

---

13. Bruce L. McCormack, review of *The Holy Spirit and the Christian Life: The Theological Basis of Ethics* by Karl Barth, *Princeton Seminary Bulletin* 15, no. 3 (1994): 312–14.

14. McCormack, review of *The Holy Spirit and the Christian Life*, 312.

15. McCormack, review of *The Holy Spirit and the Christian Life*, 312.

16. McCormack, review of *The Holy Spirit and the Christian Life*, 313.

17. Barth, *The Holy Spirit and the Christian Life* (Louisville: Westminster John Knox, 1993), 5.

creature."[18] This for Barth is an outflow of the deity and sovereignty of the Holy Spirit, who creates the continuity between God and humanity, applying what has been accomplished in Christ for humanity by the God who has thereby shown himself to be *for* humanity. Grace, says Barth, is "ever and in all relations God's *deed* and *act*."[19]

Another of Barth's disciples, Jüngel, radicalizing and yet correcting Barth at the same time (on the transcendence front), moves constructively to reorient the discussion by way of what he called the *analogia adventus*.[20] That is, he made the advent of Jesus Christ the norm for understanding God's being and human being, and the nature of the God-human relation. The analogy must really find its centre in the one mediator between God and the one true man, the man Christ Jesus. It is first the *analogia Christi*, in other words, not first the analogy of general humanity. It does, however, become the *analogia entis* for humans in Christ, that is, for those who believe (*analogia fidei*). Humans in union with Christ by faith are in correspondence with Christ and with God.

Another crucial issue in this debate has to do with mediation, the Protestant critique being that the *analogy of being* viewpoint fosters a mediator other than Christ Jesus, who alone created and reconciled humanity to God and brings those who exercise faith into ontological correspondence with God. We are therefore, as David Congdon states, "not free to reason our way to God apart from the way, the truth and the life." His "role of mediation encompasses our reason but not apart from our need for a redeemer . . . in Christ alone there exists an analogy."[21] Or to say this another way, any analogy between God and humanity/creation that does not need the incarnation is suspect. He concludes appropriately that the "doctrine of analogy is thus a correlate

---

18. Barth, *The Holy Spirit and the Christian Life*, 5.

19. Barth, *The Holy Spirit and the Christian Life*, 5.

20. For a full treatment of the work of Jüngel and Barth with respect to the analogy of being and the analogy of faith, see Spencer, *Analogy of Faith*. See also Spencer's work on Barth's ethics in light of the freedom of God (*Clearing a Space for Human Action: Ethical Ontology in the Theology of Karl Barth* [New York: Peter Lang, 2003]), as well as the work of John Webster (*Barth's Ethics of Reconciliation* [Cambridge: Cambridge University Press, 1995]; *Barth's Moral Theology: Human Action in Barth's Thought* [Edinburgh: T&T Clark, 1998]) and Joseph L. Mangina (*Karl Barth on the Christian Life: The Practical Knowledge of God*, vol. 8 of *Issues in Systematic Theology* [New York: Peter Lang, 2001]).

21. David Congdon, "Who's Afraid of the *Analogia Entis?*," *The Fire and the Rose* (blog), December 30, 2006, https://fireandrose.blogspot.com/2006/12/whos-afraid-of-analogia-entis_30.html.

of Christology."[22] In sum, the faith in reason of the *analogia entis* viewpoint, grounded in Aristotelian and Thomistic logic, stands over against the Protestant *analogia adventus fidei* viewpoint, which has its starting point not in reason but in the revelation of God in Christ. But a number of questions arise from these deliberations.

Do Catholic social ethics governed by faith in reason give Catholics a greater confidence that they can be heard in the public square? It must be said that those who adhere to the *analogia adventus fidei* can engage similarly, not with faith in reason per se but with faith that the Spirit of God is at work as they engage. A number of New Testament passages suggest that the cognitive capacity for relationship with God has been removed by the fall and that spiritual resurrection or regeneration is needed for its recovery (Eph. 2:1–10; 1 Cor. 2:14–16; 2 Cor. 4:3–6). And does this make the IQ of non-Christians lower? Apart from spiritual discernment, the answer must be no. The structural view has value in that it helps to describe human capacities and indeed human rights that have not been affected by the fall (see Gen. 9:6, which comes after the fall). These are ontological and are a consequence of the relatedness of humans to God by creation and providence, whether humans are spiritually awakened or not. I would hasten to add, however, that the amazing capacity that humans have for reason, amply demonstrated in this scientific age, does nevertheless show evidence of some deficiency, for which the world suffers. Science and its application in technology can be destructive, for example, when it functions without reference to global perspective and is exercised apart from any *relationship* with God or concern for relationship with neighbour. This accounts for the irony that humanity can place people on the moon and send robots to Mars and at the same time is capable of destroying the environment of its own planet through its technological myopia and greed. Again, therefore, relationship is seen to drive reason and rule.

RECONCILIATION

Redemption—or better, reconciliation in Christ and redemption by the Spirit, as Barth categorized them—is the grace of God bringing humanity back into the relational aspect of the *imago* (reconciliation)

---

22. Congdon, "Who's Afraid of the *Analogia Entis?*"

and then repairing its structural and functional brokenness (redemption of the human person as a child of God) to enable human persons to be and to act as he intended in the creation. Once again, it is important to stress that the nondegreed nature of the *imago* is unchanged by the fall and by redemption. Human persons who believe and are incorporated into Christ are justified and begin to be sanctified; the righteousness of Christ received by faith becomes our righteousness, and the justice by which God has worked our justification becomes our justice to be lived. Transformation begins to happen in all aspects of life in the home (in familying and sexual behaviour) and in the workplace (in the holiness and purposefulness of vocation as participation in God's work in the world toward the new creation). In the "now but not yet" of the kingdom, these restoration processes take time and are often characterized by failure. "A life of confession and slow growth" is a more realistic description than "victorious Christian living."

What is reversed by Christian conversion, according to Paul, is what we may call filial or relational. God takes the initiative, for "God was in Christ, reconciling the world to himself" (2 Cor. 5:19 KJV). The history of Jesus Christ, the Son who became one with us, is the means of our salvation. In the process by which we appropriate this by the Spirit, a regeneration, which includes illumination, reverses what Paul refers to unapologetically as the spiritual blindness of humanity without Christ (1 Cor. 2:14; 2 Cor. 4:4). The dead are made alive, and the blind are made to see. The reason that characterizes the realm of divine wisdom, and indeed the gospel, is not discerned by natural intellect and wisdom. In fact, the "message of the cross is foolishness to those who are perishing" (1 Cor. 1:18). The economy of the cross and the upside-down nature of the kingdom of God are not discernible without the work of the Spirit of God upon the image bearer's intellect. For this reason the Christian, having been regenerated and illumined by the gracious awakening of the Spirit, can in fact claim to have more insight than his or her teachers (Ps. 119:99). This should not of course become a matter of pride, nor should it be boiled down in reductionistic fashion to mean that the IQ or EQ of the Christian is higher than that of the rest of humanity. The revealed Word of God does make wise the simple (Ps. 19:7), but this must be understood in a wider sense than mere intellectual acumen and includes moral discernment concerning right living that leads to relational harmony with other humans and creation. It is this wisdom perspective, however, that the Christian is expected to bring to bear on the world in all its aspects. The path of wisdom overflows from within the community of the church to the world. It is unapologetically the ethic of the believing church, and though the church cannot within a pluralistic society expect its norms to be those of the world, it is expected to bear witness with a view to being salt and light. It is expected to be an alternative community of hope, a sign of the kingdom that has come and is coming, a witnessing communion in *ekstasis*, just like the Trinity.

Fallen humans are still capable of rational thought, horizontal relationships, and vocational, artistic, and scientific achievement, but they are incapable of divine life or relationship with God. There is a givenness of the image related to creation, though as we have seen in Protestant thought it is being given by the *analogia relationis* rather than given by *analogia entis*. It is nondegreed by *creation*. Rationality and vocation are extrinsic rather than intrinsic to the image. Fetuses with Down syndrome cannot be aborted simply because they may be low on the IQ scale. We cannot classify others as "useless mouths," as Hitler put it. All human beings from implantation to death are image bearers and with that have inalienable human rights. This is the result of the *relatedness* of all human beings to God by creation. The teleology suggested by God's desire for every human being to be saved (1 Tim. 2:3–4: "God our Savior, who wants all people to be saved"; Matt. 18:14: "Your Father in heaven is not willing that any of these little ones should perish") directs the Christian to anticipate that God may be awakening people as they bear witness to the gospel. It is incontrovertibly God's desire that all are and will be his.

This difference between the Christian and the non-Christian invites the age-old nature/grace distinction, which has been a source of contention between and within the traditions. It must be acknowledged by all traditions that nature, including all of humanity, is engraced—that is, human persons are made in the image of God, and they could not exist apart from the providence of a good God, who lets his rain fall on the just and the unjust (Matt. 5:45). The breath and life span and geographical location of every human being is in his hands and under his care, and this *sensus divinitatis* invokes the sense of morality or obligatedness as well as some awareness of God present in all human beings (Acts 17:24–27; Rom. 2). However, the distinction between common grace and saving grace is present in especially the Reformed and evangelical traditions (the Orthodox tradition makes less of this given that their view of the fall is less severe, being more like immaturity than inability). For biblical and theological reasons, the Reformational tradition strongly holds that human beings are dead in trespasses and sins and unable to respond to the gospel apart from this saving grace and that there are indeed no *points of contact* between humans in their natural state. Unlike the majority Roman Catholic and liberal Protestant view of human capacity suggested by the statement, "Grace does not destroy nature, but perfects it,"[23] the Reformed tradition insists, on the basis of Paul's teaching, that what is required is "no mere rejigging or re-polishing or repairing of human nature: but rather the crucifixion of the flesh, and the raising of the new creature. Regeneration is expressed not in the figure of repair or restoration, but of new birth, a completely new start."[24] Trevor Hart develops this line of thought by expressing further:

Nature is not, in its historical state, predisposed towards grace, but resists it. The old creation is not capable of the new creation, i.e. there is nothing in the old Adam, the flesh, which could simply be developed or extrapolated to posit the new Adam. Redemption, therefore, is not a matter of evolution, or of development, or perfection: but of revolution, crisis and crucifixion.[25]

Furthermore, Reformed theology resists developing an ontology that bridges the divine-human divide on the basis of nature, and on the other hand requires, as Alan Torrance has said, the "radical and dynamic continuity between the divine and the human that is the event of Christ."[26] The fuller outworking of reconciliation and redemption will be discussed in chapter 6 under evangelical ethics. Suffice it to say that regeneration does restore and by degree makes possible the cultivation of wisdom and a moral life that is intended to be shared with the world for whom Christ died. Suffice it to say also that ethics within the church community must be realistic in the "now but not yet" period of redemption before consummation. The saints are both justified and

---

23. Thomas Aquinas, *Summa Theologiae* I, q. 1, a. 8, ad. 2.

24. Trevor Hart, "A Capacity for Ambiguity: The Barth-Brunner Debate Revisited," *Tyndale Bulletin* 44, no. 2 (1993): 300.

25. Hart, "Capacity for Ambiguity," 293.

26. Alan J. Torrance, *Persons in Communion: Essay on Trinitarian Description and Human Participation* (Edinburgh: T&T Clark, 1996), 209.

sinners. There may be progression in sanctification, but the progress is not complete until the end. Muddled in the middle, in the now but not yet, we are neither triumphalist nor defeatist, but as those already justified in Christ, we pursue and can experience change, the degree of which varies within the tradition. The pursuit of the ethical holy life in this in-between time is humbling because we do not yet see clearly, because we continue to be subject to sinful nature (and sinful behaviour as perpetrators) and brokenness (what sinful behaviour has done to us as victims), because we cannot ever look with condemnation on others, and because we are always in need of forgiveness. The ethical holy life is pursued within a life of confession and repentance.

Redemption is the redemption *of* creation, not *out of* creation. Humans are not redeemed to become something other than human. The horizontal and sequential nature of salvation history is from creation to new creation. This is true of the nonhuman creation also, which will not burn up in a literal sense but will go through purification and into deliverance from bondage. There is, however, also an important vertical dimension to Christian reality. We are indeed seated now in the heavenly realms in Christ Jesus (Eph. 2:6). We have access by prayer to the throne room of the Father by the intercession of the Spirit and the high priestly ministry of the Son. However, this living on a heavenly plane is intended to be exercised here on earth, just as Jesus taught in the Lord's Prayer: "Your kingdom come, your will be done, on earth as it is in heaven." Thus, being "hidden with Christ in God" (Col. 3:3) is an identity and experience lived out in the ethical dilemmas and doings of earth.

CONSUMMATION

Consummation is consummation of creation and of resurrected humans, who will inhabit new creation within the immediate presence of God, who has come to dwell in the new Jerusalem on earth (Rev. 21:1–14). The beatific vision of Christ will consummate the sanctification process in glorification of the believers. All justice will be redressed. The temporary nature of marriage will be revealed. Work will continue. Many unanswered questions remain about what heaven on earth looks like, but it is certain that we will be human, not angels and not God. We will be mere humans but with a spiritual orientation and bodies that will most likely correspond morally and metaphysically to that of Jesus.

That is, just as Jesus was human and recognizable, having a continuity with who he was before resurrection, and just as there was also a discontinuity about Jesus's body in that it was oriented toward heaven, so the substance of our bodies will have continuity and discontinuity with our present bodies. This discontinuity does not mean that humans will be transhuman, but merely and fully human.

What is the relevance of the consummation when Christ returns to the moral quest? In a word, it is the telos of our moral vision. It is defined as best we can determine by complete relational harmony between us and God, between ourselves and our human neighbours, and between ourselves as human and the nonhuman creation, so fulfilling the relational reality of the *imago*. We shall know even as we are known (see 1 Cor. 13:12). It will also restore any deficits in the structural or ontological nature of the *imago* with respect to discovering the limits of what perfected human intellects can know and with respect to the healing of the brokenness of human affections. There will also be that paradoxical freedom in God's freedom to be obedient and to exercise perfect justice. This hope of the beatific vision and the transformation or glorification that goes with it is intended to purify the people of God, as 1 John 3:2–3 indicates: "Dear friends, now we are children of God, and what we will be has not yet been made known. But we know that when Christ appears, we shall be like him, for we shall see him as he is. All who have this hope in him *purify themselves, just as he is pure*" (emphasis added). Eschatology of the future kind is not intended for speculation but as an incentive to the ethical life.

It is also intended to encourage us to persevere through all the vicissitudes of life on earth, the persecutions received for faithful witness to the gospel and its ethical imperatives, the repeated failures as we battle our sinful tendencies and addictions, and the brokennesses of our emotions and affections and sexuality. Romans 8 is a specific case of such encouragement where Paul speaks of justification and glorification in the same tense and together as a *fait accompli*: "Those he predestined, he also called; those he called, he also justified; those he justified, he also glorified" (v. 30). The troubling period of the sanctification journey that comes in between justification and sanctification is omitted by Paul, as if to say in the eternal scope of things that moral formation and those ethical struggles will seem like nothing. If you are justified, take it as a given—you are already glorified! This is a fitting place to move on to speak of ethics as evangelical.

CHAPTER 6

Theological Ethics Are *Evangelical*

It is hard to imagine a better picture of what evangelical ethics means than the story in Luke 19 of Jesus's encounter with Zacchaeus, who was a pariah in Israel not just because he was an agent in taking taxes on behalf of the despised Roman imperial government but because most likely he extorted funds by taking more than was asked by the Romans. His repentance is remarkable. In the presence of Jesus and his disposition to forgive, Zacchaeus knows there are ethical implications to his repentance. You cannot follow Jesus and stay the same, ethically speaking. But the grace of God expressed in Jesus's acceptance motivated this ethical transformation. Half of his possessions go to the poor, and he pays back what the law required, four times what he had stolen. Repentance is motivated by gospel and validated by restitution.

Let us be clear that evangelical ethics is not necessarily the same as the ethics of the evangelicals, referring to the movement, which contains a wide swath of opinion on the place of ethics in the Christian life, including the opinion that it has no place. Though one would hope that evangelicals are evangelical in their ethics—that is, that they understand that ethics are *of the gospel*, that they are evangelical and not legal, that they are evangelical in that they are motivated by the grace of God and his decision eternally to be for humanity in Jesus Christ, that they are enabled only by participation in the life of God, and that they are discernible and possible because of a created moral order that has been reaffirmed in the resurrection of Jesus—this cannot be taken as a given. Even if it is true that evangelical Christians believe in theory that their ethics do flow out of their faith in Jesus, they may in fact live as practical atheists due to a dualism that separates their ethical convictions from their faith. There are also evangelicals who are antinomian in their conviction, who have the gospel and ethics in opposition. Some have made it almost a virtue to deny that ethics exists for those who are justified by faith, doing so to the neglect of repentance and the life of sanctification that includes ethics. They live without awareness of the twin graces Calvin spoke of as being inseparable but distinguishable consequences of union with Christ by faith. That is, they magnify the first grace of *justification* to the neglect of ethics, becoming antinomian, or they assume that *sanctification* (and ethics) is the means for achieving justification and become Pelagian, bound by fear.

As was stressed earlier, ethics apart from the gospel does not exist, but ethics *in* or *of* the gospel very much matters as the mark of those who have truly believed and have been transformed by conversion. Sometimes the popular emphasis that God's love is "unconditional" leads to a kind of easy-believism and an underlying assumption that I can live as I like. Of course, it is true that God's love for humanity is unconditional, but our appropriation and experience of that love are in fact predicated upon a life of faith leading to obedience. It is unconditional, not *unconditioned*. It has to be received, and it has to be lived into. The epistle of Jude expressly exhorts, "*Keep yourselves* in God's love as you wait for the mercy of our Lord Jesus Christ to bring you to eternal life," and this "by building yourselves up in your most holy faith and praying in the Holy Spirit" (Jude 1:20–21, emphasis added). Becoming a subject of the love of God will show, according to 1 John, by our human love in response to God's love, and this is expressed precisely by the keeping of God's commands: "In fact, this is love for God: to keep his commands" (5:3). In a nutshell, when the evangelical separates the gospel and morality, she or he becomes either antinomian (someone who shows "disregard or insufficient regard, for moral questions") or a moralist (someone who holds "moral conviction unevangelically").[1] In contrast to both is the biblical conviction expressed by Oliver O'Donovan that Christian ethics "is a belief that certain ethical and moral judgments belong to the gospel itself; a belief, in other words, that the church can be committed to ethics without moderating the tone of its voice as a bearer of glad tidings."[2]

Then ethics, so called, can be either a violation of the gospel or a clarification and outflow of the gospel. Ethics taught and understood the wrong way becomes legalism and an offensive affront to the gospel of grace. Ethics taught and understood the right way will be seen as an

---

1. Oliver O'Donovan, *Resurrection and Moral Order: An Outline for Evangelical Ethics* (Grand Rapids: Eerdmans, 1986), 11.
2. O'Donovan, *Resurrection and Moral Order*, 12.

essential part of the gospel, without which all talk of grace and faith is wind. That is, theology without ethics is a gnostic denial of the creational reality of life in God.

Certain theologians in the Protestant tradition have spoken eloquently and serve to highlight the interlocking, coinherent nature of theology and ethics. Karl Barth, for example, in his theology consistently refused "to isolate ethical talk of good human action from dogmatic talk of the divine achievement."[3] And in turn, for Barth, all theology was considered moral, bearing upon human action and life.[4] In light of this, Barth laid great emphasis in his ethical approach on the function and telos of the commands of God for the Christian life, though always within the framework of the gospel. Dietrich Bonhoeffer's book *Ethics* is particularly important for the distinction it makes between what one could call ethics *of* the gospel and ethics *over against* the gospel. As Bonhoeffer insists, wanting to know right and wrong was the very essence of the fallen desires of Adam and Eve! They wanted to know right and wrong apart from knowing God and participating in his life. Most ethics, whether they are Christian or not, are an attempt to articulate the good, and for the Christian to do this apart from God is simply to reenact the original sin of Adam. It was particularly the place of reason in ethical knowing, specifically reason outside of a faith-relationship with God, that expressed the essence of sin. As Bonhoeffer has so eloquently indicated, it is futile to pursue ethics or being good and doing good outside embeddedness and participation in the self-revealing God in Christ.[5] Ethics can be either the very antithesis of the gospel or the very content of the gospel. Ethics that are not grounded in who God is (i.e., the triune, covenant-keeping God) and that are not evangelical (i.e., enabled and shaped by the gospel) are an expression of self-righteousness and futility. It is this precise futility into which the fall plunged humanity in its endless obsession with right and wrong. The missional church lives into personal and communal moral formation in union with Christ, and

---

3. John Webster, *Barth's Moral Theology* (Grand Rapids: Eerdmans, 1998), 8.

4. Webster, *Barth's Moral Theology*, 18–19, 43–48. Webster corrects the impression that Barth's concern with moral theology is a late development. Barth, though reticent to speak of morality in a direct way, simply wished to recast all talk of ethics in an intensively *theological* mode of discourse. Nigel Biggar expresses similar sentiments on Barth's project in Nigel Biggar, *The Hastening That Waits: Karl Barth's Ethics* (Oxford: Clarendon, 1995), 7–13.

5. Dietrich Bonhoeffer, *Works*, vol. 6, *Ethics*, ed. Clifford Green, trans. R. Krauss, C. C. West, and D. Scott (Minneapolis: Augsburg Fortress, 2005), 47–55.

seeks to influence communal and national justice as an outflow of this evangelical orientation toward ethics.

Picking up the theme of the previous chapters, then, theological ethics, if they are biblical and theological and Trinitarian, will inevitably also be evangelical. It has already been established in chapter 2 that *Trinitarian* means that God's triune person and acts are the very foundation for ethics. That is, with respect to his person, the triune God is indeed the ground and the norm and the power for ethics, and with respect to his actions within the history of the economic revelation of God, God's acts of creation, redemption from the fall, and consummation of creation are the acts in which by grace we come to participate since our being is in union with Christ by the Holy Spirit. In other words, one can simply say that the revelation of God as Trinity *is* the gospel, and therefore the reconciling and redemptive acts of God that justify and sanctify us, including our ethical discernment and actions, are simply those in which we participate. The *ordo historia* of Jesus Christ becomes by grace the *ordo salutis* of the Christian, which includes one's ethical life, since it includes one's justification and sanctification (including ethics). The Trinity is the gospel, and the gospel is the Trinity.

The structure of this chapter is based on explanation and exposition of what is meant when we say Christian ethics must be evangelical. *First*, ethics is impossible apart from human *participation* by faith in the God who participated in our humanity, that is, who became one with us by the incarnation and lived the moral life perfectly for us, redeemed us from the consequences of our ethical failures, and restores to us both the objective reality of a moral order in Christ and an ability subjectively by the Holy Spirit's indwelling and empowering to discern the moral order and to live according to it.

Second, evangelical ethics means that ethics flows not toward a righteous position before God but *from a righteous position* given to us in Christ through whom creation has already been justified and all humanity with it (this proposition needs explanation to be sure). *Third*, ethics is only possible by the *resurrection* of Jesus from the dead and our participation in his resurrection life, for in his resurrection creation was reaffirmed and with it a created moral order that God did not permit to be destroyed. And *fourth*, ethics flows from a view of *anthropology* that properly permits the working of the gospel. Thus four words will guide our discussion of evangelical ethics: participation, justification, resurrection, and anthropology.

EVANGELICAL ETHICS ARE THE
ETHICS OF PARTICIPATION

Participation, or union, is a weighty word that for our purposes includes two movements that are at the heart of the gospel. The first is the divine movement by means of which the second person of the Trinity, the Son of God, became fully and truly human for us and for our salvation. All speech about our human action must begin with God's action to become human, to transform our humanity by the incarnation, having taken up our sinful humanity and cleansed it. He also came to stand in our place in his vicarious life of obedience for all humanity, the one Human who fulfilled the law for us, the last Adam who recapitulated a fallen humanity in which the divinely given moral order was compromised, thus threatening to undo the creation. He also came to die for us, offering up his life in a way that brought satisfaction that far outweighed our sin's debt, a substitutionary sin offering for our sin's guilt. He also ascended and lives for us now in the power of an endless life as the great high priest in heaven who represents us in all his fragrant beauty and righteousness before God. His function there is as a symbol of completed atonement and as the sustainer of the people of God until the unfinished aspect of the work of Christ is complete—our sanctification and the redemption of the creation to which as the church we are called as priests.

This is the first and most important aspect of the gospel: God participates in our humanity so that humanity represented in Christ might recover what it means to be human image bearers in both an ontological and an epistemological sense. That is, children of God by faith who are enabled to live according to God's moral order—filially speaking, children of God; forensically speaking, justified before God. Whether what Christ did in his incarnate history on earth stands good for all humans is, of course, an ongoing debate in which we will dabble in the section on justification as the grounding for ethics. What seems to be presented with perspicacity in the New Testament is that only those who repent and believe and are thereby regenerated enter into the good of what Christ has accomplished. Only those who believe may have assurance that they can pursue holiness of heart and life—that is, moral formation and moral action—without condemnation, despite the inevitable failures in their pursuit. Their objective righteousness is in Christ even as they seek to become righteous as Christ is in them by the Spirit. This is expressed poignantly by the writer of the book of Hebrews as he, with great understatement, climaxes his exposition of the atoning work of our priest, Jesus Christ: "For by one sacrifice he has made perfect forever those who are being made holy" (Heb. 10:14). Only those who believe and come alive in Christ can have a clear vision of the objective reality of the moral order. Only those who have the Spirit of Christ are then able to discern with increasing clarity the moral order and discover that they have a new being in Christ and a new ability to participate with Christ in his death and resurrection. Participation in his *death* is manifested by practices of the *mortification* of the flesh. The alternative to evangelical ethics by participation is life in what Paul calls the "flesh," which is a way of speaking of humanity on its own without God. It is the impulse to seek to assume moral responsibility by means of the independent self, without participation, in ways that become either legalistic or libertarian. O'Donovan has asserted that this does not mean that the Christian way is the happy medium between the two. These, as ways of avoiding inviting the responsibility of God, are simply "two sub-Christian forms of life."[6] Galatians 5, in contrast, describes the true freedom in Christ by the Spirit that is neither a freedom *from* the law nor a bondage *to* the law but a freedom *for* the law of God. Participation in Christ's *resurrection* implies a new capacity to see, a new sense of things, as Jonathan Edwards might say,[7] and with that comes contemplation of Christ that transforms us (2 Cor. 3:18). We are also given new desires and renewed affections as we are nurtured by the Holy Spirit's indwelling and empowering. This is *vivification* such that the graces of the Spirit, or virtues, what Paul called the fruit of the Spirit, are formed in us (Gal. 5:22–23). The fruit of the Spirit are given within a context in which believers are encouraged to stand in their moral freedom (5:1, 13), not license, by walking by the Spirit (5:16) and keeping in step with the Spirit (5:25), which is another way of saying participation in the life of the Spirit. The virtues, the chief of which is love, are developed within us as we live life in participation

---

6. O'Donovan, *Resurrection and Moral Order*, 12.

7. In 1740, Jonathan Edwards wrote retrospectively of his conversion, by which he gained a "new sense" of "the glory of the divine being" as specifically involving the Trinity: "God has appeared more glorious to me, on account of the Trinity . . . it has made me have more exalting thoughts of God, that he subsists as three persons; Father, Son, and Holy Ghost." Edwards, YE 16:800. In *Miscellanies*, 343, he states that "the revelation we now have of the Trinity," which he considers to be the chief doctrine of the faith, makes "a vast alteration with respect to the reason and obligations to many amiable and exalted duties, so that they are as it were new"(YE 13:416).

with Christ in the church, participating in the Eucharist and hearing the Word as it comes to us, again and again. It is noticeable that the New Testament seldom speaks of individual spiritual practices, but it does speak again and again of ecclesial practices. In other words, participation in Christ is participation in the church for the New Testament writers! Hearing the Word of God preached is like spring rain, whereas our individual Bible reading and study are more like a spray from a watering can. Both are essential, yet even the personal readings must have as their goal a sharing with the community, whether in a small group or with the whole congregation. One of the minimal remedies for the moral crisis of the church is for the people of God to recover from biblical illiteracy. A people of God who are saturated with the Word of God are more likely to find their way through the moral maze of our times.

The book of Proverbs provides a vivid illustration of the relationship between the practice of reading and imbibing the Word of God, one of the resurrection practices, and finding moral insight and freedom within God's created moral order as expressed in the moral law. In 2:1–11 the conditional *if* of passionate pursuit of the Word of God is first expressed in a way that reflects increasing intensity that climaxes with a mining analogy: "*if* you accept my words and store up my commands within you, turning your ear to wisdom . . . *if* you call out for insight and cry aloud for understanding . . . *if* you look for it as for silver and search for it as for hidden treasure." This is then answered twice by the promise of the gracious consequences if the condition is met: "*then you will* understand the fear of the LORD and find the knowledge of God. For the LORD gives wisdom" (2:5–6); "*then you will* understand what is right and just and fair—every good path. For wisdom will enter your heart, and knowledge will be pleasant to your soul" (2:9–10).

Moral living is a fruit of wisdom that arises from a diligent and passionate search for truth and for God in his Word. In the New Testament, Paul expresses these same connecting strands. He makes a definite connection between the way of wisdom and the fulness of the Holy Spirit in Ephesians 5:15–18, where the titular command of the paragraph, to "walk in wisdom" (5:15), is explained by the command, "Be filled with the Spirit" (5:18). The way of wisdom, the wise moral ethic, is empowered by the spiritual dynamic of life controlled and empowered by the Spirit. The life of wisdom enabled by participation in the Spirit and those ethics that go with it are worked out by Paul in 5:19–6:4, into the moral and spiritual dynamics of ecclesial worship life, marital life, family life, and life at work. Yet in Colossians 3, in a context that has all of the same ethical ramifications as Ephesians 5, Paul inserts an alternative way of saying, "Be filled with the Spirit." It is expressed as *"Let the word of Christ dwell in you richly*; teach and admonish one another in all wisdom; and with gratitude in your hearts sing psalms, hymns, and spiritual songs to God" (Col. 3:16 NRSV, emphasis added). This no doubt meant the Old Testament and whatever written New Testament documents were extant when Paul wrote this, as well as the apostolic doctrine that was known through the teaching of the apostles. Irrespective, the idea is the same. Saturation with the Word of Christ is a vital component in the formation of wise people, people who live rightly, in right relationships with the creation and their near and distant human neighbours. They reflect shalom in their marriages, in their child-rearing and parenting, and in their vocations. Paul puts the Word and the Spirit together in these two great parallel paraenetic passages of the New Testament. Pursuit of the knowledge of the Word of God on its own without the illuminating and interpreting power of the Spirit may produce the kind of Pharisaism that Jesus exposed, the pretence of outward ethical rectitude that is not matched by transformation of the heart (Matt. 22:29; John 5:39). At the opposite extreme, so-called "life in the Spirit" without the guidance of the Word of God can lead to charismatic anarchy and shoddy ethics justified by so-called prophetic words and apostolic manipulations.

But how can we put together the two movements of participation, that of the Son in our humanity and that of believing humanity in the Son? Emphasizing the one over the other has unfortunate consequences. Those who emphasize the objective realities of what has been accomplished by the history of Jesus Christ can sometimes underemphasize the need for personal appropriation of it in their own salvation history. Those who emphasize the subjective participation, the human reception and the spiritual affections and actions that are signs of true saving faith, to the neglect of the objectivity of the person and work of Christ for humanity are very likely to become introspective and lose the outwardness that gospel life and ethics bring, which is summed up in the love of neighbour. One might say that Karl Barth stressed the objective reality of Christ for salvation to the detriment of human subjectivity and that Jonathan Edwards stressed the subjective aspect of the gospel at the expense of the objective.[8] John Calvin, by contrast, may be said to have kept these realities in proper tension where both Edwards and Barth, who owed a debt to him, did not. Calvin expresses these twin graces (*duplex gratia*) of justification and sanctification as distinct but inseparable, as equal consequences of what by some is considered the most foundational reality of Calvin's soteriology, which is the believer's union with Christ (*unio cum Christi, unio mystica*) entered into by faith. What is sometimes called the *ordo docendi*, which is the order of Calvin's teaching in the *Institutes*, is sometimes employed as a way of discerning his *ordo salutis*, which is the order in which salvation occurs. Thus, because Calvin treats sanctification in the Spirit before he teaches on justification, it is sometimes concluded that this was a corrective to Luther's near obsession with justification in Christ. Thus Calvin is interpreted as equalizing the graces and combating a lack of emphasis on regeneration and the subjective work of God in the sinner without compromising the gains of Luther regarding justification.[9] Despite some controversy in the interpretation of Calvin in this area, the "inseparable yet distinguishable" nature of the graces in Christ can be affirmed by all. Calvin's soteriology may also be said to confirm that the faith that justifies the believer, leading to assurance of righteousness before God, is the same faith by which the believer is conjoined to Christ. Christ's union with humanity and the union of believers with Christ are the foundation of assurance. However, for Calvin, even faith is only possible as it is enabled by the regenerating work of the Spirit, who conjoins the

---

8. For a detailed description of these trends in Barth and Edwards, see W. Ross Hastings, *Jonathan Edwards and the Life of God: Towards an Evangelical Theology of Participation* (Minneapolis: Fortress, 2015). In defence of Edwards, sometimes he seems merely to be countering "cheap grace," as Bonhoeffer would in a later age. For example, where he anticipates the "works righteousness" accusation in *Religious Affections*, he counters that rigorous defence of justification by faith alone has "hurt" the cause of true religion in that the "effectual operations of grace in practice" are neglected in favour of "grace in contemplation" (YE 2:457–59). As he puts it, "Words are cheap," whereas "Christian practice is a costly, laborious thing" (YE 2:411). There are other times, however, when sanctification as the proof of justification leads to a conflation of the two and with that a struggle with assurance in Edwards's theology.

9. The proper interpretation of Calvin in this regard is a controversial matter. See Thomas L. Wenger, "The New Perspective on Calvin: Responding to Recent Calvin Interpretations," *JETS* 50, no. 2 (June 2007): 311–28, for a summary of opinions. I believe that in fairness to both sides of this controversy, it is still reasonable to say that Calvin did consider the two graces, justification and sanctification, to be a logical consequence of union with Christ, and as such to be inseparable yet distinguishable. Calvin's robust doctrine of sanctification is also agreed on by all, and the fact that he calls for it evangelically, as those already justified, seems abundantly clear also. See John Calvin, *Institutes*, 3.11.1; 3.13.5.

believer to Christ. The believing person who is justified in Christ must therefore inevitably also manifest sanctification by the Spirit, even if that sanctification is unfinished until the eschaton comes in fulness. Crucial to evangelical sanctification and ethics on this understanding is that they are pursued with justification already a given (for the true believer). This theme will be picked up in the following section.

One way to keep justification and sanctification together yet distinct, as has already been implied, is a Trinitarian one. We must embrace *both* subjective life engendered within us by the Holy Spirit *and* the objective realities of salvation history in the Son. The focus of our attention in the ethical life will, however, be the christological one. We do not grow morally and ethically by focusing on ourselves, even our own growth or lack of it. We grow by looking away from ourselves to the Christ whom we imitate (2 Cor. 3:18), whom we imitate not as an impossible and cruel quest but as those in union with him. Intimacy with Christ ("I want to *know Christ*—yes, to know the power of his resurrection and participation in his sufferings, becoming like him in his death," Phil. 3:10 [emphasis added]) in contemplation of Christ ("We all, who with unveiled faces *contemplate the Lord's glory*, are being transformed into his image with ever-increasing glory, which comes from the Lord, who is the Spirit," 2 Cor. 3:18 [emphasis added]) in the personal-ecclesial life ("*I* want to know," "*we all* with unveiled faces") is a good description of what it means to engage in ethics evangelically. In 2 Corinthians 3, the work of the Spirit who brings freedom is emphasized, whereas in Philippians 3, it is the objective history of Jesus Christ in which Paul wishes to participate. Both justification in Christ and sanctification by the Spirit are needed in the balanced ethical life.

One way in which to integrate the two aspects of participation is that suggested by George Hunsinger. The Spirit is the key agent in this integration, but specifically Hunsinger begins with the Spirit's role as mediator of communion in the man Christ Jesus before moving to speak of the mediatorial role of the Spirit in the human believer. In essence, the Spirit's role in "originating and maintaining the incarnation," that is, in beginning and maintaining "the communion between Christ's deity and his humanity," and then in sustaining the communion between the incarnate Son on earth and the Father in heaven, becomes the model and ground for the "loving bond between Christ and believers by which they are incorporated into him as a community, as the body of which he himself is the head."[10] It is on a Trinitarian and incarnational basis that the Spirit brings about the participation of the believers with God. As Hunsinger expresses it, "The mediation of the Spirit thus moves in two directions at once: from the eternal Trinity through Jesus Christ to humankind, and from humankind through Jesus Christ to the eternal Trinity."[11] This is helpful both for its prioritizing of the Spirit's work in the Trinity and in the incarnate Son and for its demonstration of a connection between the mediation between the divine nature of the Son and humanity and between the Son and our individual humanity. It still does not answer the mystery of how some human persons are by the Spirit conjoined to Christ by faith whilst others reject God. The correspondence between the Spirit in each participation does suggest a correspondence of his work in applying the atoning work of Christ to those he regenerates. The mystery that remains cannot overshadow the reality that evangelical ethics is carried out by those who are conjoined to Christ and his body, the church, and who have entered into his history to make it their own personal history, and who are therefore justified in Christ and are being sanctified by the Spirit as they live life in the Spirit.

In sum, we may say there are actually *two* great dynamics of the gospel that are crucial to ethics as evangelical, two messages of the evangel, if you like: the dynamic of being already justified in Christ by faith as you pursue Christian ethics with much imprecision and with much failure; and the dynamic of the Spirit's work within you that is transforming you little by little, as you imitate Christ in community with his people. The second dynamic has begun to be considered under the first topic of participation. Justice is a crucial aspect of what the life of the justified means, as they are not just accredited righteousness but are made righteous. The first dynamic now comes under consideration.

EVANGELICAL ETHICS ARE THE ETHICS OF JUSTIFICATION

If recent scholarship of John Calvin is anxious to say that justification is a *fait accompli* in Christ (*and* that it is distinct from yet tied irrevocably

---

10. George Hunsinger, "The Mediator of Communion: Karl Barth's Doctrine of the Holy Spirit," in *The Cambridge Companion to Karl Barth*, ed. John Webster (Cambridge: Cambridge University Press, 2000), 179.

11. Hunsinger, "Mediator of Communion," 179.

to sanctification by the grounding of both in union with Christ), this suggests that for the justified person, the pursuit of sanctification, including ethics, is a pursuit in freedom. It is not a pursuit of wise and holy living in order to one day gain justification. It is a pursuit *from* justification, not *toward* it. It is true that from the perspective of our human subjectivity we may gain *assurance* of our justification by the presence of faith in us, of holy and loving affections, and of their expression in good actions. But from the divine standpoint, justification is a reality pronounced over our heads. It is a reality brought about by the history of Jesus Christ, which precedes our history and our experience. No one in the tradition has grasped the importance of justification as a reality in the history of Jesus Christ as deeply as Karl Barth, and therefore no one has expounded more convincingly the freedom of the pursuit of ethics. That is, evangelical ethics is never more evangelical than it is in the Christocentric soteriology of Karl Barth.

Barth's Evangelical Ethics

Barth's ethics, which are integrated within his theology throughout *Church Dogmatics*, and which were introduced but never completed in *The Christian Life* in IV/4,[12] have a definite Trinitarian structure, already revealing ethics as evangelical. Ethics is the command of God, and specifically the command of God the Creator (Father), the command of God the Reconciler (Son), and the command of God the Redeemer (Spirit). Although there are differentiated, distinct ways of viewing the ethics of each of the persons of the Trinity, there is also a coinherent oneness. The primary emphasis in Barth's ethics is on the Son and his reconciling work, and this too gives evidence of ethics as evangelical, for it already assumes that those pursuing ethics and just living are those in need of reconciliation, those in need of justification, and who have indeed received it in the history of Jesus Christ:

> With it we have reached the central theme of special ethics. . . . The divine command is also the command of God the Reconciler and is directed also to the man who by him is reconciled to God, the sinful man to whom as such God is faithful in Jesus Christ and gracious

---

12. Karl Barth, *The Christian Life*, in CD IV/4, Lecture Fragments, trans. G. W. Bromiley (Grand Rapids: Eerdmans, 1981).

in his faithfulness. . . . We stand before the center, the source of all the reality and revelation of God and man—Jesus Christ, who is not only the ontic but also the noetic basis of the whole of Christian truth and the Christian message.[13]

The evangelical nature of ethics is grounded in the premundane covenant of grace, which for Barth is not the selection of some individuals among others, in the secret counsels of God, but the decision of God to be *for* the creation and the humanity he determines to create, and to be for them specifically by the incarnation of the Son and his reconciling work. This is the core of the good news that invites us into the life of God and obedience to his commands, that God is for humanity, for each human, for his creation, and for the vocation of the human within creation as his regent (Barth's third grace that he adds to Calvin's two). The evangelical nature of ethics in this triune God who is for us is reflected also in the three aspects of the human person in relation to the triune commanding of God in Barth's ethics: we are in the relation of creature to Creator, sinner to Reconciler, and heir of eternal life to Redeemer.[14] Each reflects good news. God's commands as *Father* invite us to be human, fully human as he intended us to be, and his commands are good for they help us to be human rather than subhuman or superhuman—or one might say, to be embodied rather than disembodied persons trying to be everywhere at once, and to consider as primary the embodied reality of our sexuality. In light of the fall and of our imperfections as we try to be the humans called to the vocations he calls us to, we need to be in relation to the *Son* as sinners who are reconciled, and we need to be in relation to the *Spirit*, who empowers us to pray and to be obedient in the Christian life and who hastens us toward what awaits fully redeemed human persons.

Having looked at the umbrella reality of reconciliation that is the context in which he pursues the ethical life, we turn now specifically to Barth's doctrine of justification. A brief consideration of his theology of justification will highlight the necessary backdrop to ethics that are evangelical.

---

13. Barth, *Christian Life*, 9.

14. This was summarized by Nigel Biggar, "Barth's Trinitarian Ethic," in *The Cambridge Companion to Karl Barth*, ed. John Webster (Cambridge: Cambridge University Press, 2000), 216.

Justification in Barth

One sometimes feels like one has taken "an excursion into a dogmatic Wonderland in which familiar values and assumptions are turned on their head"[15] when grappling with Barth's theology of justification, sanctification, reality, and experience. *Justification* is the effective sentence that has fallen on Jesus Christ instead of on sinful humanity. It is a verdict passed on all humanity, "over their heads." It is an event in Jesus Christ prior to and apart from the faith of those for whom it was accomplished. Faith is man's subjection or reception of this verdict. Even faith is the "gift of the Holy Spirit, however, and the actualization within the Christian of her being as it is in Christ."[16]

Barth, like Luther, however, places greater emphasis on the work of the One for the many—that is, on justification *in* Christ even more so than justification *by* faith. For Barth, justification is not a state but a history, that of the man Jesus in whom God has justified his creation by putting it to death and raising it up in a new form. For Barth, justification is an alien history that we then discover to be our own.

It is a refreshing exercise to consider in more depth Barth's doctrine of justification by faith that transcends Calvin's for two reasons. The first is the christological view of election Barth espouses, which makes justification a divine reality not for any particular preselected elect but for all humanity, indeed the whole cosmos. The second is that it makes justification a reality pronounced over all of creation. As God's "Yes" in reversal of the "No" over the attempt of the first Adam to undo God's creation, it reaffirms humanity and creation. This makes election beyond mere human experience. It is a reality transition. It is appropriated by faith, and though this may be thought of as being "an experience," the reality apprehended is actually something *beyond* our experience. It is an acceptance of a reality accomplished in Jesus Christ for us. Assurance of salvation is not so much attained by the inward look where the ups and downs of our faith and our pursuit of the holy and ethical life are discouraging at best. The reality of our inner souls is that we have encountered the gospel in Christ but have not yet been perfected. The grace of God

---

15. Trevor Hart, *Regarding Karl Barth: Essays toward a Reading of His Theology* (Carlisle, UK: Paternoster, 1999), 58n40.

16. Adam Neder, *Participation in Christ: An Entry into Karl Barth's Church Dogmatics* (Louisville: Westminster John Knox, 2009), 53.

is a "hastening that waits."[17] Assurance is gained by looking in another direction than the self altogether—to the God-in-Christ who is for humanity, to Christ who stands in our place, to Christ who is holy for us as our great high priest and in whom we are righteous always.

Where Barth differs from his Reformed heritage is that he avoids conditionalism and holds creation and covenant[18] together closely and therefore also the covenants of grace and redemption. He also avoids the tendency to differentiate two separate dispensations in the relationship between God and humanity—one on the basis of nature and the other on grace. For Barth, creation is the external basis for the covenant, and the covenant is the internal basis for the creation; consistent with the christological-incarnational hermeneutic, both are viewed through the lenses of "their common telos in the self-revelation of God in Jesus Christ."[19] Christ fulfils the covenant from both the side of God and the side of humanity; likewise, Christ is the fulfilment of creation, from both the side of the Creator and the side of the creature. As Hart has observed, discussion of creation and covenant paves the road for Barth's discussion of justification.[20] Another way to say this is that in the covenant of grace, God elected the Son to create humanity and the creation, and he elected thereby also to reconcile humanity as an ontological whole in his Son who would become human in order to recapitulate and represent humanity. The notion that election is centred in Christ is very much a biblically justifiable proposal in light of the fact that election is almost never mentioned without reference to Christ. First Peter 1, which refers to the elect community of God in verse 1 ("Peter, an apostle of Jesus Christ, To God's elect"), for example, speaks also of Christ as the elect one in verse 20 ("He was chosen before the creation of the world . . ."). In Barth's theology, Christ is both the *subject* of divine election, as divine Son, with the Father and the Spirit, and the prime *object* of divine election, and with him not some individuals but all humanity, whom he became one of by the incarnation. Barth acknowledged that some would believe and some would not, and therefore that

---

17. This phrase is a reference to Biggar's work on Barth's ethics, *The Hastening That Waits*. It captures the notion that the work of God in Christ in human persons awaits completion, whereas justification is already a reality.

18. Barth, *CD* III/1, 42–50.

19. Hart, *Regarding Karl Barth*, 50.

20. Hart, *Regarding Karl Barth*, 51. Hart cites *CD* III/1, 369–70.

in some mysterious sense there will be evidence of individual election, but the primary sense of election was christological and communal. This naturally carries over into Barth's view of justification.

For Barth, justification is *ontological, christological,* and divine *reality*. First, it is *ontological*. Barth would not have embraced the opinion expressed by Alister McGrath that the Christian doctrine of justification "constitutes the real center of the theological system of the Christian Church."[21] In Barth, the critical article of the church is "not justification as such, but its basis and culmination: the confession of Jesus Christ . . . the knowledge of his being and activity for us and to us and with us."[22] In light of what he believed about creation and covenant, Barth does not interpret God's pronouncement over creation that "it is good" as an aesthetic reference, or even as consonant with some divine blueprint. Rather, Barth maintains that the creation is declared "right" insofar as "it is *capax infiniti,* able to be taken up by God in the incarnation and brought concretely to its telos in fulfilment of the covenant."[23] This divine assessment of creation anticipates an ontological aspect of justification that, for Barth, determines the forensic (i.e., that which is related to law, sin, and justice). God, as Creator and Lord of the covenant, has a "right" over his creatures and covenant partners; in Christ, the elect man, God establishes humanity's right to exist by putting to death that which contradicts his purpose in creation, replacing it with the new creation. Justification is not simply a declaration of righteousness with respect to the law; more fundamentally, it is God's purpose for us as creatures and covenant partners. Sin is primarily an ontological condition, and God judges that condition in Christ on the cross and reveals his sentence on man by the resurrection so that just as sin is ontological, justification is also ontological, resulting in the establishment of new creatures and faithful covenant partners who can truly be assessed as "good." Most importantly, the existence of this new humanity as good is not in the realm of "potential" or "as if" but in actuality.[24] For Barth, ontological justification means that we are not merely treated as if we are just; we actually *are just* in God's eyes.

---

21. Alister E. McGrath, *Iustitia Dei: A History of the Christian Doctrine of Justification* (New York: Cambridge University Press, 1986), 1:1.

22. Barth, *CD* IV/1, 527.

23. Hart, *Regarding Karl Barth*, 51.

24. Barth, *CD* IV/1, 542–43.

Crucial in Barth's theology of ontological justification, second, is the fact that it is also *christological*. Its location is in the history of the incarnate Son of God, Jesus Christ, and only secondarily, as echoes, in the histories of individual men and women. Barth develops this thought in his consideration of the doctrine of election in *Church Dogmatics* II/2, in which Jesus is the "Elect Man" in whom our being is entwined and through whom God's purposes for humanity are focused. The key concept that allows Barth to see Christ as representative of humanity in an authentic sense is the central and pivotal notion of *homoousios* by which the Christ is one in his human nature with God but also with humanity. He as the one Man is identified as the one in whom all things were created in the beginning and in whom all continue to live and move and have their "being."[25] Thus we have our existence only in relation to him. This relationship is deepened by the fact that the Creator takes flesh and becomes a human person and fulfils his own creative and covenantal purposes. Thereby, our identity and being are no longer determined solely by our relationship to God but by our relationship to this Man, *Deus incarnatus*, in such a way that "his particular history is the pre-history and post-history of all our individual lives."[26]

For Barth, this christological-incarnational interpretation has profound implications for his view of reality or actuality. Rather than a mere abstraction, the divine intention for justification becomes a concrete actuality in Christ, in whom the eschatological future has been historically fully realized. Thus this ontological and christologically centred justification is for Barth, third, *a reality*.

The fact that justification is a concrete historical actuality in Christ causes Barth to relegate the realm of individual experience to the level of anhypostatic abstraction. For Barth, justification is not a state at all; it is a history. In particular, it is the history of the man Christ Jesus, in whom God has justified his creation by putting it to death and raising it up in a new form. The good news of the gospel is that Christ's history is also our history. As an individual discovers the reality that she is already justified in Christ, she is not merely in a "state" but rather is plunged into a reality transition. She is called to live in the awareness that *true reality is the supreme reality of what has taken place in the history of Jesus.*

---

25. Barth, CD III/1, 29–30.
26. Hart, *Regarding Karl Barth*, 59, citing Barth, CD III/1, 27.

Therefore, justification as Barth viewed it is an alien history that we discover to be our own, "which projects us into the crisis of eschatological transition, living out the Kingdom of God in the midst of the world, living by faith in that reality which lies beyond our experience, but which stands over against us as our reality nevertheless."[27] Whereas the issue of human individual experience apart from our relation to Christ is an anhypostatic abstraction, as Dalferth notes, "our world of common experience is an enhypostatic reality which exists only insofar as it is incorporated into the concrete reality of God's saving self-realization in Christ."[28] As Hart states, "Precisely what we must not do . . . is simply to ask after our own intrinsic and natural state, what we are in and of ourselves apart from Jesus Christ, since reality proper, the 'really real' is not to be found here."[29] For Barth, reality is christologically understood; it is our ontological relatedness to Jesus Christ, whose history—death and resurrection—is ours. Barth's input on the locus of reality is unique as, for Barth, the only determiner of what is ultimately real is the concrete history of the one Man, Jesus of Nazareth. In this manner, Barth radicalizes Luther's *simul iustus et peccator*. From within the framework of his ontology of relation to Christ, Barth is enabled to attribute reality to both the *totus iustus* and the *totus peccator* in a manner in which the *simul* has credibility. In ourselves, we are still sinful and guilty people. In Christ, we are righteous—new creatures and faithful covenant partners set free to live as such.

The distinction between "being" and "experience" is critical in Barth's reasoning. Our "being" exists within the *iustus-peccator* tension. The history of Jesus Christ is objective to our "experience" rather than our "being." As Barth would say, the depths of our "being" have been changed by the justification that God has brought about in Christ, but this reality is not locatable within our experience; it is something God has brought about by his electing grace, made concrete in Christ and irrespective of our experience of it. We are called away from self-experience and called into discovering ourselves "in Christ" and his situation.

Questions naturally arise. Is justification a process in Barth? Clearly

---

27. Hart, *Regarding Karl Barth*, 62.

28. Ingolf U. Dalferth, "Karl Barth's Eschatological Realism," in *Karl Barth: Centenary Essays*, ed. S. W. Sykes (Cambridge: Cambridge University Press, 1989), 29.

29. Hart, *Regarding Karl Barth*, 60n40. See also John Webster, "'The Firmest Grasp of the Real': Barth on Original Sin," *Toronto Journal of Theology* 4 (Spring 1988): 19–29.

no. It is a glorious reality that is ours in God. Will all humanity be justified according to Barth's theology?[30] Faith is required to appropriate justification in his theology as in the New Testament. And how did Barth view the capacity of the unbelieving human to hear the gospel and ethical witness of the church? On the one hand Barth had a well-known aversion to natural law, to anthropologies that did not take the fallenness of humanity into account, and to the insidious dimension of human culture. Sometimes his emphasis on the one Man, Jesus, has led to the critique that his anthropology was an epiphenomenon.[31] But this is to gravely misunderstand Barth, for seen through christological eyes, humanity actually rises to its intended glory. Thus, on the other hand, Barth's ontological understanding of the atonement and justification, coupled with his universal view of the election of God to be for humanity in Christ, led him to have every reason for the church to be a witness. If all human persons were at least by divine desire and design the elect of God, they were to be treated with dignity. Oliver O'Donovan, who reflects Barth's theological ethics to a significant degree (O'Donovan emphasizes the resurrection more than the incarnation and has a higher view of the ontological capacity of the human, if not the epistemological),[32] makes a comment that reflects the views of both theologians in their treatment of the human being. In discussing the Great Commandment and what neighbourliness means, O'Donovan speaks of the neighbour as "a being whose end is in God," and insists that repudiation of evangelism, which includes its ethical consequences, is "a simple refusal to take the neighbour's vocation seriously."[33] Barth believed the church should be a witness to the ethics of the gospel. Central to this is the fact that God had become a neighbour to humanity by means of the incarnation; this was itself an important exhortation for the church. Despite his realistic hamartiology, Barth did exhort the church to be present and to speak in gospel tones in the public square, something he believed the church in Nazi Germany failed to do well.

---

30. See Bruce McCormack, "The Ontological Presuppositions of Barth's Doctrine of the Atonement," in *The Glory of Atonement: Biblical, Historical and Practical Perspectives*, ed. Charles E. Hill and Frank A. James (Downers Grove, IL: Apollos, 2004), 346–66, for an excellent discussion of New Testament on this matter.

31. Hans Urs von Balthasar, *The Theology of Karl Barth*, trans. E. T. Oakes (San Francisco: Ignatius, 1992), 243.

32. O'Donovan, *Resurrection and Moral Order*, 86–87.

33. O'Donovan, *Resurrection and Moral Order*, 229.

Nigel Biggar has written extensively on the theological rigor with which Barth developed the good life in *Church Dogmatics*, the core being the living presence of God-in-Christ to his creatures,[34] with the concepts of human freedom and of created moral order being important also, as in O'Donovan's work. Barth urges the life of prayer as vital to discerning and carrying out right human action. Biggar even points out Barth's discriminating willingness to hear moral wisdom that came from outside of the Christian church.

What justification gives to the person in Christ is an identity-in-freedom, which is a significant theme for evangelical ethics.

Ethical Freedom in Barth

The idea of human freedom in the realm of ethics is closely connected to the identity of God, who loves in freedom; to the identity of humans in the one Human, Jesus Christ; and to the justification of said humans in Christ.

Adam Neder in his book on participation in Christ in the theology of Karl Barth states that the taproot of Barth's theology is

> the confession that God's gracious action toward the world is concentrated "in Christ," who is both the saviour of the world and its salvation, the giver of grace and grace itself. Not since the apostle Paul has one phrase so dominated a theologian's work. According to Barth, revelation, election, creation, reconciliation, and redemption all take place "in Christ," and their meaning and content may be rightly apprehended only in him. In fact, the very being of humanity itself is objectively included in the being of Jesus Christ, and is likewise subjectively (i.e. by individual people) realized in him. In these acts of inclusion and realization, the creature is incorporated into a depth of fellowship that is nothing less than participation in the being of God. Statements such as these are at the heart of Barth's theology. Yet they cry out for explanation.[35]

The starting point for the identity-in-freedom of humanity is indeed in Christ and therefore in the triune God. In the opinion of Karl Barth,

---

34. Biggar, *Hastening That Waits*.
35. Neder, *Participation in Christ*, xi.

if we want to discover specifically who the human being is, as well as our personal identity, we do not in the *first* place look at or into ourselves or our personal histories, nor even to the empirical sciences. We must learn all we can from these sources, but these are not, as Barth interpreter Wolf Krotke says, appropriate for "*establishing theologically* what it is that constitutes the essential character of the human."[36] For that, we do not observe human beings in general or human beings in history, but we turn first to the very inner being of the triune God, and in particular to his *freedom to love.* In freedom the triune God eternally elected the Son to become human, and in the Son therefore, he elected freely to be *for* the humanity he would create, such that in Christ, humanity is the covenant partner of God. Barth goes so far as to say that "Jesus is the divine disposition which precedes all history, indeed the creation of the world."[37] From the beginning God is not undisposed or "neutral"[38] toward his creation and humanity, for he exists eternally in his covenanting will, which is his will to be incarnate in Jesus. As such, the divine disposition is to create and redeem creation and human persons to live in a freedom derived from him, through the Son.

Barth's well-known radical christological renovation of the doctrine of election was motivated by his perceived concern that the classical Reformed doctrine of election, which includes the arbitrariness of the *deus absconditus,* cannot provide assurance. Edward T. Oakes relates how Barth actually transformed Calvin's (and Augustine's) version of predestination by grounding election in Christ.[39] Oakes comments, "He alone is the primal object of the Father's election. It is in him that the family of man is summoned to election. And the individual is summoned to his own personal and private relationship with God only as a part of this family."[40] Thus, in Barth, election is the very best news of the gospel. God has in his freedom, in the very act of the eternal generation of the Son that defines the immanent Trinity (some Barth scholars would say) and at least in the eternal covenant of God, chosen the Son to become

---

36. Wolf Krotke, "Karl Barth's Anthropology," in Webster, *Cambridge Companion to Karl Barth*, 159, emphasis original.

37. Barth, *CD* IV/3.1, 230.

38. Barth, *CD* IV/1, 42.

39. Edward T. Oakes, "Predestination in America," *Nova et Vetera* (IJT) 8, no. 3 (Summer 2010): 683–702. For more on Barth's critique of Calvin's doctrine of predestination, see John E. Cowell, *Actuality and Provisionality: Eternity and Election in the Theology of Karl Barth* (Edinburgh: Rutherford House, 1989).

40. Balthasar, *Theology of Karl Barth*, 175.

human,[41] to become Jesus, the one Man who defines humanity in its freedom, the one Man in whom God has chosen all humanity. This primal decision in God from all eternity thus made Jesus of Nazareth the prototypical human, after whose image we have been created. By his participation in humanity as an entity, in the Son, God imparts that intended identity-in-freedom to humanity, at least by design. It is entered into by human participation in Christ.

In the freedom of God's act of election, the Son is both the *electing God*, a free agent in his nature as a person within the Trinity, and also the *elect man*, receiving freedom vicariously for humanity. As Robert Osborn has stated, this ensures both that Jesus, as the electing God, is the "beginning of all God's ways" and that he, as the elected man, is "the goal and fulfillment of God's eternal will . . . the event in which God's eternal will is actualized. The creation comes from Christ, and it is fulfilled in him."[42] Osborn clarifies by saying that as "Jesus is at the beginning and in the middle, he is also at the end. . . . Whatever comes to man in the freedom of God and in the fulfillment of his eternal will comes first of all to Jesus as *the* elected man."[43] This is the very heart of the gospel for Barth. He is, in his christological expression of election, defending it against "all non-Christological interpretations of divine and human freedom in orthodox Calvinism and Lutheranism, and in philosophical versions of the same in modern Protestantism . . . he is endeavouring to correct deterministic construction of God's freedom on the one hand and existentialistic, indeterminate constructions of human freedom on the other hand."[44]

But what does this communicate about our human identity? What we are elected for in Christ is *freedom*. I venture to say that this is the most crucial descriptor of identity in Barth's anthropology. It is *derivative*, a freedom *received*, received from the freedom of God to be God, his

---

41. What exactly this means for the essence of the triune God is a hotly debated topic among Barth scholars and, principally, Bruce McCormack and George Hunsinger. For an able summation of the controversy, see Phillip Cary, "Barth Wars: A Review of *Reading Barth with Charity*," *First Things*, April 2015. The issue is whether Barth intends to convey that the divine act of electing the Son to be incarnate (*incarnandus*), in which the Son participates as electing God, actualizes the being of the immanent Trinity (McCormack), or as Hunsinger sees it, that this is a decision made within the covenant of grace involving the *Logos asarkos*.

42. Robert T. Osborn, "Karl Barth: Freedom in Christ," chapter 4 in *Freedom in Modern Theology* (Philadelphia: Westminster, 1967), 118.

43. Osborn, "Karl Barth: Freedom in Christ," 118.

44. Osborn, "Karl Barth: Freedom in Christ," 118.

freedom to love, his freedom to elect Jesus and all humanity in him. Yet it is *real*, for the end goal of that election is the creature living in freedom. This is not freedom of a modern kind that says, "I can do or be whatever I want." The free creatures live into their identity-in-freedom, paradoxically by being bound to the freedom of God in Christ, and are never more themselves than by being in union with him. This theme of identity in Christ and what Barth describes as "freedom *for*" and "freedom *from*" and a "freedom *for freedom*" cannot be fully developed here.[45] Suffice it to say that entering into our identity as the beloved of God in Christ by the Spirit is that which is core to freedom for holy affections and righteous and just actions. It is by faith that we appropriate what is ours already in the One who loves in freedom. It invites the life of prayer as the source of our healing and our moral formation and our ethics. It inspires us to treat the other believer who is our neighbour with this same dignity, and it innervates our holistic mission toward those who by God's desire are already his. It involves freedom from the devil, freedom from sin's power, and spontaneous joy in Christ. There "is a unity of freedom which is the very essence of Barth's view of freedom" that gives to freedom a spontaneous joy, so that "when I do *what* Christ gives me to do, there is no contradiction, but the occurrence of the original, the possible, the most joyful; there is freedom. . . . To be free in, for, and through Jesus is to be free indeed. In a word, Jesus is both the goal and ground of freedom, subject and object, alpha and omega."[46] This freedom for freedom given us in Christ sets us free to be participants in the prophetic office of Christ, as witnesses to Christ in the world by the preaching of the Word of God.

Summing up the contribution of Karl Barth to evangelical ethics are the notions of identity that brings freedom in Christ for ethics and a *fait accompli* justification in Christ as we pursue the moral life of justice. We turn now to a related subject that furthers the concept of ethics as evangelical, that of the resurrection of Christ, the moral order of creation that it reaffirms, and the work of the Spirit of resurrection.

---

45. See Osborn, "Karl Barth: Freedom in Christ," for this exposition.
46. Osborn, "Karl Barth: Freedom in Christ," 173. This reflects Barth, CD IV/3, 49ff.

CHAPTER 7

Theological Ethics Are *Resurrectional*

EVANGELICAL ETHICS ARE THE ETHICS OF RESURRECTION

Every aspect of the saving history of Christ from incarnation to ascension is vital to his saving work in both its ontological and forensic aspects and therefore to the evangelical ethical life. However, Oliver O'Donovan has expressed the opinion that, with regard to ethics in particular, the *resurrection* should be emphasized the most. This is because the resurrection of Jesus is especially the gift that "carries the promise of ethical illumination with it."[1] This conviction is seen by O'Donovan as a *theological* proposition in that it is not stated directly anywhere in the New Testament but is rather implied in various texts (1 Peter 1:3; Col. 3:1) and from the biblical narrative as a whole in the context of which it is seen as "God's vindication of his creation and so our created life."[2] It derives crucially from the Pauline meaning of Christ's resurrection for humanity. It is God's "final and decisive word on the life of his creature, Adam,"[3] reversing the first Adam's choice of sin and death and reaffirming in the last Adam, Jesus, God's first intent that Adam should live, an "affirmation that goes beyond and transforms the initial gift of life,"[4] as is reflected in 1 Corinthians 15:45, "'The first man Adam became a living being'; the last Adam, a life-giving spirit." The initial intent of the Creator before Adam sinned to create a world in which humanity "has a place"[5] was affirmed by the resurrection of the last Adam. Up until the time when Christ rose from the dead, it would have been possible to

---

1. Oliver O'Donovan, *Resurrection and Moral Order: An Outline for Evangelical Ethics* (Grand Rapids: Eerdmans, 1986), 13.
2. O'Donovan, *Resurrection and Moral Order*, 13.
3. O'Donovan, *Resurrection and Moral Order*, 13.
4. O'Donovan, *Resurrection and Moral Order*, 13–14.
5. O'Donovan, *Resurrection and Moral Order*, 14.

imagine that God had given up on his creation. But when God the Son becomes one with creation and humanity and is raised from the dead, creation is reaffirmed. The creature's attempt to uncreate creation is overcome in the resurrection of the last Adam. The deviance of the will of the first Adam was not permitted "to uncreate what God created,"[6] and the hope of salvation in Christ is not to be redeemed *from* creation (gnostic), but it is the redemption *of* creation.

Resurrection Reaffirms a Moral Order in Creation

In particular for theological ethics, O'Donovan wishes to emphasize the moral order present within creation and reaffirmed by the resurrection. This moral order includes the natural law, which means that for O'Donovan ethics is more than the "command of God" ethics in Barth, the Word of God heard from outside of ourselves, but is instead a moral order within the human person as made in the image of God.

In his emphasis on the resurrection, O'Donovan does not wish in any way to diminish the importance of the death of Christ or any other aspect of his saving person and history. He validates the typical pattern in the New Testament of placing ethics within the call for participation with Christ in his death, involving mortification or abnegation, and the call for participation in his resurrection involving vivification and transcendence. But he insists that these participatory aspects in personal ethics, or the aspects of criticism and revolution in social ethics, can become negative if they are not understood from the perspective of "the centre," which is a "world-order" reaffirmed by resurrection.[7] What he means by this is that there is an underlying order given by God to humanity as humans so that in both the mortification and the vivification, the goal is *being human* as God intended this within the order he gave to humanity. Without the resurrection, he argues that the cross and the ascension would collapse "together without their centre" and "become symbols for a gnostic other-worldliness."[8] Furthermore, O'Donovan argues that the resurrection is representative for *all* humanity as 1 Corinthians 15:22 indicates: "All will be made alive." This broadens the scope of ethics to the world as signalled by this universal resurrection and as vindicating the created order. The created world order was of course taken up into

---

6. O'Donovan, *Resurrection and Moral Order*, 14.
7. O'Donovan, *Resurrection and Moral Order*, 14.
8. O'Donovan, *Resurrection and Moral Order*, 15.

the Son by way of the incarnation, but its fate and the redemption and resurrection of humanity were assured by the resurrection of this representative man.[9] This gives evidence that God has been faithful to his creative order and that it will, in the end, have humanity in its proper place within it.

Resurrection Moral Order as Evangelical and Public

This is crucial to ethics as evangelical. In opposition to those who make a distinction between kingdom ethics and creation ethics, O'Donovan states that the resurrection event that was the sign of the kingdom was also the sign of the reaffirmation of creation. If kingdom ethics were to be entertained in opposition to creation, this would be a fundamentally dualistic eschatological kingdom bearing no resemblance to that of the New Testament. And creation ethics considered apart from the kingdom of God would not be evangelical ethics since the good news that God had acted to fulfil his purpose for creation would fail to be heard. O'Donovan states flatly that in "the resurrection of Christ, creation is restored and the kingdom of God dawns."[10] The resurrection reaffirms the moral order of creation that is the realm of the kingdom of God.

For this reason O'Donovan thinks of ethics as public and not esoteric, as standing over all humans, who cannot just decide whether to opt in or out. The voluntarist nature of Western moral thought since the Enlightenment makes it difficult to accept that there is a moral order of this kind. The popular understanding in the West has been that morality is a function of the human will necessary for order in individual and social life.[11] Such a thing as moral reasoning becomes subservient to the decision of the will, and no matter how reasonable an ethic may be, it is still seen to be a matter of free human self-determination.[12] This describes the ethical way of being in most Western democracies today in which the individual and their autonomous choices are the strongest ethic. There is no real objective way to resolve ethical disagreements in such societies since they simply reveal "clashes of commitment"[13] by individuals or groups. Christians have often imbibed the same

---

9. O'Donovan, *Resurrection and Moral Order*, 15.
10. O'Donovan, *Resurrection and Moral Order*, 15.
11. O'Donovan, *Resurrection and Moral Order*, 16.
12. O'Donovan, *Resurrection and Moral Order*, 16.
13. O'Donovan, *Resurrection and Moral Order*, 16.

presuppositions and may function in this manner themselves ethically, especially if the moral law has no place in their gospel theology. They may also abandon the public square, believing that there is no moral law or moral order that applies to all of humanity if it is not accompanied by faith. Since on this account ethics is seen to be esoteric and only for people of "faith," they believe they can lay no claim on those who are not Christians, who after all do not have any reason to respect their marriages or the life of their neighbour.[14]

Since it is abundantly clear that many unbelieving people do respect their marriages and the lives of their neighbours and often care for creation in ways that shame the Christian church and have work ethics that may be better than those of Christians, and since non-Christian cultures often reflect good ethics in many aspects of human life, this latter view is obviously mistaken, as O'Donovan shows.[15] This viewpoint is wrong because it fails to take creation into account and with it "the reality of a divinely-given order of things in which human nature itself is located."[16] This is what the resurrection has reaffirmed. This is not to deny the fact that humanity has bucked this order or to deny that human nature is fundamentally flawed. "Yet," says O'Donovan, "this order stands over against us and makes its claim upon us." It is objective, simply something "there," and since humanity has a place within it, it issues its summons to every human person, and the fact that we can live in it is good news. The moral order is not something that either the Christian or the non-Christian can choose to opt into or out of since it is a reality God has given and then reaffirmed in the resurrection of Jesus in a created, human body.

A "Created Moral Order" in the Tradition

This notion of ethics related to a human nature with its creation-ally given virtues in a created moral order is present in the Christian tradition in both its Eastern and Western sectors. If this is considered to be Pelagianism, it may be pointed out that even Augustine "spoke constantly" of such a human nature. He speaks, for example, of having as the object of his hatred the unrighteousness of an unrighteous man who

---

14. O'Donovan, *Resurrection and Moral Order*, 16.
15. O'Donovan, *Resurrection and Moral Order*, 16.
16. O'Donovan, *Resurrection and Moral Order*, 16.

at the same time is the object of his love "in respect of his humanity" and of seeking to free him to discover the "human nature itself."[17]

Significantly, this tradition of a moral order present within human nature, as endorsed by O'Donovan, stands in contrast to the main thesis of Alasdair MacIntyre's *After Virtue* and moral theologians in his train who have baptized his Aristotelian approach. Whilst sharing in common with MacIntyre a critique of the voluntarism of modernity, O'Donovan believes MacIntyre's polarization of the options to this to be "wayward and historically unjustified."[18] He believes that Stoicism with its morality of law, assumed by MacIntyre to be a "Judaic" ally in that sense, and Aristotelianism, which offers a teleology akin to that in Christianity, are in fact only "ambiguously related" to the Christian faith. Stoicism in its "life according to nature" (*to kata physin zên*) understanding is considered by MacIntyre to be deviant from the best classical teleological traditions and an anticipation of modernity. O'Donovan points out that the earliest tradition of Christian moral thought owed very little debt to Aristotle, and that its influences culturally were rather Platonic and Stoic, though he believes it is easy to overestimate these influences. Importantly, they were definitely in the *realist* mode, not the voluntarist. The most obvious source for this early Christian tradition, O'Donovan insists, was the reading of the Bible! Moreover, this reading communicated that ethics was more than just a "series of naked commands," which is a decidedly modern way to treat the Jewish Torah, and one from which MacIntyre, in O'Donovan's opinion, has "not emancipated himself."[19] O'Donovan finds in Augustine a supporter for his contention of the existence of a moral order in the creation and of the presence of an ontological grounding in the human person for an "ethic of nature." For O'Donovan, even the thought of Aquinas is best seen as a continuation of the patristic tradition to which he appeals and "only secondarily as an Aristotelian revision of it."[20]

A Created Order and the Fall

The viewpoint that there is an ontological grounding for the moral order that stands over humanity does not neglect the reality of humanity's fallenness. There are two aspects to this fallenness: humanity's "per-

---

17. Augustine, *Contra Faustum*, 19.24, cited in O'Donovan, *Resurrection and Moral Order*, 18.
18. O'Donovan, *Resurrection and Moral Order*, 18.
19. O'Donovan, *Resurrection and Moral Order*, 18.
20. O'Donovan, *Resurrection and Moral Order*, 18.

sistent rejection of the created order" and "an inescapable confusion in his perceptions of it."[21] This latter aspect makes following the Stoic way of "life according to nature," in an uncritical way, unreliable. There are moral characteristics of certain societies that may impress us in their consonance with the moral order, and others that may appal us for their neglect of this order. It is important to acknowledge, on the one hand, the reality that humans, as fallen, have rejected knowledge of their Creator such that the moral order has become opaque and obscure, whereas, on the other hand, the rebellion of fallen humanity does not and cannot succeed in "destroying the natural order to which he belongs."[22] Crucially, however, it is not to Stoicism that one turns to find assurance that this is true but rather to divine revelation especially expressed in the resurrection of Christ, which reaffirms that order.

By way of example, O'Donovan asks whether the prohibition of incest or of racial discrimination in a society is a faithful reflection of the created order of God. Skeptics might say that it is convention rather than nature. O'Donovan indicates that we can only know this "by taking our place within the revelation of that order afforded us in Christ."[23] The epistemological challenges for "an ethic that is 'natural,'"[24] as in it is obvious to all, are significant in light of the fall. However, O'Donovan affirms that this does not mean that there is no *ontological* ground for such an ethic, as if there were no "objective order to which the moral life can respond."[25] Any level of certainty we may have about this created moral order is ultimately dependent on God's self-disclosure by revelation through his Word and his works.

Ontology and Epistemology in the Moral Order

Keeping creation and redemption together, as one should, and as is often not the case in some evangelical theology and preaching, is a vital aspect to O'Donovan's case for evangelical ethics of the resurrection. Both creation and redemption have ontological and epistemological aspects. The created order has with it a natural knowledge, and the new creation with its ontological order has with it revelation in Christ.

---

21. O'Donovan, *Resurrection and Moral Order*, 19.
22. O'Donovan, *Resurrection and Moral Order*, 19.
23. O'Donovan, *Resurrection and Moral Order*, 19.
24. O'Donovan, *Resurrection and Moral Order*, 19.
25. O'Donovan, *Resurrection and Moral Order*, 19.

When creation and redemption are polarized, as in modern theology, we are asked to choose between "an ethics that is revealed but has no ontological grounding and an ethic that is based on creation and so is naturally known."[26] Redemption and revelation are thus polarized and are, as a consequence, "robbed of their proper theological meaning as the divine reaffirmation of the created order." "If, on the other hand," O'Donovan continues, "it is the gospel of the resurrection that assures us of the stability and permanence of the world which God has made, then neither of the polarized options is right."[27] This means that it is only by means of revelation that "we can see the natural order as it really is, and overcome the epistemological barriers to an ethic that conforms to nature."[28] This does not exclude a certain amount of "natural knowledge," which is "part of man's created endowment," but O'Donovan asserts categorically that it is "only in Christ that we apprehend the order in which we stand and that knowledge of it with which we have been endowed."[29]

That is, theological ethics must assume some roots in a universal human nature on an ontological basis but also be prophetic in that it looks to divine revelation for its ultimate answers. On the basis of the polarization spoken of, it will either advocate for a voluntarist "faith-ethic," which emphasizes Christian distinctiveness and acknowledges no human roots and expects no morality from secular society, and which is therefore isolated from it in subcultural communities of irrelevance, or opt for "an autonomous morality on which all [people] of good will can agree."[30] The former view is held by some Catholic moral theologians, and I suspect many evangelicals also. The latter view, which is held by one school of Catholic ethics, is grounded in a natural law ethic to which it is assumed all humans have epistemological access. Its naivete is exposed by the reality that Catholic autonomists and secular Western liberal ones are in anything but "cheerful agreement" on all kinds of ethical issues such as abortion and euthanasia. One reason for that is that, at the end of the day, Catholic or Protestant adherents to natural law as the basis for dialogue do not ultimately appeal to natural law but to natural law as revealed and confirmed in Holy Scripture.

---

26. O'Donovan, *Resurrection and Moral Order*, 19.
27. O'Donovan, *Resurrection and Moral Order*, 19.
28. O'Donovan, *Resurrection and Moral Order*, 20.
29. O'Donovan, *Resurrection and Moral Order*, 20.
30. O'Donovan, *Resurrection and Moral Order*, 20.

A Theological Ethic of Engagement

Over against an autonomous natural ethic that excludes revelation, and over against a faith-ethic that isolates, a moral theology of the resurrection is a theology of *engagement*: it engages with human persons and societies on the basis that there is an ontological moral order in creation, including in the being of all humans, that has been reaffirmed by the resurrection of Christ; it is therefore an ethic of realism, not voluntarism; it engages on the basis that there is some natural knowledge that is present within all humans made in the image of God. It engages realistically, however; that is, it is not naive about the fallen nature of humanity and culture and the limits and distortions of its perception, and it is therefore prophetic and costly; it engages in an evangelical way, for its basis of appeal is the reaffirmation of the created order (not escape from it as in isolationism) in the resurrection of Jesus; it engages humbly but boldly in that it unapologetically acknowledges divine revelation through the written and living Word as that which confirms the ethic of nature and clarifies human epistemological distortions in an ethic of nature.

EVANGELICAL ETHICS ARE ETHICS OF THE HOLY SPIRIT

A basic assumption of evangelical ethics of the resurrection is that its empowerment comes from the *Spirit* of the resurrection. The Holy Spirit is the gift given to the people of God to bring the perception of the moral order so that the veil that prevents epistemological clarity begins to be removed. The Spirit brings people from death into the life of the resurrection in participation with the crucified and risen Christ, thus giving them the power to live no longer according to the independence and corruption of the flesh but now according to the Spirit. This life in the Spirit leads in a "by the way" kind of way to the ability to be obedient to the moral law (Gal. 5). Yet life in the Spirit stands in contrast to life "under the law," which did not permit subjective participation in the life of God. Apart from the Spirit, the resurrection of Jesus, the reaffirmation of creation, its moral order—indeed, all the good news of the gospel—remain merely objective to us.

Already we have noted the ontological *objective* reality of justification, which is a result of the life, the death, and the resurrection of Christ *and* the objective reality of the created moral order. We stressed the assurance that comes from the objective christological realities and even chided too great an emphasis on subjectivity. However, here we wish to affirm emphatically the grace of *subjectivity* enabled by the Holy Spirit through whom we do indeed have faith, assurance, and freedom. Paul speaks of this on many occasions but perhaps nowhere more clearly than in 2 Corinthians 3 where Paul affirms the deity of the Spirit, his lordship, and his ability to open our eyes to contemplate Christ and be transformed progressively from one degree of glory to another. That is, the Spirit frees us. The notion of pursuing the ethical task is not one of bondage. It imparts moral freedom, ironically, as we have noted earlier, by submission to the freedom of God. The human person under the influence of the Spirit does not lose agency but rather is given the freedom to respond as a moral agent to what God has done for her. "Work out your salvation with fear and trembling," Paul says, "for it is God who works in you to will and to act in order to fulfill his good purpose" (Phil. 2:12–13). Karl Barth's notion of *concursus* describes well this Pauline concept that divine and human agency are compatible, not conflictual. He doesn't reduce "the scope of our free will," but rather divine agency is the precondition for our will, which is prepared by the Spirit to confront "the real challenge of the divinely created order."[31]

This freedom in the Spirit is the essence of evangelical ethics and the most convincing manner in which to communicate it to a world in which the holy grail of freedom by casting off the moral order leads only to bondage. The creation reality of shalom granted by God, specifically the Spirit of God, when we live within his moral order is an important evangelical ethos with which to communicate ethics in our culture. Young people need to know that none of God's commands are killjoys. The command of God to keep the sex act within marriage between a man and a woman seems like a stark and definitely outdated "old school" prohibition in a culture where being a virgin on a show like *The Bachelor* is considered just weird. Yet the deep emotional, physical, and spiritual consequences of promiscuity plague our culture. Sex between two consenting adults, the ethic of the day, is not the swapping of bodily fluids. In the created moral order, it is an interpenetration of embodied persons, something indelible. Exercising restraint is not a virtue much

---

31. O'Donovan, *Resurrection and Moral Order*, 23.

known in this culture, and it definitely doesn't feel like shalom! It is almost impossible to envisage the true shalom of a relationship in which the gift of a pure body is given each to the other. The promise that it is possible by the Spirit's empowerment to find true sexual freedom, which includes *experiencing* contemplative sexuality within celibacy through relational intimacy with God and friends, without expressing it in the physical act of sex outside of marriage—this is evangelical ethics. This prophetic message will not be received well everywhere!

But what are the *subjective* realities enabled by the Spirit? The Spirit both enables a present experience of the kingdom of God (which is also the kingdom that *is* creation) and is the *earnest* of full eschatological participation in the moral order (Eph. 1:13–14) in a new creation that the resurrection has made possible. This "now but not yet" dimension leads to a sense of realism about "the times between the times" when clarity is not always lucid, the obedience of the people of God is compromised, and attempts to be salt and light are often incomplete.

In sum, the moral order cannot be lived into by the faith community except by the Spirit, who regenerates and incorporates the people of the resurrection into the church as the community of the resurrection, which is then empowered by the Spirit to be morally formed and ethically guided and also to speak evangelically. Its witness to the gospel and the moral order of the resurrection, given the epistemological blindness of a culture of fallen humans, is only offered in faith that the Spirit will be at work to make it accessible and influential.

And how do we bring the objective realities together with the subjective? The gospel is neither the gospel of the Spirit alone nor the gospel of Christ the Son alone. Pertinent to the first, the New Testament writers did not tell the churches to which they wrote that because the Spirit had come, now they could bear the burden of the ceremonial law and circumcision and food laws, as if Christ had never fulfilled them. O'Donovan comments that this emphasis on the "inward moral power of the Holy Spirit unchristologically" led revival movements in the history of the church from Montanism onward into the "most terrible legalism."[32] His point is that we must not "credit the Spirit" with "power or freedom which is not that of Jesus Christ." The resolution of the objective and subjective aspects of the gospel lies in showing that "the

---

32. O'Donovan, *Resurrection and Moral Order*, 24.

freedom realized in *our* subjectivities by the Spirit is the same freedom as that which Jesus first achieved in *his* subjectivity—'objectively' from our point of view."[33] In other words, our "being-in-Christ" is contemporaneous with the gift of subjective freedom we are given. The freedom the Spirit gives us is already Christ's freedom in which we participate. In yet other words, there is an ontological reality about us as those who participate in the authority of Christ's freedom by the Spirit within the created order. We are constituted "sons and daughters of God," not slaves, by virtue of our union with Christ. Of course, the work of the Spirit is perichoretically bound up with that of the Son, for by the Spirit we are made sons and daughters and cry out, "Abba, Father." This flow of thought reflects that of Paul in this important section of Romans 8:

> The Spirit you received does not make you slaves, so that you live in fear again; rather, the Spirit you received brought about your adoption to sonship. And by him we cry, *"Abba,* Father." The Spirit himself testifies with our spirit that we are God's children. Now if we are children, then we are heirs—heirs of God and co-heirs with Christ, if indeed we share in his sufferings in order that we may also share in his glory. (8:15–17)

The heirship that comes with sonship implies that we can now not only accomplish by grace what we could not before but also now do things we were not before permitted to do.[34] This authority was the kind that Jesus exercised when he declared all foods clean and claimed that he was "Lord even of the Sabbath" (Mark 7:19; 2:28). This makes Christian ethics distinct from obedience to the law of the old covenant, even though there are continuities. One difference is the new subjective moral power under the new covenant, and another is precisely the participation of the Christian in the authority that was shown in the history of Jesus Christ.

Careful nuancing is required here. With the end of the era in which the law functioned as the pedagogue guiding humanity in its infancy by way of inhibitions, the coming of Christ brought about the "adult sonship" of humanity in the new humanity. O'Donovan asserts that this

---

33. O'Donovan, *Resurrection and Moral Order,* 24.
34. See O'Donovan, *Resurrection and Moral Order,* 24.

new humanity therefore came into a different relation to the natural order but insists at the same time that the created order itself did not change. As contained in this idea, one might similarly say the moral law and its goodness did not change (Rom. 7:12). Rather, in contrast to the fallen first Adam, humanity in Christ was "for the first time" able to assume its "proper place" within the created natural order, "no longer subservient but humble and proudly in command (Gal. 3:23–4:7)."[35]

Thus there are three consequences of this: (1) the power to obey the moral law; (2) the assurance of our justification in Christ, who perfectly obeyed and fulfilled the law in all its aspects even as we imperfectly pursue conformity to the natural order, that is, to Christ; and (3) the positive concept of creativity, of making "moral responses creatively." This Christian freedom, endowed by the Spirit, gives the Christian "the authority to designate the character of the reality which he encounters, not merely to adhere to certain designations that have already been made for him," but as an authoritative moral agent to decide "what a situation is" and what is demanded "in the light of the moral order."[36] This involves interpreting *new* situations not before encountered, probing their meanings, and making moral judgments with humble confidence. This might be considered to be similar to the "naming" authority given to the first humans (Gen. 2:19), reflecting their lordship over the natural order.

This dimension of what it means to participate as sons in the authority of Christ in creative discernment is an important one for many aspects of ethics, especially bioethics and medical ethics in which the creativity of image bearers to be God-like has brought many advances and much relief of suffering, and at the same time there has been a need for defining the limits when the temptation comes to move from being image bearers to being those who challenge the authority of God, thus becoming God usurpers, not image bearers. Barth might suggest that every ethical situation is new, not just those that are generated by new technologies, but the latter are certainly included in his situationism. Barth would insist we must hear the Word of God from outside of ourselves in these new situations. O'Donovan would not disagree but might insist that there is a discernible moral order, which is more than the Word of God but never in contradiction of it, that may be particularly important when a situation is

---

35. O'Donovan, *Resurrection and Moral Order*, 24.
36. O'Donovan, *Resurrection and Moral Order*, 24.

not immediately analogous to any biblical text or situation. O'Donovan is careful to qualify the freedom of the sons of God with precisely the moral order that stands over them, and to clarify that the freedom that the Spirit imparts does not mean that authority has been "withdrawn . . . from the rest of the natural order which confronts"[37] humanity. That is, freedom and authority in the Son and by the Spirit do not justify the kind of situation ethics that Joseph Fletcher had in mind or a Christianized version of it in which morality has no rules. Such a version of creative freedom breaks down into "mere improvisation, dominion become domination."[38] The reality of the created order exists, and humanity's confrontation of it is as a cosmos that is not "without form and void," but rather one in which God has already spoken his "Let there be . . ."

Over against Anders Nygren's view of Christian *agape* as that by which the Christian can imitate the divine in a *creatio ex nihilo* manner, O'Donovan insists this is the prerogative of God alone. Our task as image bearers and heirs of God in Christ is that of response in freedom to the objective reality of the created order. This is the proper love of the people of God (Gal. 5:6). Love has moral content reflecting the moral order of the creation. O'Donovan sums up by saying, "Love is the overall shape of Christian ethics, the form of the human participation in created order." It is a love "ordered and shaped" by the order discovered in its object, which includes the moral law, just as Christ's lordship did not overthrow the moral law or the "given order of things," but rather in fulfilment of the task given to the first Adam, his task was to "call things by their proper names," which he did with love.[39] Love, as it is expounded in the Scriptures, cannot exclude the concepts of *wisdom*, which is the intellectual apprehension of the created moral order, including the law, and *delight*, which is the affective response to that order for what it is and in light of the fact that it is. Such love is in response to the presence of the prior love of God within us and toward us and is a manifestation of our union with the humanity of Christ, who delights in all that God has planned and created.[40]

In sum, Christian ethics are evangelical because they are ethics of the resurrection. This is not just because the resurrection was the seal of the Father's approval, leading to the justification of human believers

---

37. O'Donovan, *Resurrection and Moral Order*, 25.
38. O'Donovan, *Resurrection and Moral Order*, 25.
39. O'Donovan, *Resurrection and Moral Order*, 26.
40. O'Donovan, *Resurrection and Moral Order*, 25.

(Rom. 4:25, "He was delivered over to death for our sins and was *raised to life for our justification*" [emphasis added]), but because in the body of Christ, the creation was reaffirmed and with it both its mental order and moral order. As those justified, we can by the Spirit live within and according to that moral order and do so despite the imperfection of our attempts to do so. The law of God in itself lacked the power to inspire our conformity to it in light of the weakness of the flesh, and so God did this himself, "sending his own Son in the likeness of sinful flesh to be a sin offering." He thus "condemned sin in the flesh, in order that the righteous requirement of the law might be fully met in us, who do not live according to the flesh but according to the Spirit" (Rom. 8:3–4). Having become one with Christ in his humanity and in his death and resurrection, by the regenerating and uniting work of the Holy Spirit, people in Christ and in a reaffirmed creation are enabled to live within its moral order and within the moral law that gives it expression. Christian moral thought is thus very much part of the Christian gospel.

A RESURRECTIONAL ANTHROPOLOGY FOR THEOLOGICAL ETHICS THAT ARE EVANGELICAL

To specify that ethics must be evangelical is a nice thing to say. It would seem, though, that more than one great tradition of moral theology might claim that their ethics are evangelical, that is, in accordance with the gospel. Whose position reflects best the notion of *evangelical* ethics? For Karl Barth, for example, *grace* in the matter of moral living comes to us through the Word of God heard from outside of ourselves. For Oliver O'Donovan, *grace* through the living and written Word does come to us from outside of ourselves, *and* it is encountered by a created moral order present by grace within the human person made in the divine image. That is, graced *hearing* is accompanied by graced *being*, that is, a resurrectional anthropology and moral order. O'Donovan's model proposes an ontological reality to the being of humanity made in the image of God that is unchanged by the fall and reaffirmed by resurrection but that still acknowledges an epistemological deficit as a result of the fall. O'Donovan is a *via media* between Karl Barth's divine command ethics, in which both the ontological and epistemological aspects of the image of God are denied and in which human subjectivity is downplayed, and the natural law model of Aquinas and the Catholic tradition he inspired, in which human subjectivity is prominent, a subjectivity that is grounded in a view that honours both the extant ontological and epistemological aspects of the image of God after the fall, while downplaying hamartiology, thereby glossing the epistemological blindness of the fallen human mind and heart. Proponents of this view might, in light of the *analogia entis*, say that all humans even after the fall are still engraced in this double sense and think of this as good news for humanity. Proponents of this view think that natural law minimizes the difference between the Christian and the non-Christian with respect to ethical understanding, deliberation, and action. The chief concern in this latter position, as is already evident, is that the gospel *of Christ* is not needed in it. It is at best a preevangelical ethic, but most likely in all truth, it is an unevangelical ethic, one that does not need the gospel of the incarnation, the vicarious life and death and resurrection of Jesus, to function.

Of the two moral theologians in the Protestant tradition whom we have mentioned, it may be said that each *does* require the gospel for his ethics to work. One of the few differences between Barth and O'Donovan is that Barth is decidedly less convinced about the existence of a created moral order than O'Donovan.

Barth

Thus where O'Donovan speaks of the moral *order* (which does include the moral law), Barth prefers to speak only of the moral *law*, or the command of God. For Barth *every* moral situation is new, and one cannot know in advance what one is to think or do. In this existential moment, Barth does not so much appeal to an extant moral order but invites the moral theologian principally to look away from themselves and to encounter the unpredictable situation with the Word of God, the moral law. Barth is nervous even for the Christian to speak of a human capacity. Participation in Christ is a reality also outside of ourselves, enacted by the participation of the Son in humanity at the incarnation. Justification is not a human experience but a reality transition effected by God in Christ. The human responsibility of the believer is prayer that looks away from the self and obedience to the command of God. Barth was not confident, this side of the *eschaton*, of spiritual formation or a *habitus* (ingrained dispositions and habits) within the human person. Participation in Christ is an again and again encounter with Christ, not a settled internal experience.

O'Donovan

Thus O'Donovan might claim that *evangelical* means not just that we have the Word of God that comes to us from outside ourselves but also that we are able to receive it and have the categories mentally and morally to process it by grace. The following is a summary description of O'Donovan's understanding of the created moral order and how it may be differentiated on the one hand from the natural law view of ethics and on the other from a gospel view of ethics that does not permit in the human subject the "capacity"[41] to discern and to do the good.

"Natural law" is not quite the same as "created order" or "natural order" in O'Donovan, "despite points of strong sympathy"[42] with the more realist accounts of natural law theory. The chief point of differentiation is that natural law inherently assumes a universality of both being and knowledge; that is, the law is within the being of human persons and therefore epistemologically accessible to them. This tradition is rooted largely in Thomas Aquinas, for whom the "primary principles are authenticated by their universal self-evidence alone."[43] The implications of this seem to be that the gospel is not required for moral knowledge in human persons. O'Donovan wishes to distinguish clearly between the ontological and the epistemological universality of natural law, a move already made by Renaissance and Counter-Reformation thought. Claims of natural knowledge were, on this account, assigned a very secondary position. "Natural right," which involved the capacity of a "rational nature," became preferable to Aquinas's "natural law," with its more subjective implication. The most notable opponent of natural law came in the theological ethics of Karl Barth in the twentieth century. On the one hand O'Donovan affirms the *epistemological* positions of this greatest of twentieth-century theologians, but he regrets the failure of

---

41. In the conflict between Barth and Brunner on human capacity, Brunner made a distinction between the formal and material capacity, which Barth disliked. Trevor Hart in his discussion of the differences between them with respect to any "point of contact" between God and the fallen human suggests that these two theologians from the same stable might have agreed in less charged times that fallen humans have "the capacity to receive the capacity" just as Lazarus, when called to arise by Jesus, had no capacity to raise himself up yet had a body with the capacity to receive the capacity for resurrection. See Trevor Hart, "A Capacity for Ambiguity: The Barth-Brunner Debate Revisited," *Tyndale Bulletin* 44, no. 2 (1993): 290–91. This is discussed below in clarifying O'Donovan's view.

42. O'Donovan, *Resurrection and Moral Order*, 85.

43. O'Donovan, *Resurrection and Moral Order*, 86. This is expressed in Thomas Aquinas, *Summa Theologiae* II-I, q. 94, a. 2. O'Donovan does acknowledge that Aquinas speaks of "secondary principles" that are obscured by sinfulness of character and action.

Barth to distinguish between the ontological and epistemological aspects in this discussion. O'Donovan believes that Barth compromised the doctrine of creation in his refutation of even an ontological aspect of divine law within the human being. O'Donovan sides with Brunner in this regard, who acknowledges that fallen humans have "the capacity to receive the capacity"[44] for knowledge of God and moral clarity. This left Barth dependent completely on the ethic of "divine command," which is "interpreted in the existentialist way as particular and unpredictable," leaving Barth with "too thin" a grounding for "the extensive responsibility for moral deliberation."[45]

A Place for Natural Law and a Moral Order

The crucial decisive issue in determining what of natural law is accessible to human persons is anthropological and specifically hamartiological. The claim that knowledge is "exclusive" for those who have encountered the gospel and are in Christ relates to the fact that the image of God in human persons has become defaced. But this does not imply that the image of God has been obliterated in human persons who have not been regenerated or that they have no knowledge of justice and the law at all. Human persons as created in the image of God have *being* that is not obliterated by the fall, just as the cosmos in its order was not obliterated by the fall. Thus, in one sense, unregenerate humans are devoid of all knowledge, and there is a sense in which they retain some knowledge. The first meaning is that knowledge of the natural order, which is moral knowledge, is contingent upon obedience, that is, "loving acceptance of it and conformity to it." It can only be known by participation. Whatever moral knowledge the unbelieving person or post-Christian culture may have is distorted without it. There is, in the second sense, still an ability to read the created order and a partial knowledge that is retained in fallen image bearers such that "an unbeliever or a non-Christian culture does not have to be ignorant about the structure of the family, the virtue of mercy, the vice of cowardice, or the duty of justice."[46] Thus, for O'Donovan, moral knowledge is a "natural function of man's existence."[47] However, there is a real sense in which this partial

---

44. Hart, "Capacity for Ambiguity," 290–91.
45. O'Donovan, *Resurrection and Moral Order*, 87.
46. O'Donovan, *Resurrection and Moral Order*, 88.
47. O'Donovan, *Resurrection and Moral Order*, 88.

knowledge is really no knowledge at all, for "unless the created order is grasped as a whole" and in particular the relation of the Creator to the creation as the ground of its intelligibility, that is, if God is not known, then "the order of reality is not truly known at all."[48] Thus unregenerate humans have a rational capacity for knowledge, but as Romans 1:18 indicates, the truth is suppressed by the fallen human heart. In that relational sense, the image of God was lost and is only received again by regeneration. The fragmented knowledge that the human person has as a human *being* is also not something onto which true knowledge may be built when the person believes, as if grace completes nature.

Thus, on the one hand, the Christian moral thinker does not need to deny the moral convictions and structures that exist in non-Christian or post-Christian cultures, or even to show that they may have come from Christian influence (though in certain post-Christian cultures they do, so much so that these societies often do not realize they live on borrowed capital). But, on the other hand, they must not simply embrace the perspectives of these cultures, tempting though this is when this Christian moral thinker "happens to belong"[49] to this culture and participates in it. Barth and Bonhoeffer would be emphatic on this point given the uncritical acceptance of Nazi culture among the German Christians. One can understand Barth's more severe hamartiology and his less complimentary estimate of humanity in its moral capacity. O'Donovan's account does protect against what Barth feared, whilst allowing a generous view of image bearing as an ongoing reality grounded in being. O'Donovan warns that the Christian moral agent must come at culture and its moral structures "critically, evaluating them and interpreting their significance *from the place where true knowledge of the moral order is given, under the authority of the gospel*."[50]

Warnings of Enculturation

Where one sits on these fine hamartiological and anthropological nuances that differentiate Barth and O'Donovan is secondary. It is most important to hear the warnings that both offer regarding the indiscriminate enculturation of the contemporary church on all kinds of moral issues. This is particularly urgent when the positions the church needs

---

48. O'Donovan, *Resurrection and Moral Order*, 88.
49. O'Donovan, *Resurrection and Moral Order*, 89.
50. O'Donovan, *Resurrection and Moral Order*, 90, emphasis added.

to take often have an element of the "outrageous" in our culture. The attitudes and sentiments that Barth encountered among Christian theologians in the era in which Nazism took hold in Germany is evocative of attitudes of certain evangelical theologians and churches in our time. The church seems to be rushing headlong into cultural accommodation on many ethical issues in the area of sexuality or jumping onto political bandwagons with leaders who profess allegiance to Christ for political benefit! What then? Does the church not engage with the cultural crises of the day and remain irrelevant? We must respond as Barth did by engaging and answering from the church's "Christian centre . . . the Word of God, or Jesus Christ, crucified and risen," and "who stands as Lord."[51] Or as O'Donovan puts it, Christian theology "cannot allow itself to speak *from*" the cultural crisis or the cultural belief system, but "only *to* it,"[52] with the exposition of the prophetic Word of God in critical reproof and exhortation. It must be willing to accept what Jesus accepted for his prophetic ministry to humanity. Culture does not take well to the upending of its premises and the exposure of its idolatry. The risen Christ still bears nail scars in his hands, and those in union with him must bear scars too for faithfulness to his Word.

Barth's famous disagreement with Emil Brunner may have had a harshness to it that seems unkind and unfair. Brunner's view that there is a distinction to be made between the formal and material capacity of unredeemed humans seems similar to saying the ontology was untouched by the fall, but the epistemology was fatally affected by it. O'Donovan has pointed out, however, that whereas one might permit such an interpretation based on Brunner's *Nature and Grace*, his political thought as expressed in *Justice and the Social Order* gives clear evidence of a "coalition of classical and biblical elements" in the construal of his "modern notion of justice."[53] In this he is deemed to be comparable to [William] Temple in his theology of Christendom and Tillich in his correlationist approach to "the 'questions' of our existence and the 'answers' of the Christian message."[54] The problem with these approaches is that they have created the impression that the "theological task" has always

51. Karl Barth, *The German Church Conflict*, trans. P. T. A. Parker, Ecumenical Studies in History 1 (London: Lutterworth, 1965), 28.

52. O'Donovan, *Resurrection and Moral Order*, 90.

53. O'Donovan, *Resurrection and Moral Order*, 90.

54. O'Donovan, *Resurrection and Moral Order*, 90.

been seen "as a discreet exercise in cultural accommodation,"[55] and the liberation theologies simply take this to an extreme.

If there is a universally shared theology that came from the apostles, and if there is, as O'Donovan suggests, a moral creation order that transcends culture, then how does that leave room for "moral learning" given that new situations arise in ethics with technological developments like in-vitro fertilization and sex-change operations, for example?

A Place for Moral Learning

Moral knowledge, says O'Donovan, is not cumulative in the manner that items of information are accumulated. If it were, there could be new ethical knowledge that could be added to the divine revelation of moral knowledge given to the apostles. The church would be required on each occasion of this "new" knowledge to make an absolute choice to either acquire or reject this understanding of something not already given in the faith once received. Rather, moral learning "is a grasp of the whole shape of things,"[56] O'Donovan states, and "one cannot *add* moral truth *to* moral truth; one can only *repent* false perceptions of the moral order and turn to truer ones."[57] Learning moral truth is a lot like Christian conversion. It does involve the "unlearning of errors," involving multiple repentings.[58] However, like sanctification this repentance is grounded in prior justification, that is, it is grounded in grace already given in Christ. It is not mere accumulation of knowledge. Moral learning is a knowing better of what "we already know in *outline*,"[59] a constant penetrative and explorative thinking of a reality that we already know in an abstract way "but which contains depths of meaning and experience into which we must reach."[60] The "new" events of history may be radically new, but our evaluation of them comes by way of the knowledge of the moral order brought with us.

The moral issue arising from something new like in-vitro fertilization, for example, and what its legitimate uses might be does not arise because of "questions the technique has put to us," but because of "questions which we have put to the technique" arising from the moral order we

---

55. O'Donovan, *Resurrection and Moral Order*, 91.
56. O'Donovan, *Resurrection and Moral Order*, 91.
57. O'Donovan, *Resurrection and Moral Order*, 92, emphasis original.
58. O'Donovan, *Resurrection and Moral Order*, 92, emphasis original.
59. O'Donovan, *Resurrection and Moral Order*, 92, emphasis original.
60. O'Donovan, *Resurrection and Moral Order*, 92.

bring to it. We may need to speak of parenthood in new ways, but this will be informed by the moral order we know. We find the known of the created order within the unknown of each new situation, and we engage in each conflict between right and wrong by ongoing repentance of old forms and a turning again and again to the right and the good. A realism about the presence of old and wrong moral thinking in the world and the need of ongoing repentance of the idols and evils of it is awakened when we consider the cross of Christ. There we see the stark contrast of the "true human life and the misshapen human life," between "the order of creation as God intended it and its distortion."[61] At the cross the false excluded the true and the Son of Man was deprived of the basic "form of participation which is the precondition for other forms."[62] Although "God reversed the crucifixion" and "vindicated the true over the false," this did not change the reality "that the corrupted order had in itself the tendency and the capacity to destroy the uncorrupted, and so to defend itself against all correction or amendment."[63] The *resurrection* was the last word, however. It reaffirmed the creation order, and it makes possible joyful and obedient participation in Christ and the creation order, but the abiding message of the cross is that this life will be lived in conflict for the faithful people of God and moral perspectives grounded in this order. O'Donovan perceptively and succinctly reminds us that we "are not invited now to live in the created order as though there had been no cross," and "the resurrection body of Christ bears nail-prints."[64] Conflict is a given in the life of Christian discipleship and may involve, as with Jesus, suffering including sacrifice of "created goods" that might be our "right."[65] This exclusion may come from others, or it may arise within our own selves as we struggle with our own physical challenges in a fallen world.

O'Donovan cites the example of someone who "may be ill-endowed psycho-sexually to enjoy the fulfillment and responsibility of sexual life in marriage,"[66] and is tempted to make a compromise with respect to the moral order in some way or another. Whereas sometimes compromise of a secondary kind may under certain circumstances be permitted,

---

61. O'Donovan, *Resurrection and Moral Order*, 94.
62. O'Donovan, *Resurrection and Moral Order*, 94.
63. O'Donovan, *Resurrection and Moral Order*, 94–95.
64. O'Donovan, *Resurrection and Moral Order*, 95.
65. O'Donovan, *Resurrection and Moral Order*, 95.
66. O'Donovan, *Resurrection and Moral Order*, 95.

O'Donovan stridently makes the point that "striking bargains with the world is not the *imitatio Christi*." Rather, followers of Jesus are "called to bear his cross, to 'mortify' those aspects of their own nature which are inclined to compromise 'upon the earth' (Col. 3:5, AV). They are called to accept exclusion from the created good as the necessary price of a true and unqualified witness to it."[67] This may apply in a timely way to the issue of the Christian disciple with homosexual desires who chooses to refrain from homosexual sex, in so doing being excluded from the created good of having sex as the necessary price of bearing witness to what that created good is, an act between a man and a woman within the covenant of marriage.

Conflict without compromise toward the risen Christ and the created order is the order of the day even in "new" situations. This does not preclude the reality that all ethical deliberation involves adapting moral laws to the specificities of the moral field or situation and therefore a secondary "compromise" that is between the ideal and the real. This is simple casuistry, which is unavoidable. But this is not so much a compromise as it is a discovering of "the right qualification for one's general rule of action, which will recognize the *truth* about the circumstances in which one has to act."[68] Complete disconnection from society would be necessary if this were not the case. Yet faithfulness is the call of the Christian disciple—no matter how difficult the context or how "limited the choices," this is faithfulness in imitation of the faithfulness of Christ, who was both deeply connected to his society and faithful all the way to the cross.[69]

O'Donovan speaks of a second area of secondary "compromise" that relates to how the Christian church or disciple may engage in the public square and speak to what should be "norms for the conduct of public life."[70] A more complete discussion of how the church should express itself morally in the public square can be found in chapter 9. For now it will suffice to say that the church as the community of the risen Christ, in its standards and moral life together, should provide a witness to the created order, albeit it may be an "oblique and indirect witness."[71]

---

67. O'Donovan, *Resurrection and Moral Order*, 95–96.
68. O'Donovan, *Resurrection and Moral Order*, 96, emphasis original.
69. O'Donovan, *Resurrection and Moral Order*, 96.
70. O'Donovan, *Resurrection and Moral Order*, 97.
71. O'Donovan, *Resurrection and Moral Order*, 97.

O'Donovan thinks of this as a subsidiary concern for Christian moral thought and that its primary mode should be existential rather than legislative. Compromise, in the form of realism and moderation, is endemic to the process of devising norms for public life based on those of the church's life. But a faithful witness is called for nevertheless, one often requiring self-denial of goods that may be our rights, as modelled by the cross of Christ.

In favour of O'Donovan's proposal of the reality of a created moral order are its roots in the Old Testament. The concept of the moral order in the created cosmos is part of the wisdom of the wisdom literature of the Old Testament. To break the moral standards of the law of God, to violate the social dynamic between parent and child, is to disturb the moral order. This is a recurring theme in the commentary by Bruce Waltke on the interpretation of the book of Proverbs. The Lord is the agent upholding this moral order,[72] so this is not a pantheistic concept. There is an "unbridgeable gulf between human and divine righteousness: indeed, no one is fully pure before his Creator." Waltke adds therefore that "the LORD is more than a guarantor of the moral order. He intervenes between a person's thoughts and schemes and their enactment so that he emerges as the one who directs and implements a person's life."[73] The actions of God when the moral law is disturbed are not always readily discernible, however, and reductionistic opinions about what is happening in the life of people are to be avoided, as the book of Job reveals. With reference to Proverbs 1:18, Waltke states that here "the iniquities themselves set and spring the trap leading to death." As elsewhere in the book, Waltke notes that "no distinction is made, nor is any tension felt by the sage, between the LORD who upholds the moral order and the moral order of act-consequence itself. . . . No thunderbolt from heaven strikes him down." "Rather," he asserts, "sin *will catch him* . . . like a hunter's trap, here displaying a figurative use of 'capture.'"[74] On the positive side, those who develop the "trait of mastering the moral order" are those who are morally formed. As such, they are enabled to "have control over their emotions (29:11) and to rule fools (11:29)," and "they are a source of joy to their parents (15:20;

---

72. Bruce Waltke, *The Book of Proverbs, Chapters 1–15*, New International Commentary on the Old Testament (Grand Rapids: Eerdmans, 2004), 82, 207, 324, 483, 519, 533.

73. Waltke, *Book of Proverbs*, 15.

74. Waltke, *Book of Proverbs*, 324, emphasis original.

Theological Ethics Are Resurrectional ▪ 165

23:24), are themselves protected (13:14), and bring healing to others."[75] The wisdom expounded in the book of Proverbs is to be proclaimed in the public square, for that wisdom reflects the moral order of creation. This is reflected in Proverbs 1:20–21, for example: "Out in the open wisdom calls aloud, she raises her voice in the public square; on top of the wall she cries out, at the city gate she makes her speech." The wise in every era are encouraged to speak there, even if they are not heard and even if the presence of evil leads to attempts to annul the good and the true and the beautiful. This anticipates the topic of chapter 9, which is the responsibility of the Christian and the church in the public square.

---

75. Waltke, *Book of Proverbs*, 94.

CHAPTER 8

Theological Ethics Are *Sexual*

S exual ethics belongs within theological ethics because sex relates especially to the core of human being and because orthodox Christian positions on the controversial issues of our time related to sex do in fact have a deep theological grounding.[1] Prior to launching into a discussion of this theological grounding of Christian sexual ethics, it is important to say that Christian ethics may be distinguished from pastoral care but must never be separated from it. Human persons, made in the image of God, no matter how deeply broken and fallen, can in Christ and the power of the gospel find redemption and the beginning of restoration toward wholeness and holiness. We may now proceed to discuss the theological ethics of sexuality.

It seems to me that what is most lacking in the church's discussion of sexuality is content and clarity on the *meaning* of sex and of marriage[2] and therefore on the joy that is sex, given it comes from the being of God. The tragedy of the triumph of views of sex that are grounded in secularism is that this is a mindset within which sex has lost its deeper meaning. In a pre-Christian culture, the early gentile church was not surprised at what the culture believed and practised in its promiscuous Greek setting. The church did ultimately have an influence on it from the inside out, from church to world. In what is now a post-Christian culture,

---

1. In a book on theological ethics, it may seem strange that sexual ethics should be discussed and even given its own chapter. It could have been reserved for a book on applied ethics alongside other applied ethical topics like bioethics, ecoethics, and so on. The Trinitarian anthropology laid out in previous chapters comes into play in this area of human being and ethics. Not all of the detailed ethical issues can be covered here; those await a book on applied ethics.

2. Some exceptions to this are the work of Dennis Hollinger, *The Meaning of Sex: Christian Ethics and the Moral Life* (Grand Rapids: Baker Academic, 2009); Christopher Ash, *Marriage: Sex in the Service of God* (Vancouver: Regent College Publishing, 2003); Vigen Guroian, "An Ethic of Marriage and Family," in *From Christ to the World: Introductory Readings in Christian Ethics*, ed. Wayne G. Boulton, Thomas D. Kennedy, and Allen Verhey (Grand Rapids: Eerdmans, 1994), 322–30; and Gary Inrig, *Pure Desire: Moral Sanity in a Sex-Saturated Culture* (Grand Rapids: Discovery House, 2010).

it is not surprising that cultural narratives about sex and marriage are in conflict with biblical narratives. The need for the church's influence is critical once again. Despite the confusion around sexuality within secular modernity, humanity maintains a deep awareness of the wonder and spirituality of sexuality and romance. It seems thus that humanity cannot deny its creation in the image of God and the role that sexedness plays within that, even though they may not be aware of the source.

Here then is a summary of some cultural narratives of our time:

- My body is mine, and I am entitled to and have the right to use it as I please (a narrative of individualism born of modernity).
- The act of sex is morally fine as long as there is mutual consent (the idea that sex embodies a surrender of the *person* who belongs to the other person by covenant relationship is strange).
- The act of sex can, for some, simply be the exchange of bodily fluids with no lasting relational impact or spiritual meaning.
- Promiscuity is simply a consequence of the evolutionary biological realities of survival of the fittest, and whatever is natural must therefore be good,[3] a notion that stands in contrast with the idea that humans are more than their animal instincts and are capable of controlling them as a result of having been endowed with the image of a faithful God who calls his image bearers to faithfulness.[4]
- It is just "old school" to think that sex before marriage between two people who love each other and who live together is wrong.
- Marriage is a contract in which I am entitled to become more self-realized and more fulfilled, and if it does not deliver, I may—or even *should*—leave it.
- People, even children, have the right to choose their own gender because gender is a socially imposed *mental* construct that can be disconnected from the *body*. Gender desires trump biology (which is a gnostic concept).

---

3. Popular Jungian psychologist and pseudo-theologian Jordan Peterson expresses this understanding of male sexuality grounded in social Darwinism and bourgeois individualism. Peterson follows Jung with respect to the idea that all humans have a "shadow" side where evil is present and that no one, not even Christ, has been exempt from this.

4. Karl Barth's insistence that the nature of humanity is defined *first* by God's election of humanity in Christ, and *not merely evolutionary theory*, is what gives humanity its capacity to be in control of its sexuality, as well as to engage in scholarship and science and music as image bearers of the God of wisdom, knowledge, creativity, and beauty.

- If someone has desire (even "orientation") toward someone of the same sex, they should act out their desires in same-sex sex acts—that is, the distinction between same-sex attraction and same-sex sex acts is not a real distinction.
- "Hospitality," or inclusion, means that no moral standards can be imposed on people, not even by Jesus (this relates to the postmodern concept of "alterity"[5]).

None of this will surprise anyone remotely in touch with contemporary Western culture.

What *should* be surprising is that many of the people of the church have imbibed those narratives indiscriminately and have become so enculturated that they think and behave no differently than the culture does and have no rationale or motivation for being or doing otherwise. The only thing that can upend these cultural narratives and provide meaning to sex in its given goodness, enabling healthy singleness and marriage, is the biblical narratives and their theological inferences. That the world is fallen is not a novel concept. The church has to focus on its own life and health, simply because of a *theological* reality: the church is married to Christ for the sake of the world. Paul's teaching about what gives marriage its meaning is this: "This is a profound mystery—but I am talking about Christ and the church" (Eph. 5:32). The healing of the people of God with respect to sex—in light of their enculturation and because every one of us has brokenness in this area in this fallen world—is a "vital ecclesiological matter," as Vigen Guroian has said.[6] That is, marriages and families form important subsocieties of the church, so if they lose their way, that is, "their sense of belonging and purpose within the community of faith," then "the church is weakened; and lessened in its ability to witness to Christ and his kingdom," which is a "great loss to a world in need of redemption."[7]

The core of this understanding of the church is the doctrine of the

---

5. Alterity has to do with the unconditional acceptance of the "otherness" of a person. For a discussion of this, see Brian Treanor, *Aspects of Alterity: Levinas, Marcel, and the Contemporary Debate* (New York: Fordham University Press, 2006). Jean-François Lyotard speaks of "incredulity toward metanarratives" as the very definition of postmodernity, and these grand narratives are in postmodernity replaced by the "petite narratives" of each person. Every other is truly other, and is to be heard, but no other is wholly other.

6. Guroian, "Ethic of Marriage and Family," 322.

7. Guroian, "Ethic of Marriage and Family," 322–23.

Trinity, for the church is an icon of the Trinity, and marriage is, in turn, an icon or image of the church. Union is what characterizes the centre and source of the cosmos, the holy Trinity (the perfect eternal union of three persons of irreducibly differentiated identity[8]); it is what characterizes the church as the harbinger of the new creation (a differentiated union between Christ and the church), and it is what characterizes two persons in the oneness of marriage (differentiated by their sex). Interestingly, sexual intercourse for the Eastern Orthodox is described as *synousia*, a term that means consubstantiality, a word first used for the oneness of essence in the eternal union of the three differentiated persons of the Trinity. The husband and the wife are joined together to be an "ecclesial entity" in what is the first good of Christian marriage—the *union* of persons, one body made up of two persons differentiated by their sexedness. In "freedom and sexual love and through their relationship to Christ [they] image the triune life of the Godhead"; they "express the great mystery of salvation in Christ's relationship to the church."[9] This is the *meaning* of marriage, and it is far removed from modern views of marriage as a contractual commitment that can be entered into by persons, no matter which sex.

Our expressed ecclesial conviction that the church is *communio* in *ekstasis* when it comes to ethics is confirmed in Guroian's thought. The home of ethics is *first* the church, which is the recipient of divine revelation and the community in union with the triune God and its icon on earth. The church cannot impose its virtues and values on the culture, but it can influence it toward them. Sexual ethics, healthy singleness, and healthy marriage must be birthed and practised with integrity, wholeness, and joyful shalom in the church, and as such become a bridge for ethics *from* the church community of hospitality and in prophetic speech *to* the world. Hospitable families living in shalom have a significant missional influence in our very broken culture. Single people who have learnt the contemplative and relationally other-oriented nature of sexuality, a concept that will be discussed below, can be a source of hope for lonely people and demonstrate that celibate single life can be

---

8. Reducing persons to "relations," as we have indicated in chapter 2, is inappropriate in light of the revelation of persons in the economic Trinity. See also Wesley Hill, *Paul and the Trinity: Persons, Relations, and the Pauline Letters* (Grand Rapids: Eerdmans, 2015); and Hill, "Divine Persons and Their 'Reduction' to Relations: A Plea for Conceptual Clarity," *International Journal of Systematic Theology* 14, no. 2 (2012): 148–60.

9. Guroian, "Ethic of Marriage and Family," 324.

a life of fulfilment, as Jesus himself has shown. Our approach must in this way always be evangelical.

More broadly, what gives sex its meaning, then, is simply an application of all that has been said in this book: sex and sexual ethics must be theological, Trinitarian, biblical, evangelical, ecclesial, personal, and so on. The narratives that flow from these considerations will indeed upend the narratives of contemporary culture by offering a *meaning* emphasis that will run throughout this chapter. A brief list of these narratives will counter those expressed above:

- My body belongs first to God and is the temple of the Holy Spirit (1 Cor. 6:19), and I am responsible to use it with accountability to my ecclesial and human community, for I am a person-in-relation, and my sexual nature is given that I might seek to move out of myself toward God in contemplation and toward my fellow human in friendship and community.
- The act of sex embodies a surrender of the *person* that comes from belonging to the other person only by covenant relationship—lifelong faithfulness of the spouses to each other within the covenant of marriage mirrors the covenant faithfulness of the triune God to humanity in Christ, and it is within this lifelong commitment that children and grandchildren are birthed in a stable environment and legacies are left, that is, where shalom emerges, where the good of sex within faithful marriage becomes apparent. This is not to say that God does not work redemptively when there is breakdown from the ideal, but the ideal, or "the good," remains the ideal nevertheless.
- We do not so much *have* a body as we *are* a body (animated by soul or spirit), and so the act of sex is between two *persons* in covenant and has lasting physical, emotional, and spiritual meaning.
- The idea that sex before marriage between two people who love each other and who live together is wrong *is* "old school" and is gladly acknowledged to be "old school," for it is as old as the creation of humanity by God and God's institution of marriage. Marriage since its inception has always involved a holistic leaving of the original family, a covenantal and public cleaving to each other, *before* there is a joining of two bodies as the climax of the marriage act (Gen. 2:24; Matt. 5:31–32; 19:1–12; Eph. 5:18–33).

- Marriage is *between a man and a woman,* who alone can reflect the notion of union between sexually differentiated persons that mirrors the church and the triune God.
- Marriage is a lasting *covenant,* not a contract. Each partner comes into the union to die with Christ to self, as modelled by and in participation with the sacrifice of Christ for his church (Eph. 5:22–33),[10] and to live in mutual submission to the other.
- The exceptions that may legitimate divorce are adultery (Deut. 24; Matt. 5; 19), abuse, and neglect (Ex. 21).[11]
- People, even children, do not have the right to choose their "gender," as if gender is something disembodied. Sexedness is actually an embodied reality that must be given priority over "gender identity," though compassion must be extended toward people who for various reasons struggle with gender dysphoria (a state of dissatisfaction, anxiety, or restlessness around sexual identity), especially those who are intersex.[12]
- In light of the above, with the exception of intersex where the wrong sex may have been chosen by doctors or parents, transgenderism should be discouraged.[13]

---

10. Vigen Guroian establishes that in the Orthodox view there is no hierarchy of Christian life as in the Roman Catholic Church in which celibacy is designated "a higher state of Christian living than marriage." To the contrary, "married life and the raising of a family has been described at times within the Orthodox tradition as a more difficult and courageous vocation than that of celibacy." Guroian, "Ethic of Marriage and Family," 328. This entrance into the kingdom comes by way of "crucifixion (*askesis*)" (330).

11. Space does not permit a full discourse on divorce, a discourse that involves complex exegesis of a number of passages (Gen. 2:24; Ex. 21; Deut. 22:13–21; 24:1–4; Matt. 5:31–32; 19:4–6; 1 Cor. 7:10–16; Eph. 5:21–33, to name a few) and a multiplicity of views in the tradition (Catholic, Patristic, Erasmian-Reformed [adultery exception], Preteritive [Augustinian], Betrothal, Consanguinity [F. F. Bruce], David Instone-Brewer [neglect/abuse and adultery exceptions], and the "Grace" view [Larry Richards]). See especially David Instone-Brewer's groundbreaking work *Divorce and Remarriage in the Church: Biblical Solutions for Pastoral Realities* (Bletchley, UK: Paternoster, 2003).

12. True gonadal intersex in which persons are born chromosomally with the genotypes XXY, XYY, or XO and have phenotypes (physical features) of both sexes.

13. Research shows that the psychological angst that accompanies gender dysphoria is not greatly relieved by sex-change surgery. See the work of former Johns Hopkins chief psychiatrist Paul McHugh and the findings of the US National Transgender Discrimination Survey, referenced by Rick Thomas, Christian Medical Fellowship (UK), "Gender Dysphoria" (2016), https://www .cmf.org.uk/resources/publications/content/?context=article&id=26419 and references therein. See also Mark A. Yarhouse, *Understanding Gender Dysphoria: Navigating Issues in a Changing Culture* (Downers Grove, IL: IVP Academic, 2015). Irrespective of how troubled persons are and what persons do to relieve this, the church must remain committed to their care *and* their discipleship and healing in community.

- Persons with same-sex desires are not permitted by God to act out their desires in the same-sex sex act *since* human desires are not reliable guides for morality[14] (whether one is same-sex or opposite-sex attracted), and *since* such an act is disordered with respect to the creation of humans who in their maleness and femaleness together reflect the image of the triune God,[15] and *since* the plain sense of Scripture in both the Old and New Testaments condemns it.
- There is a distinction to be made between same-sex attraction and same-sex sex acts, just as there is a distinction between opposite-sex attracted single persons who can abstain from acting out their attraction.
- "Hospitality" in a biblical sense is different from postmodern alterity in that the invitation to belong in the church is an invitation to belong to Christ and therefore to discipleship and discipline.

The grounding of these narratives will be our subject matter for the remainder of the chapter.

Space does not permit a long *biblical* section with detailed exegetical content. So-called traditional moral teaching on sex and marriage is based on interpreting the biblical narrative and its texts using normal interpretation (which means grammatical, historical, rhetorical, canonical interpretation) or the plain sense of Scripture that is perspicuous for the people of God. Attempts to derail the fruit of this interpretation, which is built on more than twenty centuries of tradition, may simply be called revisionist.[16] There is no trajectory, for example, of an improvement in

---

14. Just as the desires of pedophiles for sex with children do not justify their sex acts of adults with children.

15. Mark MacDonald, Indigenous bishop of the Anglican Church of Canada, attributes the "widespread ambivalence and reluctance among Indigenous Anglicans to change the marriage canon to allow same-sex marriage" to their faith in the authority of Scripture and their strong doctrine of creation in which marriage is viewed as "a unique communal ceremony, designed and practiced to express a worldview where the difference between man and woman is an embodied portrayal of an essential aspect of how Creation works." Mark MacDonald, "On the Marriage Canon," *Anglican Journal* 145, no. 6 (June 2019): 5.

16. See the work of Robert J. Gagnon in exposing this revisionism: Robert A. J. Gagnon, *The Bible and Homosexual Practice: Texts and Hermeneutics* (Nashville: Abingdon, 2002); Gagnon, "Leviticus and the *Times*," *First Things*, August 1, 2018, https://www.firstthings.com/web-exclusives/2018/08/leviticus-and-the-times; and Gagnon, "No, God Isn't Transgender," *First Things*, August 15, 2016, https://www.firstthings.com/blogs/firstthoughts/2016/08/no-god-isnt-transgender. See also the helpful work of Iain Provan, *Seeking What Is Right: The Old Testament and the Good Life* (Waco, TX: Baylor University Press, 2020); and Gordon J. Wenham, *Story as Torah: Reading Old Testament Narrative Ethically* (Grand Rapids: Baker Academic, 2004).

how God views the same-sex sex act across time and in the movement from the Old Testament to the New. These biblical moral mandates include what has been stated above. It should be emphasized that a strong case may be made that the primary good of marriage is "union with the other."[17] Procreation is a secondary good, though, and as such must feature in our understanding of what marriage means. Space does not permit detailed pastoral ethics and care for the sexually broken (which in a fallen world includes all of us!) nor a consideration of every detailed sexual ethical issue. These situations await a detailed pastoral ethical treatment.

Ethics often hinges on "vital distinctions" and "fine-tuned nuances."[18] Thus let me be categorical up front about some core theological convictions to avoid any confusion once we dive into the intricacies and nuances of what follows. I believe that the historic, ecclesial, orthodox revelation of who *God* is in his fundamental disposition of benevolence or goodness toward humanity in Christ forms the basis of all ethics, including sexual ethics. Inherent in this is what *humanity* is: we are made in God's image as persons who are not completely defined by their sex, but who cannot be defined apart from their embodied sex. These realities of a theological and theo-anthropological nature transcend all ages and all cultures, be they temporal or geographical. Said another way, I believe that the nature of the covenant-forming, relational Yahweh—revealed in the New Testament to be the covenant-ratifying, relational, triune God—in the person of Jesus Christ, stands as the theological paradigm for understanding the nature of humanity. The justification for this analogy is the concept of the image of God, especially as intended by God in his eternal councils to be fulfilled in the one Man who defines humanity, the man Jesus Christ.

What follows, then, is a sustained argument for the meaning of sex and marriage in light of the fact that what the *image of God* means in the creation narrative is described by the author of Genesis in a relational way that is defined by sex. Genesis 1:27 is the archetypal statement on what humans are and on their meaning as creatures made in the image of God: "So God created mankind in his own image, in the image of God

---

17. Guroian, "Ethic of Marriage and Family," 324. See Wayne G. Boulton, Thomas D. Kennedy, and Allen Verhey, eds., *From Christ to the World: Introductory Readings in Christian Ethics* (Grand Rapids: Eerdmans, 1994), 319, for a summary of biblical perspectives.

18. Dennis Hollinger, *The Meaning of Sex: Christian Ethics and the Moral Life* (Grand Rapids: Baker Academic, 2009), 172.

he created them; *male and female he created them*" (emphasis added). Genesis 2:24 speaks of marriage as an institution given by God and expressed in language of union: "That is why a man leaves his father and mother and is united to his wife, and they become one flesh." Who is the God who is imaging himself in humanity, and what are human persons as sexed beings if they are his image?

THE MEANING OF SEXUALITY IN LIGHT OF THE TRIUNE GOD AND HUMAN IMAGE-BEARING

Peter Kreeft once said in his inimical way, "No, we do not think too much about sex; we think hardly at all about sex. Dreaming, fantasizing, feeling, experimenting—yes. But honest, look-it-in-the-face thinking?—hardly ever."[19] This chapter is really about the role of sexedness (our being male and female in society, our being male or female in society[20]) in our existence as human persons *made in the image of the triune God*. As humans made in the image of a specifically triune God who is three persons differentiated by irreducible and noninterchangeable identity, in one communion, sharing the same essence, we too are persons differentiated by our irreducible and noninterchangeable identity, which includes our embodied sexual nature (whether we are male or female) as those in communion with God and our fellow human persons. The complementary relationality of sexedness is suggested by the fact that it is as male and female *together* that humanity reflects the image of God, but it is also as persons *differentiated* by our sex that we image God. To recap a concept in chapter 2, perichoresis in the Trinity does not just define the oneness of the communion and essence of the Trinity (each is in the other). It also validates the irreducible identity of the persons

---

19. Peter Kreeft, "Is There Sex in Heaven?," in *Everything You Ever Wanted to Know about Heaven but Never Dreamed of Asking* (San Francisco: Ignatius, 1990), 117.

20. I prefer the term *sexedness*, the fact that human persons have embodied sex organs, to *gender*, which is a new construct since the sexual revolution of the 1960s, and even to *sexuality*, which means many things including behaviour. By *sexedness* I mean simply that human beings are identified by their embodied sexual characteristics, that human sexual identity is grounded in biological sex and not socially constructed. To do otherwise is to challenge "the prerogative of the Creator" and elevate "the experience of the individual to a god-like role in the arbitration and definition of reality and morality." I am indebted in this regard to the work of my colleague, historian Sarah Williams, who wrote this in a personal communication: "Tolerating the autonomy of the individual in this area is now insisted upon in law to such a degree that the underlying presuppositions are becoming almost completely impossible to challenge." She concludes, "This is a tyranny disguised as a freedom."

(each is not the other). By way of analogy, the *imago trinitatis* suggests that we as humans belong to each other and are interdependent but that we have a differentiated identity of which embodied sexedness is a part.

These conclusions are reached by reflection on what biblical revelation in its totality portrays about the self-giving God in Christ, in whose image we are made. They are also discovered in consideration of the grand biblical narrative that includes our *creation* as sexual beings who are "very good"; the *fall*, which distorts that goodness in all kinds of ways; the *redemption* in Christ by the Spirit, through whom healing and holiness may be found; and the *consummation* of the healed and holy body-soul unity of persons in the new creation. The telos of this consummation, that is, our future existence as earthy and embodied persons, not only inspires healing in the "not yet" but enables us to find the ultimate meaning of sex *now* by noting what its ultimate fulfilment in heavenly existence will be *then*. In sum, in light of the high dignity of sex as the subject of the creating, reconciling, and fully redemptive (eschatological) actions of God, this account is an invitation to *experience* ourselves as sexual beings, even though we may not be engaging in sexual action. It will be about discovering our sexual nature as that which moves us out of ourselves toward the human other in fulfilling relationship, and toward God in contemplative worship—where ultimate satisfaction is found.

Justifying the Divine-Human Analogy

Why can the statement that God is Trinity, a statement about God (theology proper), be used to provide insight into the identity (theological anthropology) and the ideals (ethics) of human existence? Of course, making any analogy between who God is and who we are as human beings needs to be done with great care so that neither his transcendence nor his immanence is disrespected.

For example, human persons do not and cannot reflect *perfectly* either the personhood-in-relation of God or the completeness of relationality of the divine persons, which is a communion of mutually internal coinherence. In this vein, the term *community*, in my opinion, ought not to be used of the divine being (as it suggests a gathering of three individuals and therefore tritheism, not Trinity) but only for the social existence of human beings that echoes the Trinity. *Community* is an appropriate term for human persons who reflect and even approach the likeness of the divine communion but can never achieve it.

Yet Scripture assures us that we *are* the image of this God, that we do *echo* divine persons-in-communion. The view of the interpersonal self as constituting the image of God is profoundly consonant with the view of humanity presented in the biblical story. As already noted, all human persons in a *nondegreed* way reflect the image of God and are therefore an *analogy* of the relational and personal God by grace (*analogia relationis*).[21] Though we cannot be mutually internal to one another like the Father and the Son ("I am in the Father and the Father is in me," John 14:10 NRSV), we are from birth, and even before it, formed by the other, and we live out our lives in interdependence. Human persons in community are sexed persons in community. We are persons, remarkably unique persons, and as such, sexed persons of one of only two possible sexes. In the sexed nature of human beings, there is a core ontological aspect of the *imago* that enables the relational reality of the interdependence that characterizes the *imago*. By grace, redeemed humans can move into a *degreed* aspect of image-bearing by way of healing of sexual brokenness and the deepening of relationship with God and humans.

There are three bridging concepts, all grounded in Scripture, that justify the analogy between who God is and who we are, including who we are as sexed persons. These are our *modelling* of and our *participation* in him, both of which are grounded in *Christ*, the *incarnate Son*. Consideration of each is followed by noting the specifically sexual nature of human persons made in the image of God.

Image by Modelling

The bridging concept of the *modelling* of human personhood and community after divine personhood and communion is present in a great deal of Trinitarian theology since Karl Barth.[22] A key argument for the validity of the modelling bridge is the historical legacy of the term *person* and its meaning. This legacy is not Western, Cartesian individualism

---

21. The relationship between divine and human personhood is analogous, not univocal. The nexus of the relations of the person of Christ as the Son of God within the Trinity and his relationship as man with all humanity, for Barth, expresses the appropriate analogy between God and humanity by a technical term, the analogy of faith (*analogia fidei*) or relations (*analogia relationis*).

22. Theologians who express this reality in the recent past are cited in John Witvliet, "The Doctrine of the Trinity and the Theology and Practice of Christian Worship in the Reformed Tradition" (PhD diss., University of Notre Dame, 1997), 260, and include Peter Van Inwagen, Lesslie Newbigin, and Wolfhart Pannenberg.

("I think, therefore, I am") but the fourth-century Trinitarian debates ("I am because you are"), in which it became clear that, by sheer divine grace, human personhood was analogous to divine Trinitarian personhood.[23] It seems logical to assume that personhood must include the sexedness of persons as Trinitarian image bearers.

Image by Participation

There is a second bridging concept: the concept of *model* is in fact only possible by means of the idea of the *participation* of human persons and communities in the divine communion.[24] The only reason we can and do model the triune God is that we are in relationship with him (at least in relatedness to him if not in Christ) such that we participate in his life, personhood, and communion! These bridging concepts absolutely go together.

The very concept of humanity being in the image of God, going back to Adam and Eve, was contingent upon relationship with God and participation in divine life through the mediation of Christ. John Calvin surmised that even Adam, before the fall, imaged God only because he was in participation in the preincarnate Christ.[25] It is not a bridge too far to suggest that Adam and Eve imaged God *in the goodness of sexedness* that is included in the pronunciation of humans as "very good."

Image through the Incarnate Son

The alienation from God of humanity in the fall caused the image of God to be defaced, distorted, and broken, including sexually. The promise of the gospel of the God who is for humanity is concerning the Son who was eternally elected to become one with us, a sexed human person, "the image of the invisible God." How could we bridge

---

23. See Alan Torrance, "On Deriving 'Ought' from 'Is,'" in *The Doctrine of God and Theological Ethics*, ed. Alan J. Torrance and Michael Banner (London: T&T Clark, 2006), 193–94; and Colin Gunton, *The Promise of Trinitarian Theology* (Edinburgh: T&T Clark, 2003), 87–92. See also John MacMurray, *Persons in Relation* (London: Faber & Faber, 1961), 17, 69, 213. John MacMurray is important in this regard, Gunton suggests, because this unique ontology and *imago* theology seems to arise out of an implicitly Trinitarian reflection. Of special importance for Gunton was Coleridge and the Trinitarian foundations reflected in several of his works (see MacMurray, *Persons in Relation*, 98–100).

24. See Christoph Schwöbel, ed., *Trinitarian Theology Today* (Edinburgh: T&T Clark, 1995), 124–27, and T. F. Torrance's tightly argued exposition of the "onto-relational" understanding of personhood in both God and humanity in T. F. Torrance, *Reality and Evangelical Theology* (Philadelphia: Westminster, 1982). See also John Witvliet, "Doctrine of the Trinity," 259–60.

25. John Calvin, *Institutes of the Christian Religion*, 2.12.1; 2.12.6.

the divine-human divide without confusing God and humanity in order for the image to be restored? This third and most important bridging concept is, in fact, a bridging *person*. We affirm, with Alan Torrance, the "radical and dynamic continuity between the divine and the human that is the event of Christ."[26] Thus, emphatically, the analogy or modelling is grounded not in univocity, but in Christ, by way of the Bonhoefferian/Barthian *analogia relationis*.

In union with the last Adam, the covenant partner of God for us, we can be re-created, forgiven, children of God, and begin to find healing for our sexual brokenness and find our sexual desires to be reordered. This is the core of an evangelical sexual ethic. By the operation of God's grace in our lives, through faith, when we come into union or participation with Christ, which is already real as far as God is concerned, the image of God is restored gradually in us. What we must affirm here as a result of the eternal decree of God to become human in Christ for humanity is that all humans, irrespective of their sexual brokenness, are made in the image of God and deeply loved by him.[27] This eternal electing love of God for every human person also compels us not to treat other human beings as sex objects and not to objectify and degrade them through pornography. Objectification of other human persons is *not* harmless.

In sum, the image-bearing nature of humans moves beyond mere modelling; it is actually a participation in the divine love and life, in Christ, the one Man for all humanity. The Spirit, by regenerating and indwelling and incorporating us into the new humanity, enables human persons in ecclesial community to participate in the life of God, beginning the healing and shalom of the kingdom that has come and empowering the sexual wholeness and holiness that theology proper and Christology affirm.

In the Son's *participation with us*, he enacted reconciliation and redemption from fallenness and sin, including sexual fallenness and sin,

---

26. Alan J. Torrance, *Persons in Communion: An Essay on Trinitarian Description and Human Participation* (Edinburgh: T&T Clark, 1996), 209, emphasis original. Oliver O'Donovan has confirmed this specifically christological grounding of the analogy in *Resurrection and Moral Order: An Outline for Evangelical Ethics* (Grand Rapids: Eerdmans, 1986), 238.

27. Emil Brunner wished to distinguish between the image of God as formal (all humanity) and material (in regenerate people), but Karl Barth (*Nein!*) was nervous of this because it made the issue of image bearing contingent upon human capacities, rather than the design of God. And to do that made it a facile step to disqualify people with questionable intellectual or physical or sexual capacities from being human (Hitler's "useless mouths"). Trevor Hart, "A Capacity for Ambiguity: The Barth-Brunner Debate Revisited," *Tyndale Bulletin* 44, no. 2 (1993): 290–91.

forgiving and reconstituting us as sons and daughters of God. In *our participation in his humanity* by the Spirit, we move toward the recovery of the degreed image of God in all aspects of our being. The *model* that Jesus provided of a sexual being for whom sex was completely contemplative (other-orienting), drawing him out to the Father and to other human persons in holy friendship, someone who did not require the act of sex to be a fulfilled human person, is attainable to some extent in this life through our participation in his life and love. It begins to heal us now. When we as Christians see Christ face-to-face and are glorified, we will be healed and find the ultimate fulfilment of the pleasure that sexuality signals now, which is joyful communion with the triune God.

Explaining the Divine-Human Analogy with Respect to Sex

But why as human persons is our sexedness, in particular, so important for imaging God? This question leads us to the core of the *meaning of sex*.

The fact that humans are sexual beings in a binary way,[28] that they are beings who are *not* interchangeable with respect to sex, speaks to something particular about *who God is*. Ray Anderson expresses it this way:

There is at least an intentional correspondence . . . between the intrinsic plurality of human beings as constituted male and female and the being of God in whose likeness and image this plurality exists. . . . Quite clearly the *imago* is not totally present in the form of individual humanity, but more completely as co-humanity. It is thus quite natural and expected that God himself is also a "we."[29]

Anderson is, in this respect, reflecting the theology of Karl Barth, who believed that the sexual nature of humanity as it is expressed by

---

28. Even the tragic occurrence of intersex that affects 0.015 percent of the population in a manner in which the subject has both male and female elements does not affect the claim that biologically human beings are binary with respect to sex. See Alex Byrne, "Is Sex Binary?," ARC Digital, November 1 2018, https://arcdigital.media/is-sex-binary-16bec97d161e. The claim that there are eighty-one genders can only be true if the multiplicity of "genders" is dissociated from the embodied sex of the subjects in gnostic fashion. The claim that there are five sexes is also spurious in that anomalies become a standard. The reference point for anomalies is always the binary. I recognize that the binary concept in human sexuality is strongly challenged in our time.

29. R. S. Anderson, *On Being Human: Essays on Anthropology* (Pasadena, CA: Fuller Seminary Press, 1982).

the description of the image of God in the prototypical statement of Genesis 1:27 is understood as a *reflection of the covenant-forming and covenant-keeping nature of God*. For example, Barth identifies humanity as essentially male and female, and suggests that being man or woman (distinctively) has no meaning apart from the human community in which there are both men and women. We do not know ourselves as male apart from the presence in the world of the female, and vice versa.[30] Barth's point is that *the only valid human differentiation that is ontological about us is our sexuality*. Persons are human first, but crucially, as human, this includes their sexual nature as male or female. That is, sex does not define a human person, but a human person cannot be defined apart from her or his sex. The presence in humanity of both females and males, in their distinctness and in their community, is crucial to the imaging of God. And this appears to be an eternal reality.

When discussing Genesis 2, Barth grounds this differentiation within the created order *as a revelation of the covenant unity* of man and woman, whereby the woman is created as "helpmeet" for man, through whom and for whom he discovers himself as male, and both together as human: "He can only be an I through and for this Thou. The Thou which is not an I and is therefore constitutive for the I is woman. Thus man in his divinely created sexuality *is a similitude of the covenant*, which rests upon the fact that God Himself does not will to be alone but with man and for him, with and for His people."[31]

It is important to emphasize that this imaging of the divine being in the marriage covenant between a man and a woman does not imply that single people do not image God in their binary sexual beings. The image is pronounced over humanity in Genesis chapter 1 without reference to marriage or the act of sex. Chapter 1 has to do with the maleness and femaleness of *humanity*. It is chapter 2 that introduces the institution of marriage as a covenantal reality within which the *act* of sex may be legitimately practised. Single and married persons simply image God in different ways. Stanley Grenz has written that in our nonsexual relationships as single people, we reflect the inclusiveness of the love of God in our friendships, whereas in marriage we mirror the exclusive nature of the love of God, that is, his covenant faithfulness to his people, and

---

30. Karl Barth, CD III/4, 117.
31. Barth, CD III/4, 149, emphasis added.

we do so in a manner that reflects the distinctiveness of our sexedness in oneness.[32]

In sum, whether in singleness or in marriage, in human relationality the male and female binary plays an important role. Humanity functions as cohumanity in its being male and female together, and by humans being male or female individually. Human relationality structured in this sexual binary manner has correspondence to God and his covenant partner. Barth gleaned this from the primal passage on the image of God in Genesis 1:26–27. Barth notes that God created humans to relate as man and woman in Genesis 1, even before marriage and sex are mentioned in Genesis 2, "because he is not solitary in himself, and therefore does not will to be so *ad extra*."[33] Commenting on Barth's thought, Krotke states that "this is because what is manifest in the irrevocable differentiation and relatedness of man and woman is that in order 'to be God's partner in this covenant man himself requires a partner'" and "cannot be understood as God's creature without this partner."[34] The relation of man and woman as sexually differentiated within society and in marriage as an *ordered relation* is a concept much ignored in contemporary evangelical anthropology and has obvious ramifications for the same-sex marriage debate. This, in turn, influences all human relations to be based on partnership as "nearness with differentiation." Without the "I and Thou" of human encounter as male and female, the human is not human.[35]

Thus far, then, we have pointed to a correspondence between the triune God[36] and humans as sexed beings, which, though not univocal, is analogous. It is specifically made analogous by the coming of the Son as a sexed human person. Christ is the bridging model. Crucially, this analogy has to do with an ontological concept, not numbers. The fact that there are three persons in the Godhead and that humans have *two* differentiated entities, male and female, is neither here nor there when it comes to the analogy between the Trinity and sexed human

---

32. Stanley J. Grenz, *Sexual Ethics: An Evangelical Perspective* (Louisville: Westminster John Knox, 1990), 252.

33. Barth, *CD* III/2, 324.

34. Barth, *CD* III/1, 290; W. Krotke, "Karl Barth's Anthropology," in *The Cambridge Companion to Karl Barth*, ed. John Webster (Cambridge: Cambridge University Press, 2000), 168.

35. Barth, *CD* III/2, 289.

36. My conclusions are not dependent on which model of the Trinity in the tradition one prefers, nor do they ignore the profound and unapproachable mystery that will always characterize the ineffable relational Being of God.

persons. It is the concept of *differentiated and complementary and non-interchangeable plurality within unity* that is the issue. It is "otherness and oneness" that describe who God is. Otherness in a communion of equality and oneness. To be crystal clear, sexedness is *not* an imaging of God as Father, the Spirit as Mother, and the Son as offspring, nor should we make any attempt to read sexedness or gender back into the Trinity.[37] The differentiation that human persons echo, including their distinct sexedness, is simply the reality within the Godhead that there is a differentiation of persons who are characterized by irreducible identity, as well as their interpenetration as persons and their oneness of essence and equality and communion.[38] They are not male and female in any embodied or substantial way. We have been created male and female not to reflect gender in the Godhead but simply to reflect oneness with difference and the coinherence and interanimation of the divine persons. *Our* differentiation is sexedness. *God's* differentiation that we echo is that of persons who are differentiated (by their mutual eternal relations *and* in their economic roles) yet completely mutually internal, and one, and equal. They are persons, *not* individuals defined in an Enlightenment way, as per Sarah Coakley's concerns.[39] They are persons-in-relation within a communion of love and an equality of divine essence. The sacred echoing of this in gendered human existence has some crucial implications for inhabiting our sexual being, spirituality, and ethics.

---

37. Sarah Coakley makes helpful advances with respect to a Trinitarian ontology (persons not to be reduced to relations, deriving meaning of the Father from above, not below, etc.) and the spirituality of sex. An appeal to the Spirit as a feminizing influence in the Trinity seems to move in the direction of ascribing "gender" to the persons, however. See Sarah Coakley, *Powers and Submissions: Spirituality, Philosophy and Gender* (Oxford; Malden, MA: Wiley-Blackwell, 2002), 62–64, 120–121; and Coakley, *God, Sexuality, and the Self: An Essay "On the Trinity"* (Cambridge: Cambridge University Press, 2013). Kevin Vanhoozer's reluctance to use Trinitarian relations to speak to human social relations, including gender roles, is understandable (*Trinity without Hierarchy: Reclaiming Nicene Orthodoxy in Evangelical Theology*, ed. Michael Bird and Scott Harrower [Grand Rapids: Kregel Academic, 2015], 2).

38. My viewpoint has much in common with that of Hans Urs von Balthasar who spoke aptly of an appropriate Christian personalism understood as the "fundamental interrelatedness of persons—as a meaningfully understood *imago Trinitatis* would have demanded." He speaks of the human as the "personal *imago trinitatis*." His inclusion of sexedness in the *imago Dei* or *trinitatis* as reflective of the differentiation of the persons of the Trinity is, I think, fundamentally correct. Hans Urs von Balthasar, "On the Concept of Person," 24, https://www.communio-icr.com/files/balthasar13-1.pdf.

39. Sarah Coakley, "Persons in the 'Social' Doctrine of the Trinity: Current Analytical Discussion and 'Cappadocian Theology,'" in *Powers and Submissions: Spirituality, Philosophy and Gender*, 109–30.

THE IMPLICATIONS OF THE DIVINE-HUMAN ANALOGY

Ontological Implications

So what is the meaning of sex in light of this analogy? We image God by relational participation in his life and being in Christ, by the Spirit. And we image God *particularly* as we relate to other humans in ways that are true to our characteristics as embodied women and men.

Goodness

In light of its Trinitarian and covenantal roots, the meaning of sex relates first to its goodness. Despite some views of it in the patristic and medieval church, sex as understood in biblical revelation is fundamentally a good thing. It is derived from the good triune Creator and pronounced as good, indeed, "very good," given that it was part and parcel of the humanity God created on the sixth day. The Song of Solomon is an echo of this goodness. This perspective is the first message the church needs to communicate. Our prohibitions on who can have sex and when, legitimate though they are, are not the first thing that should be heard from Christians and the church. As that which echoes the Godhead in which each divine person indwells and animates the other, sex drives us out of ourselves into relationship, and it thus should be celebrated. As that which gives to women and men their womanness and manness, respectively, it is to be a source of awe and wonder. Furthermore, the actual practice of sex within the warranted limits of the marriage of a man and a woman is meant to be joyful. God is not against pleasure, which is built into his design of the proper relatedness of male and female intimacy. Echoing the mystery of the triune being of God, it is mysterious, and that mystery seems only to grow within long-term covenantal marriage. The interpenetrative perichoresis of the divine persons is one of sublime joy and love that spilled over into creation, that spawned its reconciliation, and that will produce a new creation of that ecstatic and erotic joy! The beauty and goodness of sex are an echo of this. Kreeft gives voice to these sentiments in an articulate way:

> This spiritual intercourse with God is the ecstasy hinted at in all earthly intercourse, physical or spiritual. It is the ultimate reason why sexual passion is so strong, so different from other passions,

so heavy with suggestions of profound meanings that just elude our grasp. . . . Human sexuality is that image, and human sexuality is a foretaste of that self-giving, that losing and finding the self, that oneness-in-manyness that is the heart of the life and joy of the Trinity. That is what we long for; that is why we tremble to stand outside ourselves in the other, to give our whole selves, body and soul: because we are images of God the sexual being. We love the other sex because God loves God.[40]

The goodness of God must also influence how we see the *prohibitions* God places on sex acts. It is the goodness of God that directs him to prohibit the practice of intercourse outside of covenantal marriage between a man and a woman. He desires shalom for humanity. Sex is too powerful a force to be practised outside of the safety and security of this covenantal, permanent bond between a man and a woman.

Identity

The second creational, Trinitarian perspective that has consequences for our sexual being is identity. To summarize what has already been stated, our sexual nature is crucial to our *identity*, as this is grounded in the triune God. Genesis 1:27 indicates that being male and female as humans is an integral part of being reflectors of the image of God. Maleness and femaleness together convey the image of God. And the attraction of male for female and female for male is a reflection of the attraction and communion that the persons of the Trinity have for each other. The reality in God that is reflected in the sexed nature of humans is that the persons of the Trinity are equal in that all three are God but that they are as persons *irreducibly distinct in their identity*, such that the Father is not the Son nor ever will be, and the Son is not the Father, and the Spirit is not the Son.

Our identity, therefore, including its binary sexual nature, as it reflects the identity of God in his differentiated oneness, has profound consequences for our formation as sexual beings and is the standard against which fallenness is defined. It is also crucial for the ethical decision about whether same-sex[41] sex is permissible. Because it violates the

---

40. Kreeft, "Is There Sex in Heaven?," 132.
41. The terms *heterosexual* and *homosexual* are a product of the nineteenth century with particular social agendas. In this regard, I refer you to an article by Michael Hannon, "Against

imaging by differentiated human persons of who God is, sex between persons of the same sex is a disordered act. It runs contrary to the creational givenness of maleness and femaleness. Scripture, when it is not subject to modern revisionist readings, in both the Old and New Testaments, is crystal clear about the wrongness of same-sex sex acts. The severe judgment of God upon these acts may be hard to understand until they are seen in light of these Trinitarian perspectives that help to explain why. For, as Kreeft insists, "sexuality is 'the image of God' according to Scripture (see Genesis 1:27), and for B to be an image of A, A must in some way have all the qualities imaged by B. God therefore is a sexual being"[42] (though God does not possess sex organs!).

This eternal perspective simply reinforces the importance of sex to our identity. But it also reinforces the importance of sex to our whole personhood, viewed as a body-soul identity. While we insist that the bodily nature of sex is what determines a person's sex (sexedness), we also suggest that sex goes deeper into the inner nature of the human person. Kreeft expresses this spirituality and eternality of sex, affirming we have sexual souls, and that this idea is "the only alternative to either materialism or dualism."[43]

Relationality

The third creational reality that influences our sexual existence is relationality: movement toward the other. The precise goodness or joy of sexuality that is a consequence of creation in the image of the triune God of grace is that it drives us to relate as equals—it drives us out of ourselves and into relationship with others—but it drives us to do so as persons with distinct personhood of which sexuality is a very significant part. This is a reality that transcends genitalia, though it will govern their functioning. James Houston has in his *Trinitarian Spirituality* stated that "to know the Triune God is to act like Him, in self-giving, in inter-dependence, and in boundless love."[44] He also expressed the sentiment

---

Heterosexuality," *First Things*, March 2014. The Scripture knows nothing of orientation but only the behaviour of sodomy.

42. Kreeft, "Is There Sex in Heaven?," 123.

43. Kreeft, "Is There Sex in Heaven?," 120.

44. James Houston, "Trinitarian Spirituality," lecture, part of a lecture series by Edwin Hui and James Houston, "The Trinity and the Christian Life," Regent College, 1992. See also Coakley, *God, Sexuality, and the Self*, for her encouragement of a reconception of the relation between sexual desire and the desire for God, specifically using prayer as a means to discover how this relation

that maleness and femaleness were essential for humanity to be the image of a triune, eternally intimate God. To be an artistic expression of God, we needed to be male and female, and this takes us beyond the biology and psychology of sex to its spirituality.

Spiritual Implications

The design of God in creating the sexual drive was not just pro-creation, therefore. It was to drive humans to seek him and to seek community, to move them outside of themselves, and to provide the reward of its pleasure within the context of covenantal relational inti-macy. Sexuality presses us toward the very core of Christian spirituality: to love God and to love neighbour. Paul Stevens expresses this well:

> Therefore God-likeness is a social reality. True spirituality is inter-personal, relational. Relationships are pathways to God. So the purpose of human sexuality is not merely for procreation, or for the mutual blessing of covenant partners, though both are good in themselves. Sexuality was designed to be first and finally contem-plative so that we would seek God Himself. Whether we marry and procreate, or remain as singles celebrating sexual diversity in a co-sexual community, sexuality is designed to turn us toward God, to make us prayerful, and to evoke our faith.[45]

Sexuality, as we noted in chapter 4, is an other-orienting energy that drives us outward to seek relationship with others. This is the greatest key to healthy sexuality, whether we are single or married. The issue of coming to terms with our identity as sexual beings in a healthy God-honouring way is as much a challenge for married people as for singles. Disordered sexual desires are the common lot of all human persons. In fact, married people who do receive the privilege of acting out their sexuality in the sex act can often mask the fact that they are not healthy sexually. Good sex in marriage is sex in the context of respectful, mutual, and whole-personed intimacy, and it finds its proper place when marriage partners are satisfying their core longings in God.

This outwardly orienting purpose of sexedness helps to explain

---

has an intrinsic connection to Trinitarian theology. This speaks to the contemplative practices to which we refer.

45. Paul Stevens, *Disciplines of a Hungry Heart* (Wheaton, IL: Harold Shaw, 1993), 68–69.

why singleness does not make singles any lesser humans. Richard Rohr, Catholic monk, makes this point well:

> God seemingly had to take all kinds of risks in order that we would not miss the one thing necessary: we are called and even driven out of ourselves by an almost insatiable appetite so that we would never presume that we were self-sufficient. It is so important that we know that we are incomplete, needy, and essentially social that God had to create a life-force within us that would not be silenced—not until 10 minutes after we were dead, they told us novices![46]

This helps to understand how people can be single (including those with same-sex desires) and not sexually active but still sexually whole and fulfilled. Noted Christian leader John Stott, who was single all his life, commented that "sexual experience is not essential to human fulfilment. To be sure, it is a good gift of God. But it is not given to all, and it is not indispensable to humanness."[47] If marriage were required for sexual wholeness, Jesus would have been short-changed. The single person's sexuality is expressed in his or her capacity to love and be loved. Loving does not need to be genital to be intimate. In the context of deeply caring and emotionally fulfilling and healthy relationships, sexuality can be experienced without being expressed genitally.

In fact, Jesus's teaching that there will be no marriage in heaven relativizes the importance of "having sex" in this life and ameliorates the command of God that sex acts are reserved for marriage between a man and a woman in covenant. It is a cherished axiom of our postmodern age that all humans have the *right* to have sex, whether same-sex or opposite-sex, and that deprivation in this regard is unfair on God's part or even harmful to the single person. This latter Freudian or Brownian assumption flies in the face of the good intentions of God for humanity.

Jesus's teaching suggests that the sex act as we experience it down here is limited temporally and in terms of the "fulfillment" that we look to it to bring. I believe it also suggests that the sex act only points to a fulfilment of intimacy and pleasure that surpasses it. That fulfilment

---

46. Richard Rohr, "An Appetite for Wholeness: Living with Our Sexuality," *Sojourners*, November 1982, 30.

47. John R. W. Stott, *Same-Sex Partnerships? A Christian Perspective* (Grand Rapids: Revell, 1998), 70.

is that of intimacy with God. The pleasure that will be ours in heaven must be so much greater than sex down here that the pleasure of sex down here is small by comparison. All of which means that intimacy with God is the highest source of pleasure—higher than that in the sex act—and it is thus available to all humans, single or married.

Our sex drive, therefore, whether we are single or married, should drive us to seek intimacy with God. This intimacy enables singles to handle their sexuality without sinning in the inappropriate acting out of sex in fornication, and it also helps married people not to put so much pressure on sex to satisfy desires and longings that can only be satisfied by connecting relationally in emotional, intellectual, and spiritual ways, with God and with their spouses, as well as with friends.

I would contend that our too-great obsession with sex is a sign that we thirst for something deeper. When we try to satisfy that deeper thirst for God in the sex act, sex becomes an addiction, at worst, and an imposition in marriage, at best. When we let our sex drive take us into ourselves instead of into God and others, it has lost its intended design—that of reaching out to the "other."

This points us also to the *reason* why sex is not for the self ultimately and why acts of sex that are self-focused cannot ultimately be the healthiest expressions of sex, and why even sex in marriage should not be carried out in a self-oriented way (1 Peter 3:7).

In sum, sexuality is other-orienting, or contemplative. In general we *experience* sexuality to drive us out of ourselves toward others and God. Within covenant it can be expressed as a consummation of covenant (two become one flesh), which involves a public act of leaving, a commitment to cleaving, and the pursuit of lifelong intimacy. Stan Grenz points to the incongruity of premarital sex when he states, "Sex outside of marriage . . . involves two people in a life-uniting act who do not have a life-uniting intent."[48]

Ethical Implications

All that we have spoken of so far of the nature of God as triune—as One who loves in freedom, as good and committed to the good of humanity,

---

48. Stanley J. Grenz and Roy D. Bell, *Betrayal of Trust: Confronting and Preventing Clergy Sexual Misconduct*, 2nd ed. (Grand Rapids: Baker, 2001), 83. This book on sexual failure in the pastorate should be required reading for all pastors and church elders/leaders!

as demonstrated by his self-giving act in Christ and the Spirit—we now bring to bear as the *ethos* that guides the *ethics* of sexuality.

The following are theologico-ethical conclusions related to this ethos.

(1) The ethos for ethical commands is grounded first in the *being* of the triune God who loves in freedom. When the sexes get blurred, the image of God as distinct persons in one essence and communion is not reflected and honoured in our *being*.

From the opening pages of the book of Genesis and throughout the remainder of Scripture, the sexual differentiation of embodied human beings into two sexes, male and female, images the triune God, and is taught explicitly and assumed by the writers of Scripture. Human, personal identity trumps sexual identity, meaning that defining oneself as "gay" or "straight" rather than as a bodily male or female person is inappropriate and faulty anthropology. Sexual identity in Scripture is therefore related to identifying with one's given body, male or female, not to the nature of one's sexual desires. On the contrary, Scripture is clear in its teaching and commandments that human sexual desires are disordered and must be regulated (e.g., Ex. 20:17; Col. 3:5).[49] All sexual acts, same-sex or otherwise, outside the marriage of a man and a woman are repeatedly condemned in Scripture (e.g., Ex. 20:14; Heb. 13:4). There is no trajectory from the Old Testament to the New Testament, that is, one in which what is condemned in the Old is permitted in the New, and views that argue for a trajectory are revisionist at best and fanciful at worst. These views are not controversial when measured against the ecclesial history of Christian faith and practice. The latter "old school" viewpoint, as Peter Kreeft indicates, expresses "simply the primeval platitudes known to all premodern societies; the sane, sunny country

---

49. Beneath the antinomian sensibilities of our time, writes R. R. Reno, is a "moral conviction, widespread though often tacit: that human beings flourish to the degree that they're free to satisfy their personal desires. The same conviction underwrites our therapeutic vocabulary of empowerment, the pedagogy of multiculturalism, and our paradoxical moral code of nonjudgmentalism. What makes for happiness and fulfillment—and here we enter into the metaphysical dream that defines our era—is an Empire of Desire." R. R. Reno, "Empire of Desire: Outlining the Postmodern Metaphysical Dream," *First Things*, June 2014, http://www.firstthings.com /article/2014/06/empire-of-desire. Culture, which Reno states should have the "fundamental goal of disciplining desire," is now committed to the liberation from all that represses desire: "The deepest moral law, therefore, is to be true to oneself." The inherent difficulty is that there is no way to distinguish between homosexuality, which is deemed to be fine, and "adults having sex with adolescents," which "is absolutely prohibited and severely punished—a historical anomaly." Reno ends his article with these words: "Thus runs a world that has lost its capacity to dream of something higher than desire—something to desire."

of sexual common sense by the vote of 'the democracy of the dead.'"
"Yet," says Kreeft, "in another way they are 'radical,' in the etymological
sense of the word: they are our sexual roots, and our uprooted society is
rooting around looking for sexual substitute roots like a pig rooting for
truffles. It has not found them. That fact should at least make us pause
and look back at our 'wise blood,' our roots."[50]

(2) The ethos for sexual commands is the good acts or *goodness* of
God who loves in freedom and creates and redeems also so that humans
too may love in freedom. Specifically, God puts boundaries on sexual
practices for the good, the shalom, of human persons and humanity as a
whole. The call of the Scriptures and the gospel for celibacy for all who
are not in a marriage between a man and a woman is not only possible
but can be something good, shalom-filled, and enabled by the gospel.[51]

(3) Specifically, ethics in light of the self-revelation of God in Christ
are always presented in Scripture as *evangelical* ethics. That is, they are
motivated by the gospel orientation of the heart of God. He is *for* humanity. He sent his Son, who in his vicarious humanity was perfect for us and
died to redeem us from our sins and to reconcile us to himself. It is in
union and communion with him that we find forgiveness again and again
and again, healing for our hurts, and restoration for our brokenness.
This is experienced to some degree in this life, through *practised* union
with Christ in death and resurrection, by the power of the indwelling
Spirit, toward mortification of old ways and vivification of the virtues
and holiness. I emphasize *practised* here because, apart from embodied
and ecclesial practices, Christians do not live into what is their most real
reality as God sees it. Commenting on the perversion of our desires by
original sin to make them self-oriented, R. R. Reno points nevertheless
to "something higher than the natural nobility of Aristotle's well-trained
soul." This, he spells out, is "fellowship with God" that "extends beyond
our natural possibilities." What we need therefore is "a divine repair of
our disordered desires, as well as a pedagogy that takes us beyond this

---

50. Kreeft, "Is There Sex in Heaven?," 117.
51. For helpful guidelines for the pursuit of celibacy for persons who are same-sex attracted,
see Mark Yarhouse and Olya Zaporozhets, *Costly Obedience: What We Can Learn from the Celibate
Gay Christian Community* (Grand Rapids: Zondervan, 2019). See also Ed Shaw, *Same-Sex Attraction
and the Church: The Surprising Plausibility of the Celibate Life* (Downers Grove, IL: IVP, 2015);
and the works of Wesley Hill, *Spiritual Friendship: Finding Love in the Church as a Celibate Gay
Christian* (Grand Rapids: Brazos, 2015); *Washed and Waiting: Reflections on Christian Faithfulness
and Homosexuality* (Grand Rapids: Zondervan, 2010).

world." He means "the supernatural virtues" of "faith, hope, and love," which "stretch the soul upward."[52]

The long road to sexual recovery, wholeness, and holiness is therefore a participational journey that is Trinitarian, ecclesial, and so on, and in light of eschatology, it is a lifelong journey for all of us in the "now," not ending in wholeness until the "not yet."

In this journey of practices, there will be a prime emphasis on relationality. Our experience of intimacy with Christ "expels the controlling and compulsive power of lesser affections,"[53] states Larry Crabb, who has worked hard over the years in counselling people with sexual brokenness. There is an untapped and untested depth of joy and satisfaction for our deepest thirst to be explored in experiencing communion with the Father, the Son, and the Spirit. Our first response to our thirst is often the broken cisterns that hold no real water. But when we connect deeply with other new covenant people, we connect deeply with Christ, and this moderates our sexual desires, keeps them in perspective, and enables us either to abstain from the acts of sex that are illegitimate or, if married, to fulfil our spouse and ourselves in unpressured and holistic ways. When people truly connect with each other in new covenant heart-to-heart ways, "something is poured out of one and into the other that has the power to heal the soul of its deepest wounds and restore its health."[54] Henri Nouwen similarly proposes friendship as a way to express the outward impulse of sex without the act of sex. It is "one of the greatest gifts a human being can receive . . . a bond stronger than sexual union can create, deeper than a shared fate can solidify, and even more intimate than the bonds of marriage or community . . . a unity of souls that gives nobility and sincerity to love."[55]

The expectation with respect to change will be one of *realism*. That is, this side of the eschaton, none of us is fully healed and fully holy. With Luther and Barth we insist that we are saints and sinners at the same time (*iustus et peccator*). The mark of the Christian will be *hunger* for righteousness, not fully realized righteousness in this life. The hunger must be there, however, and not a settled acquiescence to sexual sins,

---

52. Reno, "Empire of Desire."
53. Larry Crabb, "Traits of a Sexually Healthy Pastor," *Leadership Magazine*, Summer 1995, 38.
54. Larry Crabb, *Connecting: Healing Ourselves and Our Relationships* (Nashville: Thomas Nelson, 2005), xi.
55. Henri J. M. Nouwen, *Bread for the Journey: A Daybook of Wisdom and Faith* (repr., New York: HarperCollins, 2006), 7.

or theological rationalizations of the same. This means that repeated failure and confession and absolution and restoration will be the norm for all Christians, and that therefore we should expect that there will be people *struggling* with all manner of sins. The mark of the true disciple is that they are struggling, resisting, battling—and not justifying—their sin.

(4) Although evangelical ethics can only be experienced by regenerated persons, the intended scope of the gospel is for all humanity. Therefore, the church, reflecting the Trinity-for-humanity in Christ (*koinōnia in ekstasis*), will be a voice in the public square (taking the destiny of God for all humanity seriously and speaking evangelically and not legally there), and it will be a community of hospitality. Hospitality in a gospel and Trinitarian sense (the gift of the other) is, however, not the *alterity* of postmodernity (Derrida and Levinas),[56] but the hospitality that invites people, irrespective of "orientation," to the *centre*, that is, to Jesus and discipleship. It portrays unconditional love, but not unconditioned love. That is, it can only ultimately embrace into its membership those who wish to follow Jesus and the command of God, which he reiterated and reaffirmed (Matt. 5) in his ministry and through his apostles (Rom. 1; 1 Cor. 6). The church is both a *centred* set, which invites all people to the centre, Jesus, and a *bounded* set, made up of true disciples of Jesus who are committed to the Word of God in its ethical fulness. This bounded aspect means that appropriate boundaries may be placed within the church's life for the protection of the flock and especially its younger members.

This affirms the *welcoming but nonaffirming* position. That is, the church must welcome people who are same-sex attracted, who are struggling with their sexual desires, or who have gender dysphoria. We will love persons irrespective of their struggles and welcome them to work out these issues as they journey with us. However, we do not affirm "gay" sexual relations or "gay" marriage and will affirm graciously but truthfully that we consider the expression of such relations as a violation of our community standards. Rather, as in the case of persons who are heterosexual and single, we issue the call of discipleship toward the telos of celibacy. In this regard we recognize that we are countercultural in a number of important ways. Whereas the sex-saturated culture of modernity and

---

56. For an excellent discussion of true Christian hospitality, see Luke Bretherton, *Hospitality as Holiness: Christian Witness amid Moral Diversity* (Abingdon: Routledge, 2016).

postmodernity expresses the value that every human person has the right to sexual relations, we say that this is a fiction. Whereas our fragmented culture may be outraged because the church's evaluation based on Scripture and the Christian tradition insists on celibacy for persons who do not qualify for covenantal marriage, stating that it is therefore tragic for a person to have same-sex inclinations, we answer that in a fallen world the whole area of sexuality and sex is tragic as a result of the fall.

Tragic is in fact a description of the sexual experience, or lack of it, of just about every person I know in this fallen world. Some have been born intersex.[57] Some have been sexually abused, with profound emotional and relational and marital consequences. Heterosexual persons too are precluded from having sex outside of marriage. There are many single people who want to be married—this too is tragic. We live in a fallen world. We offer hope of a new creation. We encourage faithfulness more than fulfilment. For ethics done in a Christian way is not relativistic; it is not a summation of "what we do" but of what "should be done" in light of God's revealed will for us as humans. The distinction implied here between being and practice is a challenging one for our culture, as is the concomitant notion that a person can be same-sex attracted and abstain from same-sex sex acts. This relates to the cultural assumption of the "right" that all humans have to engage in sex. The biblical mandate for the practice of opposite-sex sex is actually no different; it is reserved for those in a marriage covenant between a man and a woman. In all these ways, we are countercultural—unapologetically so.

Some evangelical churches do not struggle with the nonaffirming position but rather with being welcoming. Evangelicals who rightly eschew same-sex sex acts can be guilty of failing to love the same-sex attracted person. It seems that the church finds it challenging to show concrete signs that we love people who struggle with same-sex, rather than opposite-sex, sexual brokenness. We can do that by offering a welcoming spirit, supportive counselling,[58] social support, and discipleship

---

57. Intersex persons are persons born with disordered/different sexual development (DSD). These persons have a mix of male and female biological traits that can make it hard for doctors to assign them a male or female sex. The causes are either genetic or hormonal. It occurs rarely (0.015 percent of all births). A decision is usually made by parents and medical staff as to which sex the child should become with appropriate surgery. The child can grow up to sense that they should be the opposite sex of that decided upon at birth. This is decidedly a complex ethical case requiring great compassion.

58. By *supportive*, I do not mean conversion therapy. I mean the kind that provides insight first into whether one's same-sex attraction is a permanent disposition or a temporary phase (an

groups that focus on the journey toward celibacy. If we were as passionate about loving the same-sex attracted person and bringing them into discipleship in Christ as we are about hating their sins, we might be more credible as the community of Christ.

(5) Although the act of sex is not required for persons to be human (Jesus is a case in point), when it does occur between a man and a woman, it must be within the safety of permanent covenant. This is because it is a sacrament of the triune Godhead. It is also because, as such, it unites persons, not just bodies. The biblical language of "one flesh" and "two becoming one" is not accidentally like the mystery of three persons being one in the communion of the Godhead, or of Christ and his church being "one." Sexual intercourse creates a mysterious "one flesh" bond. This is what makes adultery so wrong for married people. But it is also what makes premarital sex and cohabitation inappropriate for people who have not yet professed public covenant. The reality is that when we have sex with someone outside of marriage, we become one with them and so defraud that person's future spouse. And even if that person does become our spouse, we have violated God's express will, which is that sexual intercourse be practised within the security of covenant commitment only.[59]

(6) The primary distortion to sex that the fall brings and that the gospel corrects is a turning in on oneself—the opposite of true sex as designed by God. As Kreeft says, "The greatest pleasure is self-giving, [as] is graphically illustrated by sexual intercourse and by the very structure of the sexual organs, which must give themselves to each other in order to be fulfilled." Kreeft goes on to express the belief that heaven, while not a place for marrying, will in fact be a place for being properly sexual. By this he means that "all earthly perversions of true sexuality are overcome, especially the master perversion, selfishness." "The highest pleasure," he asserts, "always comes in self-forgetfulness." He insists that

---

increasing occurrence in today's youth culture). If it is deemed that for reasons of nature and nurture one has a permanent disposition, Christian counsel will involve guidance toward faithful Christian living in a celibate lifestyle. Even if genetics does some day reveal a genetic disposition toward same-sex attraction, this would still be the faithful Christian way. Where it is determined that the inclination toward same-sex attraction is temporary, counselling can be offered to provide insights into the dynamics of this phenomenon.

59. On the issue of how much physical contact is permissible before marriage, it should develop in a relationship in proportion to the level of commitment in the relationship. When a courtship becomes an engagement, the couple should keep the engagement short to avoid too much temptation if the couple is together frequently.

the human self "has a built-in, God-imaging design of self-fulfillment by self-forgetfulness, pleasure through unselfishness, ecstasy by *ekstasis*, 'standing-outside-the-self.'"[60] Sexuality is a constant reminder of our embodiedness, and this can either drive us into self-obsession or be a means to drive us outward to the divine and human other.

This rather mysterious notion of being sexual in heaven but not married brings us back to the heart of what sexuality is, as suggested by its creation as described in Genesis 1 and as fulfilled in the man Christ Jesus, the last Adam in the new creation. That is, sexuality is other-centredness reflected in the eternal Trinity, and it is other-centredness reflected in the man Jesus, who possessed his sexedness without ever acting on it sexually, yet who acted on its impulse to be the man in communion with his Father and his fellow humans, thus defining perfect cohumanity and perfect loving relationality.

In anticipation of the next chapter, how does the church speak in the public square about matters of homosexuality? Some theologians would say that we cannot impose our standards upon society, so beyond speaking evangelically about flourishing within God's good desires for humanity, we cannot impose Christian values on the state, especially when the state has already made same-sex marriage a constitutional right. "After all, the Bible also prohibits adultery, but Christians are not advocating for adultery laws," as Tremper Longman says. He goes on to say that he is grateful that the state and the church agree in forbidding incest or polyamorous marriages but insists that God "wants non-Christians to have a relationship with him, not simply to act like Christians."[61] Similarly, as a public Christian theologian who affirms the distinctness of church and state and who honours democracy as a political system, John Milbank restricts church marriage to heterosexuals, allowing same-sex civil unions in the state. On the other hand, Oliver O'Donovan, on the basis of a moral order in the creation, reaffirmed by the resurrection, might rather suggest that an appeal can be made from the church to society on these evangelical grounds.

---

60. Kreeft, "Is There Sex in Heaven?," 123.

61. Tremper Longman III, *The Bible and the Ballot: Using Scripture in Political Decisions* (Grand Rapids: Eerdmans, 2020), 230.

CHAPTER 9

Theological Ethics
Are *Public*

The Christian tradition has a wide gamut of opinion about whether the church should be engaged at all with the world and its morals and ethics, and if it is, what the form and tone of that engagement should look like. We begin therefore with a brief survey of the *range* of opinions. Secondly, on the assumption that this *is* something required for the church and the Christian, we offer a sustained appeal for appropriate engagement with appropriate *rationale*. This will include discussion of the nature of the church, the kingdom of God, and the state. It will also include a consideration of what the aims of this engagement are. Throughout, there will be concern and comment on the all-important question of *how* such engagement is intended to happen, that is, the *methodology* of engagement. The answer offered will be "in an evangelical and ecclesial way." The church as it functions within itself and in the public square will be guided by its Trinitarian nature. It echoes the Trinity intensively as a communion overflowing outward in love, *communio* in *ekstasis*. As such, it functions out of its missional identity and as a hospitable alternative *polis* for the world to see and enter.

THE RANGE OF OPINION

In one sense, the church *is* in the public square whether it likes it or not. Its presence is seen and felt, although the degree to which this is so may vary widely (if some churches in the West ceased to exist, would anyone in the city notice?). Furthermore, individual Christians are already in all sectors of the public square whether they like it or not. As Paul Stevens is wont to say, you don't have to send your people out; they are already out, every weekday in all the workplaces of the public square, including the political ones. Rather, "what is needed" in the life of the church and in pastoral equipping, says Stevens, "is a comprehensive biblical foundation for the Christian's life in the world as well as the church, a theology for homemakers, nurses and doctors, plumbers, stockbrokers, politicians and farmers."[1] He comments also that "without a deeper understanding of why we work, we find that life becomes bleached of meaning. We feel stuck working in dead end jobs that engage only a fraction of our gifts and aspirations."[2] Teaching the whole people of God that each is a missionary in union with the missional God is crucial for this understanding. Almost no one in the church would question that individual Christians can be, indeed, are, in the public square, including the political square, and are to bear witness there to the gospel in its fulness, acting toward the direction of the shalom it brings to the world. This is in the spirit of Martin Luther, who in addition to other great contributions to the Reformation recovered the dignity of work and vocation for the whole people of God and maintained that there was no one better to be a magistrate (politician) than the Christian.[3]

What is sometimes questioned is whether the *church* as church collectively should be engaged with politics, especially given that the separation of church and state is a valued conviction in many countries and that Constantinianism does not exist in most Western countries anymore. This separation does function as an important boundary. One way to think of this is to view the church and the state as distinct sphere sovereignties under God, as Dutch prime minister and theologian Abraham Kuyper (1837–1920) and philosopher Herman Dooyeweerd (1894–1977) suggested.[4] Christ is Lord over both spheres but in different ways. "Differentiated

---

1. R. Paul Stevens, *The Other Six Days: Vocation, Work, and Ministry in Biblical Perspective* (Grand Rapids: Eerdmans; Vancouver: Regent College Publishing, 1999), 4.

2. R. Paul Stevens and Alvin Ung, *Taking Your Soul to Work: Overcoming the Nine Deadly Sins of the Workplace* (Grand Rapids: Eerdmans, 2010), 4.

3. Martin Luther, "Temporal Authority: To What Extent It Should Be Obeyed," in *Luther's Works*, American ed., 55 vols., ed J. Pelikan and H. Lehmann (St. Louis: Concordia; Philadelphia: Fortress, 1955–), 45:96. Luther's encouragement toward engagement did not mean an indiscriminate endorsement of temporal authority, including endorsements of war. See Sarah Hinlicky Wilson, "Martin Luther, Pacifist?," Plough, October 18, 2017, https://www.plough.com/en/topics/justice/nonviolence/martin-luther-pacifist.

4. Abraham Kuyper, "Sphere Sovereignty," public address, inauguration of the Free University, trans. George Kamps, October 20, 1880. See also Richard Mouw, *Abraham Kuyper: A Short and Personal Introduction* (Grand Rapids: Eerdmans, 2011); H. Dooyeweerd, *Roots of Western Culture: Pagan, Secular, and Christian Options* (Lewiston, NY: Edwin Mellen, 2003), 49ff.; and Dooyeweerd, "The Christian Idea of the State," in *Essays in Legal, Social, and Political Philosophy*, ed. Alan Cameron and D. F. M. Strauss (Lewiston, NY: Edwin Mellen, 1997), 130–34. See also Gregory Baus, "Dooyeweerd's Societal Sphere Sovereignty: A Theory of Differentiated Responsibility," *Griffin's View on International and Comparative Law* 7 (June 2006): 209–17. The sphere sovereignty view actually simply reflects the Reformation view as expressed by both Luther and Calvin on

responsibilities" in each sphere is another way to refer to this idea. The distinction implies that partisan politics should not be bundled within but rather kept separate from the life of the gathered church.

But does the lordship of Christ over both realms and the nature of the church as the *primary* missionary of God actually allow a measure of *interdependence* between church and state rather than complete independence? If the distinction between the spheres has typically been between the creation order (state) and the redemption order (church) in this Reformed understanding, are we not concerned for these to have at least a measure of interaction? That is, a relationship not only in which each retains its own identity and governing autonomy but also in which there can be mutual exchange of perspective. In the Old Testament Israel, albeit a theocracy, prophets, priests, and kings were in different spheres, yet with much interchange. There are many cases in the Old Testament where the prophet was in the king's court to let the king know a divine perspective he may have missed (Amos 7 is a good example). Interdependence allows for some two-way communication whilst still acknowledging the boundaries.

And what would be the particular role of the church as a corporate body in the public square? What is its role in the mission of God to the village and the city and the nation and the world? Does it go beyond *being* an alternative society, the new humanity where justice and peace are present, where forgiveness and reconciliation are modelled, where the poor are fed and cared for and rehabilitated? Does it do more than *be*? If it is granted that the home of ethics is the church, does that home selfishly build up its moral character under the influence of biblical narratives and hoard its ethical insights? Or does it as the church *speak* into the culture, into science, into the political world? In recent literature, there has been much focus on two main points of view on how the church is to be in the public square: the first has a primary focus on being the community of God, an alternative *polis*, a colony of "resident aliens,"[5] and the second has a focus on being the community of God *and* speaking wisely and evangelically in the

two manners of divine rule. The two-kingdom view of the Reformers was over against the Roman Catholic mingling of church and state and the Anabaptist withdrawal from the state. See Klaus Bockmuehl, *The Christian Way of Living: An Ethics of the Ten Commandments* (Vancouver: Regent College Publishing, 1994), 89–90.

5. Stanley J. Hauerwas and William Willimon, *Resident Aliens: Life in the Christian Colony* (Nashville: Abingdon, 2014).

public square.[6] The contrast between these views is presented in a stark fashion for clarity. Transforming the world is still an agenda for the first approach, so it is not that one approach is missional and the other not. It is rather that the first is anxious to avoid the power dynamics of the public square and the culture of lobbying that characterizes politics, especially in the USA and especially with religious groups like the Moral Majority. It is not that the proponents of the Hauerwasian way, or Hauerwas himself, never speak publicly and prophetically. They do. But their first aim is the cultivation of an ecclesial ethical community of character that is a visible and hospitable presence in the culture, one that speaks with integrity by its being. Correspondingly, the O'Donovan approach does not in any way neglect the ecclesial moral formation of the people of God but is anxious to say it must also *speak* evangelically.

Theological ethicist David Zac Niringiye has actually suggested that there are *four positions*, not just two.[7] He suggests that the typologies of engagement in various Christian traditions within the scope especially of evangelicals involve a spectrum with the following identifiable positions: disengagement (separatistic, sometimes just ecclesially prioritized as in the case of Hauerwas and Willimon), cooperation (in pursuit of the common good/shalom), co-optation (indiscriminate adoption of cultural norms), and confrontation (engaging the "powers" at work in and behind society). The latter is sometimes associated solely with the Moral Majority in the USA and its method of intimidatory confrontation. Such a method or tone carries with it a use of political power that is difficult to reconcile with the way of Christ and servanthood. However, there are ways of confrontation that are much more compatible with the Christian way, that are the prophetic word of the church to the world, unapologetic and uncompromising when required, but spoken with humility and respect. Such speaking would be accompanied by the offering of a gospel alternative that the church models. One example of this is that when speaking to the issue of abortion, rather than vigilante reprisals, the church can offer its caring people or crisis pregnancy centres as a means to alleviate the challenges faced by mothers of unwanted babies.

---

6. Oliver O'Donovan, *Resurrection and Moral Order: An Outline for Evangelical Ethics* (Grand Rapids: Eerdmans, 1986), 76–97, 140–62; Alan Torrance, "On Deriving 'Ought' from 'Is,'" in *The Doctrine of God and Theological Ethics*, ed. Alan J. Torrance and Michael Banner (London: T&T Clark, 2006), 180–85.

7. David Zac Niringiye, *The Church: God's Pilgrim People* (Downers Grove, IL: IVP Academic, 2015).

An expanded nine "models of Christian influence" have been outlined by Dennis Hollinger: Christian relief, Christian alternative institutions, evangelism, prophetic pronouncements, lobbying, political parties/political groups, nonviolent resistance, Christian embodiment, and individual impact.[8]

Both of these classification systems are helpful delineations of *ways* in which the Christian church and its persons can engage. Proponents of all these views can lack an emphasis on civility (Richard Mouw[9]) or the common good (Niringiye[10]). *How* we engage is as important as the decision *whether* to engage and our intended *aim*. Richard Mouw's primary concern is the tolerance and civil dialogue that must be shown when Christians and the church engage the public square. Mouw thinks of civility as a virtue nearly extinct in American politics, including among so-called Christian politicians and lobbyists. It is a Christian virtue, one by which we may enter public discussions with strong convictions of Christian truth, an openness to learn from those with whom we disagree, and a commitment to honour the humanity of even our greatest enemy. It is neither an anaemic niceness nor a road to relativism.[11] It is a demeanour of grace, a discourse in which one's inner intensity is never permitted to overpower self-restraint or rational dialogue.[12]

David Zac Niringiye's primary concern is that the gospel necessitates an obligation not only to proclaim and demonstrate the good news of salvation but also to strive for the common good.[13] He fears that the word *mission* can be problematic because it is sometimes equated with evangelism. This problem is ameliorated if it is understood that mission is not just evangelism and discipleship, that is, fulfilment of the Great Commission, but also the Great Commandment and the cultural mandate, which entail shalom for all creation.

Helpful as all of these *methods* of engagement are (and guidance concerning the *spirit* in which engagement should happen), it seems to me that these still come under two main *philosophies* of engagement,

---

8. Dennis P. Hollinger, *Choosing the Good: Christian Ethics in a Complex World* (Grand Rapids: Baker Academic, 2002), 256–72.

9. Richard Mouw, *Uncommon Decency: Christian Civility in an Uncivil World* (Downers Grove, IL: IVP, 1992); Mouw, *The God Who Commands* (Notre Dame, IN: University of Notre Dame Press, 1991), 150.

10. Niringiye, *The Church*.

11. Mouw, *Uncommon Decency*, 21–22, 73, 112, 157.

12. Mouw, *Uncommon Decency*, 21–34.

13. Niringiye, *The Church*.

which are those referenced above (three if we include withdrawal). One calls the church to be the church, focusing on the nature of the church as God's community where wisdom is discerned by people of character who are being formed by the biblical narrative; the second calls the church to be the church as a community of character and ethical discernment and, as the icon of the Trinity, *communio* in *ekstasis*, taking responsibility to speak to the world in evangelical ways. It sees itself not so much as an alternative community but as a community that is, like the Trinity, open for human relations. In the first approach, one might say that the church emphasizes its nature as a bounded set; in the second, a centred set. In the first, although the church will be hospitable, it feels a little bit like a community that has circled the wagons. In the second, there is still a commitment of the church to being the church in all its depth, yet alongside this is a sense of missional width that includes a sharing with the rest of humanity in the cultural mandate with concern for the *common good*,[14] and dialogue and engagement on matters of justice and compassion that fulfil the Great Commandment, as well as evangelism as per the Great Commission. The church as the new humanity thus understands itself to be the harbinger of the reconciliation and redemption of all humanity. It sees itself as elect in order to have the responsibility of sharing election with the humanity with whom Christ became one, and for whom he died and rose again. It sees humanity as having been ontologically neighboured by Christ. This is an outflow of seeing ecclesiology in a Trinitarian way, one of the primary rationales for engagement in the public square offered below.

THE RATIONALE FOR ENGAGEMENT (THE "WHY" QUESTION)

The Biblical Texts and Narrative

Some important biblical texts appear to speak to the issue of whether the church should be in the public square. These must be interpreted properly in context and in the normal historical, grammatical, rhetorical

---

14. Charles E. Gutenson, *Christians and the Common Good: How Faith Intersects with Public Life* (Grand Rapids: Brazos, 2011); Mouw, *Uncommon Decency*; Miroslav Volf, *A Public Faith: How Followers of Christ Should Serve the Common Good* (Grand Rapids: Brazos, 2011). See also Richard John Neuhaus, *The Naked Public Square: Religion and Democracy in America* (Grand Rapids: Eerdmans, 1984).

way. Luke 20:20–25, for example, is the occasion when Jesus is asked whether it is right to pay taxes to Caesar. He responds masterfully by asking whose portrait is on a denarius and then saying, "Then give back to Caesar what is Caesar's, and to God what is God's." This, taken alongside Romans 13:1–7, would appear to give credence to the separation between church and state, whilst urging proper obedience to the state—as long as its commands do not conflict with God's commands, given that the authority of the state is relative and is itself under God. Civil disobedience and consequent martyrdom is a presupposition of a number of texts for Christians in the New Testament. Thus antinomianism is not justifiable. But neither is acquiescence to laws that violate the moral law of God or that outlaw evangelism. One could also interpret these passages to mean that engagement as a leader in politics or jurisprudence must be governed by the same criteria: keep church and state separate yet in dialogue; obey the moral law and inspire and command others toward justice and peace; disobey the law when it calls for actions that contradict the moral law and the ends of the kingdom of God.

A passage such as John 18:33–37 in which Jesus says, "My kingdom is not of this world. If it were, my servants would fight" (v. 36), along with Philippians 3:20 ("But our citizenship is in heaven"), may seem to justify the position of withdrawal from society. But these texts must be considered alongside a number of other passages suggesting that we also have a citizenship on earth that is to be taken seriously (Acts 22:22–29; Rom. 13:1). The very essence of what happens in the book of Acts is the coming of the kingdom from heaven to earth. The Lord's Prayer actually suggests we pray for God's kingdom to come, that his will might be done on earth as it is in heaven. The fact that during the writing of the New Testament, the church was always a fledgling and persecuted minority may account for the fact that there is very little in the New Testament about the engagement of Christians in government or politics. They were precluded from this by their refusal to worship the emperors. As the church develops and morphs into a majority in the Constantinian era, these opportunities arise and with them the temptation of compromise of differing kinds. The Scriptures have been sufficient through each successive era of the church for guiding leaders to engage with wisdom when they can.

What is the intended aim of engagement by the church? A text that is often quoted in this regard is that which speaks of the witness of Christians as "salt" and "light" (Matt. 5:13–16).

The wider context of these verses, the Beatitudes, signifies that those who live the kingdom way will be distinctive in what they value and in their lifestyles and virtues. The immediate context, however, is the beatitude on persecution, which suggests that in their distinctiveness, as they are engaged with society, they will attract attention that is not always friendly. New Testament scholar R. T. France in his commentary on Matthew suggests poignantly that it is the "visible distinctiveness which arouses the hostility of others." But he adds, "It is only those who are involved with other people who will be seen to be different and so attract persecution. Salt is of no use as long as it stays in the salt cellar. Light is no use under a bowl. . . . Disciples, therefore, must be both distinctive and involved." He concludes, "Neither the indistinguishably assimilated nor the inaccessible hermit will fulfill the mandate of these challenging verses."[15] It is by being prophetic in the culture, and in a way that is backed up by the kingdom values and the character of those who live out the Beatitudes, that people are salt and light. Clearly evangelism is included here by way of application, but a much wider scope is in view, one that makes evangelism credible. Adherence to the new values of the kingdom of heaven has an influence on society that is purifying and preservational.

Most strikingly, France affirms that the salt and the light referred to here are the communal people of God, the church: "The address is in the second-person plural not only because more than one person is being addressed, but because it is the corporate impact of a disciple community, as an alternative society, which is here in view." The idea of little candles shining each in their small corner is a product of Western individualism, whereas what Jesus had in mind is "the collective light of a whole community which draws the attention of the watching world."[16] This important text, in sum, would seem to suggest that the church is intended by its character and kingdom values and actions to be a felt presence in society *for its preservation and for its illumination*. It can also by its prophetic presence attract persecution in this age. In the fulness of the eschatological trajectory of the kingdom, the people of God will

---

15. R. T. France, *The Gospel of Matthew*, New International Commentary on the New Testament (Grand Rapids: Eerdmans, 2007), 172.

16. France, *Gospel of Matthew*, 171.

reign over the world, but not until then (1 Cor. 6:2; 2 Tim. 2:12). In the in-between time, the church has been and should be influential in justice and all moral areas . . . and persecution.

The call of the church in any age is faithfulness to shalom-sharing, the living and proclaiming of the gospel in its fulness (John 20:19–23). The results are God's concern, not ours. The church has historically done better in terms of faithfulness to its identity and calling when it has been a persecuted minority, just as it is depicted in John 20, for example, rather than when it has been the ruling political entity with a cultural hegemony. After the day of Pentecost when the Holy Spirit came upon and in his church, the disciples would in fact accomplish the impossible—the evangelization of a significant portion of their then-known world. And the shalom imparted by the risen Christ to his kingdom community was ultimately shared with a broken and alienated world. People were drawn into that gathered community of shalom, and the catalytic impact of that scattered community in turn ultimately brought shalom to the ancient and medieval world in all kinds of ways—the liberation of women, the humanization of children, hospitals, education, art, architecture, and science.

In addition to these key texts, which seem at least to allow for the influence of the church on the state, the overall canonical context of these texts, that is, the *shape of the master narrative* of the Bible, seems to encourage this engagement. This is the trajectory from creation to new creation, and within it a vision for human flourishing grounded in the fact that God loves all humanity, and his desire is for the salvation of all, which means not just eternal life but eternal life in a new creation in which shalom is finally present in fulness. In this spirit, Charles Gutenson has urged the avoidance of prooftexting on these issues and has expressed the need for proper hermeneutics, and especially the reading of the Bible as a whole story.[17] Knowing the story we are in is all important. Gutenson also speaks about common errors Christians make when they engage in political debate. The first is the tendency "to put too much trust in the political process for making the world a better place." He comments that "public policies and institutions can serve a kingdom agenda," but we can put "*too much* confidence in them."[18]

---

17. Gutenson, *Christians and the Common Good*, 12, 38, 51.
18. Gutenson, *Christians and the Common Good*, 19, 27, 51, 136, 137.

There is, in other words, a note of realism about the telos of social engagement by the church. Is it preservation of society in the spirit of the salt and light passage, or are there triumphalistic expectations that move beyond this? The role of the church as the kingdom community is to influence society toward justice and kingdom values, but "attempting to create a moral society trusting solely in the legislative process"[19] goes too far. Just getting the "right laws" in place, as Gutenson affirms, does not guarantee a moral society.[20] The Hauerwasian view would suggest that our role is not to make society a little less corrupt and humans a little less adulterous. Yet the preserving role of the church would suggest the possibility of influence according to the trajectory of God's desire for humanity. The close identity of the church with the kingdom of God, an issue we explore below, also suggests an outward influence of the church.

A second common error made by overly zealous Christians is a "tendency to be overly narrow in determining what counts as a moral issue." This narrowing of the moral agenda easily creates the impression "that we have narrowed the moral agenda in a way that serves partisan interests."[21] A closely related third common error is that "we also often get the priorities backwards or otherwise out of alignment with the teachings of Scripture."[22] Having surveyed the Scriptures, we move on to look at the theological realities that flow from the study of Scripture.

The Trinitarian Nature of the Church

Bringing into play the Trinitarian nature of ethics, some theologians have found it helpful to think of the being and the economic acts of the Trinity as the grounding for the church as a community of depth *and* of width, including social engagement. For example, Miroslav Volf expresses a primary concern for the participation of all humanity in creational shalom as what may be called the "common good," and he does so within a discussion of the nature of the church in light of the doctrine of the Trinity, as the shape of social engagement.[23] He makes a strong defence of the appropriateness of the Trinity as a model for human

---

19. Gutenson, *Christians and the Common Good*, 52.
20. Gutenson, *Christians and the Common Good*, 52, 68.
21. Gutenson, *Christians and the Common Good*, 8, 52, 68.
22. Gutenson, *Christians and the Common Good*, 136.
23. Miroslav Volf, "'The Trinity Is Our Social Programme': The Doctrine of the Triunity and the Shape of Social Engagement," in Torrance and Banner, *Doctrine of God and Theological Ethics*, 105–24.

society,[24] over against those who resist this move on the grounds that God is transcendent and not amenable to being "copied." Acknowledging that we cannot copy God in some respects, Volf affirms that we cannot abandon the Trinity in favour of God's "kingship" of power as the sole way in which we imitate God. That is, we *can* operate conjunctively, not only disjunctively, with regard to God as the triune God in light of the fact that humanity is spoken of as the image of God and that we are explicitly brought into faith and baptism in the triune name of God (Matt. 28:20) and into the triune life of God and are, as such, created "according to God's likeness" (Eph. 4:24) and explicitly commanded to imitate God (Matt. 5:48; Phil. 2:1–4; 1 Thess. 1:6; 2:14; 1 Peter 1:16). He is careful to indicate the limits of the correspondence between the Trinity and human community, which are twofold: the first is the remove between God and humanity (both ontologically and noetically); since our best human notions of what the Trinity is are less than what the Trinity actually is, we must always speak of correspondences such as "persons," "relations," and "perichoresis" as analogous and not univocal.[25] The second is the hamartiological reality that humans are sinners and historically transitory.[26] In light of this, Volf looks not first to the circular notion of the love and perichoresis of the Trinity to seek justification for correspondence but rather to the downward salvific line of the movement of the Trinity to humanity in Christ. The downward vertical line then leads to the participation of redeemed humanity in the life of the Trinity, not because we are now ontologically divine but because we have in the Son been brought into communion with God by the Spirit in our moral and character transformation whilst remaining human. In sum, avoiding any univocal comparison, we can still by way of analogy copy "God in *some* respects,"[27] as the church in his image learns from the life of the triune God by *participating* in his life, in the Son, and by the Spirit. Modelling and participation go inseparably together, as noted in chapter 8. There is thus a rationale for the church's evangelical ethical engagement with the world in a way that images the Trinity in its twofold

---

24. Volf makes a strong case for the Trinity as a model for humans and specifically human community in *After Our Likeness* and in "The Trinity Is Our Social Programme," where his main protagonist is Ted Peters (*God as Trinity: Relationality and Temporality in Divine Life* [Louisville: Westminster John Knox, 1993]).

25. Volf, "Trinity Is Our Social Programme," 106–7.

26. Volf, "Trinity Is Our Social Programme," 106–7.

27. Volf, "Trinity Is Our Social Programme," 106.

movement, outward to the world in a way that is a participation in the Son's redemptive movement, and inward, offering hospitality to those who seek to enter the community and begin their quest for Christ and discipleship.

Volf emphasizes two particularly helpful aspects of the life of the Trinity that can be "copied," and indeed must be imaged in the life of the church as icon of the Trinity. The first is *identity*, and the second, *self-donation*. The first, identity, is "inscribed in the character and relations of divine persons," and what this might suggest about "how to go about negotiating identities under conditions of enmity and conflict."[28] Volf boldly suggests that the concept of perichoresis of the persons who in the Trinity are constituted by one another so that they are persons-in-communion (persons and communion being equiprimal) serves to establish not only the *unity* of the Godhead (*De Fide*, John of Damascus[29]), but equally so, the irreducible *identity* of the persons.[30] We may say that the divine persons are personally and mutually interior to one another, as the Jesus of John's Gospel reveals (10:38; 14:10; 17:21), yet they are also decidedly *not* the other, with distinctions that include but move beyond their eternal relations. As Volf expresses it: "Every divine person is and acts as itself and yet the two other persons are present and act in that person."[31] These identities, though interpenetrated, are *irreducible* but *not self-enclosed*. The *irreducibility*, by way of correspondence in human persons, speaks profoundly to the dignity and uniqueness of human persons, who, in a fallen world and in the course of carrying out the witness of the socially engaged church in usually conflicted and even hostile situations, will need to negotiate and hold intact their identity. This involves the tension of appropriate assertiveness and deference, not "dissolving into the other or being smothered by the other,"[32] with maintenance of personal boundaries and an appropriate sense of the self. They need to know "when to enclose the boundaries of the self in order to stabilize one's identity and when to open them in order to enrich it."[33]

---

28. Volf, "Trinity Is Our Social Programme," 109.

29. John of Damascus, in *De Fide*, popularized the term *perichoresis*, which Pseudo-Cyril first extended from its christological use in Gregory Nazianzus into Trinitarian language. See Michael G. Lawler, "*Perichoresis*: New Theological Wine in an Old Theological Wineskin," *Horizons* 22, no. 1 (1995): 49–51.

30. Volf, "Trinity Is Our Social Programme," 110.

31. Volf, "Trinity Is Our Social Programme," 111.

32. Volf, "Trinity Is Our Social Programme," 111.

33. Volf, "Trinity Is Our Social Programme," 112–13.

The *not being self-enclosed* aspect of identity speaks to the nature of the person as ecclesial, as defined by the divine and human other, a concept ably expounded by John Zizioulas in *Being as Communion* as the "catholicity of person."[34] Volf sums this up by saying that a "person can be a unique image of the whole . . . only by being located in Christ and partaking of Christ's identity." Christ is "a corporate personality constituted by the many who are in him."[35] Though Volf finds fault with Zizioulas's ability to define the identity of the person, the communal and catholic nature of the person is a crucial argument for the engagement of the church with the world, for it presents the idea of a church and all its persons as being for the other, missional, not inwardly oriented.

The second way the church can model the Trinity in participation with the life of the Trinity is the concept of *self-donation*. Self-donation defines first the heart of the triune being of God, in which each person is in the other and for the other in divine perichoresis, the "making room" each for the other or, as Volf states elsewhere, the fact that the persons are "mutually internal"[36] to one another. Hospitality, one could say, is at the heart of the universe, for it is the heart of the Creator. However, Volf makes a distinction between two loves of the Trinity that are both characterized by self-donation: the dance of the free and internal love of the Trinity, the horizontal "cycle of exchange between perfect lovers,"[37] and the downward love flowing out of that love within the Godhead toward a created, sinful world with a view to its transformation. The first love is always positive, whilst the second is reactive in the sense that it is exercised in the midst of opposition. The love that was expressed vertically involved translation of divine love by way of the incarnation and life of Jesus and then a cross. Similarly, the church is to reflect the inner love of the Trinity (living "as in the day" [Rom. 13:8–14], experiencing the inner love of the Trinity) and also the outward linear love that means *engagement* by "complex and difficult *translation*"[38] in the season of incarnational, cross-proclaiming, and cross-bearing mission ("the night" of Rom. 12:13). Volf thus speaks of self-donation as the

---

34. John Zizioulas, *Being as Communion: Studies in Personhood and the Church* (Yonkers, NY: St. Vladimir's Seminary Press, 1997), 60–64.

35. Volf, "Trinity Is Our Social Programme," 112.

36. Miroslav Volf, *After Our Likeness: The Church as the Image of the Trinity* (Grand Rapids: Eerdmans, 1998), 209, *passim*.

37. Volf, "Trinity Is Our Social Programme," 114.

38. Volf, *After Our Likeness*, 209, *passim*, emphasis original.

gold that gilds concepts of Trinitarian doctrine like "plurality-in-unity" and that guides persons in human relations in the opening and closing of the boundaries of our identities: "The self gives something of itself, of its own space . . . in a movement in which it contracts itself in order to be expanded by the other and in which at the same time enters the contracted other to increase the other's plenitude."[39] This will be necessary in the practice of Trinitarian love revealed in the cross, which involves the extension of grace and forgiveness to those whose starting position is to be "caught in the snares of non-love and seduced by injustice, deceit and violence."[40] For the life of the church, this means that it must operate according to the divine welcome given by Christ (the linear downward love of the Trinity), which "translates into the *will* to give ourselves to others and welcome them, to readjust our identities to make space for them," which "is prior to any judgement about others, except of identifying them in their humanity."[41] Volf employs Romans 15:7 to strengthen this argument: "Welcome one another, therefore, just as Christ has welcomed you, for the glory of God" (NRSV). He cites the comment of Rowan Williams on this text: "Generosity, mercy and welcome are imperatives for the Christian because they are a participation in the divine activity; but they are also imperative because they show God's glory and invite or attract human beings to 'give glory' to God—that is, to reflect back to God what God is."[42]

The penultimate aim of the outward movement of the church in engagement with the world is preservation and the bringing of humans into the love of God through faith. The ultimate end is the glory of God in his triune holiness, beauty, and perichoretic love.

A particular emphasis in the work of Alan Torrance on Trinitarian ethics is that Christian witness to the state "is not to be found outside of ecclesial participation."[43] However, he is equally clear that the church's authority to have a voice in the state lies "nowhere else than in the incarnate Word," which is the "one Word of God to humanity, together

39. Volf, "Trinity Is Our Social Programme," 113–14.

40. Volf, "Trinity Is Our Social Programme," 116.

41. Volf, "Trinity Is Our Social Programme," 116. Here Volf is reiterating the sentiments of *Exclusion and Embrace: A Theological Exploration of Identity, Otherness, and Reconciliation* (Nashville: Abingdon, 1996) and Richard Hays, *The Moral Vision of the New Testament: A Contemporary Introduction to New Testament Ethics* (Edinburgh: T&T Clark, 1997), 197.

42. Rowan Williams, "Interiority and Epiphany: A Reading in New Testament Ethics," *Modern Theology* 13, no. 1 (January 1997): 42.

43. Torrance, "On Deriving 'Ought' from 'Is,'" 183.

with all that is implied by it concerning the Creator-creature relation, the nature of community and God's unconditional endorsement of the dignity of our humanity,"[44] not on the basis of some common epistemological foundation that is "universally demonstrable."[45] The church may well be able to endorse some of the "subliminal agreements which undergird human relations appropriately" within the state, but this *koinonia*, which is indeed the telos of the state, has its fundamental and foundational reality within the church. Torrance is adamant, therefore, that "the pressure of interpretation in social ethics is and must be *from* the church *to* the state."[46] That is, multiple "*points* of contact" may arise but no "single *point* of contact." An "ontology of ecclesial participation" is that which moulds social ethics and not the other way around.[47] The church will serve society best, says Torrance, "by being nothing other than the church and it is never more relevant than when it has the courage to *be* the church."[48] He sums up this argument by asserting that it "is in and through our participation alone in the One in whom and through whom there is neither Jew nor Gentile, rich nor poor, black nor white, male and female that we find unconditional warrant for affirming the unconditional value of humanity."[49] We thereby also see humanity for what it is and how best to serve it. This reminds us that the whole movement of human rights and human dignity present in many governments of the Western world does indeed owe these great foundations of social and political ethics to the church's theology of the human in community. These governments rely on borrowed capital, for they have largely forsaken any reliance on the Christian church and its theology for these warranted convictions, choosing to appeal to a vacuous secularism in which "objective" neutrality has been shown by postmodernity to be a myth.

But does this decidedly ecclesial approach not create incipient isolationism on behalf of the church? Torrance counters this, first because its very ground of existence is the inclusive *missio trinitatis*. That is, it has its being or hypostasis in a radically inclusive *ekstasis* toward the secular world. It has its very being in a love that transcends its own boundaries.

---

44. Torrance, "On Deriving 'Ought' from 'Is,'" 183.
45. Torrance, "On Deriving 'Ought' from 'Is,'" 183.
46. Torrance, "On Deriving 'Ought' from 'Is,'" 183.
47. Torrance, "On Deriving 'Ought' from 'Is,'" 183.
48. Torrance, "On Deriving 'Ought' from 'Is,'" 183.
49. Torrance, "On Deriving 'Ought' from 'Is,'" 184.

In fact, it is when the church seeks to establish a "foundationally secu-lar ethic" or a "non-descript religious ethic" that it ironically becomes isolationist, because "it relativizes its grounds for loving enemies or people from different theological or ethical or religious traditions and cultures."[50] Torrance insists that ethical witness on any other basis than this Trinitarian approach, including "a nature-grace model in the form of a two-kingdom, law-grace, state-church dichotomy,"[51] has resulted and will result in the church becoming deeply compromised by being implicated in policies that are incompatible with the mind of Christ.

But above all, this Trinitarian approach inspires and empowers the "living out of God's unconditional affirmation of the weak, the confused, the alienated, and most significantly, the guilty"[52] to whom it offers the good news of forgiveness and reconciliation. It affirms the dignity of all human persons irrespective of age or race or religion or orientation and offers forgiveness for the sin of all and seeks reconciliation of all in light of its grounding in the reconciling person and work of Christ.

The Trinitarian approach to engagement in the public square and especially its distortions are summed up well by Richard Mouw in *The God Who Commands*. He begins a chapter on theological ethics with the troubling observation that "Christians play favourites with the members of the Trinity."[53] Daniel Migliore has also made the point that the Trinity fully considered is the context for the refinement of conceptions of divine power and, indeed, the harmonizing of all the attributes of God, including those that are seemingly conflicted.[54] The corollary is that neglect of one or more of the persons of the Trinity leads to an imbalance in theological ethics.[55]

In sum, a significant rationale for the engagement of the church comes from its nature as conjoined to the communion of the triune God, which is the communion of love in ecstatic overflow to humanity.

---

50. Torrance, "On Deriving 'Ought' from 'Is,'" 184.

51. Torrance, "On Deriving 'Ought' from 'Is,'" 184.

52. Torrance, "On Deriving 'Ought' from 'Is,'" 184.

53. Mouw, *God Who Commands*, 150.

54. Daniel Migliore, *The Power of God* (Philadelphia: Westminster, 1983), 77.

55. This is a point made also by H. Richard Niebuhr, who stated that Christianity might well be characterized as "an association, loosely held together, of three Unitarian religions." For example, a "unitarianism of the creator" (Father) results in engagement that is unchristological and unpneumatic, focused purely on the common good and social justice with no concern for evangelism. See H. Richard Niebuhr, "The Doctrine of the Trinity and the Unity of the Church," *Theology Today* 3 (1946): 372–76.

THE HUMAN CAPACITY TO HEAR AND REASON (TRINITARIAN THEOLOGICAL ANTHROPOLOGY)

A further rationale pertains to the conclusion reached in previous chapters on the capacity of the non-Christian to perceive the moral order and the moral law rationally, albeit not with gospel clarity or empowerment. It relates to good creational, incarnational, and resurrectional theology that reaffirms the created moral order, and the image of God in humans in its relational, structural, and functional aspects. It asserts that even though non-Christians are not in relationship with God, they are in relatedness to the God who never lets them go, and indeed who has entered into humanity as an ontological entity to justify them and all creation in Christ. The gospel of the triune God declares that God is *for* humanity. Our engagement in the public square must be there, and it must reflect not a sectarian superiority but a God who is *for* humanity, all of it.

Engagement of the church and of the individual Christian is in keeping with the relational/related nature of the image of God and therefore, not surprisingly, with the second part of the Great Commandment by which Christians are called to love their neighbour, the neighbour whom God himself has neighboured by the incarnation. Karl Barth offers the term *mitmenschlichkeit*, translated as a human "with-ness," conveying an interrelatedness that describes this notion of *in relation*—fellow persons mutually giving and receiving assistance with gladness.[56] The church is challenged to model and reflect communal life that overcomes both the rampant *individualism* of modernity and, paradoxically, the frightening sense of *collectivism* brought on by overpopulation, anonymity, and the loss of true community in the disembodied relationships that social media fosters. Individualism discounts "the embedded webs of interlocution,"[57] and collectivism collapses in on personhood—extremes both rooted in society's impoverished theology.[58] Thus, a perichoretic understanding of personhood provides the necessary relief for both individualism and collectivism,[59] as we have noted earlier. As Colin

---

56. Karl Barth, *CD* III, study ed., ed. G.W. Bromiley (London: T&T Clark, 1960), 258, 263.

57. If self is viewed as drawing purpose out of itself and seeking "relationships" only insofar as they are "fulfilling," it ignores the embedded webs of interlocution. Charles Taylor, *Sources of the Self: The Making of the Modern Identity* (Cambridge, MA: Harvard University Press, 1989), 38–39.

58. Colin E. Gunton, *Father, Son, and Holy Spirit: Toward a Fully Trinitarian Theology* (Edinburgh: T&T Clark, 2003), 53.

59. Human persons do have irreducible identities (as do the divine persons), and humans are individualized in at least three ways: physicality, personality, and gender.

Gunton emphasized, "If the notion of perichoresis helps us to rethink [these extremes], it is by virtue of the fact that, although it envisages close relatedness, it never does so to the detriment of particularity."[60] *Otherness* and *relation* are held in tight juxtaposition. "Only where both are given due stress is personhood fully enabled."[61] The nature of the church as the icon of the Trinity precisely calls us to reflect and communicate this personhood in communion, however imperfectly.[62] But the failure to be the coinherent community of the church and to speak evangelically to culture and to hospitably invite the world into its fellowship is a denial of these Trinitarian realities.

Another angle on this is to affirm that all human persons are the recipients of *common grace*, which encourages moral dialogue. Jesus actually refers in the parable of the shrewd manager to the "people of this world" being "more shrewd in dealing with their own kind than are the people of the light" (Luke 16:8). Crucially, the evangelical nature of ethics insists that ethics must be couched within the gestalt and ethos of the gospel. Surely, therefore, the church's or an individual Christian's engagement for the common good or even prophetically must be contextualized within the gospel, and it is a proper expectation that the Holy Spirit will be at work in these interactions, to illumine and regenerate those who hear it. They might, as Barth would emphasize, have no capacity to hear apart from the Spirit's enlivening work, but we will with Brunner (and Barth also) insist that they have "the capacity to receive the capacity" and that our words will be accompanied by the work of the Spirit. Acts 17 provides evidence that even in the natural state, the person who does not know the one true God has an awareness of transcendence that directs their attention toward caricatures of God. God never leaves them, for each lives and moves and has their being in him, and God is always, like the Prodigal Father, looking for those who might "seek him and perhaps reach out for him and find him" (Acts 17:26–28). The being and speaking of the people of God in the public square concerning justice and righteousness are, in other words, missional, for the church is that by identity in the triune missional God

---

60. Colin E. Gunton, *The One, the Three, and the Many* (Cambridge: Cambridge University Press, 1993), 169.
61. Colin E. Gunton, "Trinity, Ontology, and Anthropology: Towards a Renewal of the Doctrine of the *Imago Dei*," in *Persons, Divine and Human: King's College Essays in Theological Anthropology*, ed. Christoph Schwöbel and Colin E. Gunton (Edinburgh: T&T Clark, 1999), 59.
62. Stanley Grenz, *Theology for the Community of God* (Grand Rapids: Eerdmans, 2000), 232.

in whom it participates. That participatory awareness will keep its engagement respectful, humble, oriented toward shalom or the common good. But it will also anticipate the working of the Spirit as it reflects its incarnational life as the body of Christ on earth.

The debates about how the human person is enabled to be responsive to the law or the law within the gospel come to roost here, and without recapitulating them, we will simply say that whether we opt for the Thomistic natural law view grounded in the *analogia entis* or prefer the *analogia fide* or *relationis* or *adventus* of the Bonhoefferian/Barthian school, the church and the Christian must speak.

What then shall we make of those who are not Christian? And how is the Christian to engage in the public square in a post-Christian age where Christian convictions are not welcome and communicate Christian ethics in ways that make sense to others? Whilst both excoriating the indiscriminate enculturation of many in the German church and appealing that culture had placed their Saviour on a cross, Barth, along with Bonhoeffer, urgently expressed the need for the church to speak out and engage ethically in the public and political arena during the rise of the Nazi regime on the basis of the *analogia fidei*. On what basis could he hope for that to have any influence if there was no capacity for the population to hear? For Barth, the incarnation of Christ played a critical role in theology, including anthropology. Barth's confidence to engage his culture was not based so much on creational grounds or on the basis of any capacity related to natural law, but rather on the basis of the reaffirmation of creation by the incarnation and resurrection of Jesus. God has become a neighbour to humanity in that his Son has become fully human. It is on the basis of the "ethic of neighbour" that Barth can engage the world. It was the "neighbour concept" in Barth that for him meant that Christians could engage in the public arena. As Ray Anderson states, "One implication of Barth's theological ethics is that Christians can and ought to be able to participate in the setting of moral agendas and even in morally committed actions that affect the social and public lives of human beings, side by side with those committed to a different theology of the church and with a different ideological view of political and economic structure."[63]

---

63. Ray Anderson, *The Shape of Practical Theology: Empowering Ministry with Theological Praxis* (Downers Grove, IL: InterVarsity Press, 2011), 153–54.

THE CREATIONAL VOCATION OR MISSION OF THE CHRISTIAN AS HUMAN

Some evangelicals historically have been concerned only with evangelism and disciple making. Their philosophy has been that only new birth will bring moral transformation to people and societies. The zeal for evangelism is always commendable, and there is truth in their view. The trouble is that it is not the whole truth, and failure to see the Great Commission within the wider context of the biblical story and the wider commands of God, the Great Commandment, and the cultural mandate leads to dualisms and pietistic isolation from people and societies. The first command of God is the cultural mandate, and this involves all that it means to be human, to care for the creation, to exercise justice, and to live well in communities. This is the business of the Christian, because of all people they have been, in Christ the true human, restored to be fully human image bearers, who participate in ruling and in relationship.

The second command of God is crucial also to what happens in church and in state: loving the neighbour whom God has neighboured in Christ. The third comes at the centre of three concentric circles represented by these three Great Commands of God, and it is most convincingly carried out by people who are becoming fully human and who have shalom in their work and homes and church lives. In turn, the telos of making disciples will be to help them to love their neighbour in society and to rediscover what it means to be human in all the places where they have been broken—in their work and home and sexual lives. The mission of the people of God is their very identity, an identity they gain by being in union with the missional God and the *missio Dei*. God, who is known because of his sendings (*missio*), the sending of the Son, the giving of the Spirit, invites the people of God to bring to completion the mission of the Son by the power of the Holy Spirit (John 20:19–23). The essence of the life of the church is to gather to commune deeply through Word and sacrament with the missional God in order to be sent widely into every square inch of the world for the glory of God.

Disengagement neglects what Christians are called to do by way of that creational vocation aspect of mission—which is as image bearers to rule relationally as cocreators and codevelopers of the earth by tending it and caring for it, bringing shalom, the "good" (which is what God pronounced on creation, and which the advent of Christ for the reconciliation of all things has and will restore). The mission of the Christian is first this! And in this they can share with other humans, Christian or not. The Christian gospel is not merely "spiritual." It is inclusive of all that is, at all times. So when a human being, Christian or otherwise, engages in action that brings shalom—nourishing the health of the environment and bringing peace in relationships—that person is doing the will of God for humanity, and Christians can affirm and encourage and participate in it. That includes in medicine, politics, education, and all fields of endeavour. Lesslie Newbigin spoke not only of modelling kingdom reality within the church but also of the whole people of God working out creational kingdom reality in "the whole public life for Christ and his kingdom."[64] What is often missing is a relating of mission to ethics—the whole people of God as scattered and not just gathered. "The missionary encounter with our culture for which I am pleading," Newbigin writes, "will require the energetic fostering of a declericalized lay theology,"[65] which includes enabling Christians to "share with one another the actual experience of their weekday work and to seek illumination from the Gospel for their secular duty." This in turn will enable them to bring kingdom perspective to all aspects of human life that include ethical dimensions. But because it is contained in gospel living and not legal condemnation, it will be evangelical ethics. Orthodoxy and orthopraxis together in Christians is what grants them credibility to speak and be heard in the public square.

Naturally concerns might arise that the boundaries of the church and the state might be compromised. There are wise applied ethical principles that relate to how the church may behave in its gathered capacity. For example, it is very unwise for any church to be aligned with one political party in countries where there are multiple parties, often populated by leaders who are Christian. There might in a large church, for example, be a number of politicians from different parties, and each might conceivably receive the prayers of its people, but the church is not an appropriate place for campaigning and dialoguing on these matters. In the country of Canada, it is not ethical for a church (which is registered as a nonprofit organization) to use its building for meetings of a political party. But these wise principles should not prevent

---

64. Lesslie Newbigin, *The Gospel in a Pluralist Society* (Grand Rapids: Eerdmans, 1989), 231.
65. Lesslie Newbigin, *Foolishness to the Greeks: The Gospel and Western Culture* (Grand Rapids: Eerdmans, 1988), 142.

individuals from running for office or prevent pastoral leaders or elders from offering wise general guidance based on broad ethical principles in many areas that relate to an election for the benefit of the people of God. And the church certainly must on occasion speak beyond partisan politics to ethical and moral principles that relate to justice for all human persons. The idea that the church would be unengaged or not open is simply a contradiction, for it is the church of the open Trinity, the icon of the Trinity, that is open for human relations, in the incarnation and by the Spirit. The church is the body of Jesus, who was the Man for others. The gospel is that God is for humanity, and that includes justice!

Among the many answers to the meaning of humanity is the Christian claim, as Tom Smail has said, "that the ultimate has revealed himself in all his ultimacy and also in all his human accessibility in the incarnation, death, and resurrection of Jesus Christ, that the ultimate is in fact the triune and tripersonal God."[66] He affirms the "virtue of Pannenberg," who, in his desire to use accessible reason to speak universally, "insists that that Christian claim must be made and defended not in the closed ghettos of faith but *in the public forum*, where believers and unbelievers alike ask the ultimate questions about the life of the world and their own."[67]

The Universal Character of Divine Election

The doctrine of election in its severe particularistic form has been used to justify isolation of the elect from the world—and even as a means of expressing nationalistic hubris and separatist apartheid as in South Africa and in the United States in its pilgrim origins, which recur in Moral Majority politics. Related to the love of God for all humanity expressed above, to fail to be engaged ethically in an evangelical tone is to misunderstand the nature of election and the missional nature of Israel and the church. These entities are not ontologically different from humanity, nor is the relationship of God to Israel then and the church now ontologically different. The election of Israel reveals and defines the universal relationship. Election was not for bearing privilege but for discharging responsibility.

Lesslie Newbigin had some perceptive things to say on election, consonant with the point of view that it is the best news of the gospel. In *The Open Secret*, Newbigin speaks of election, "the doctrine that permeates

---

66. Tom Smail, *Like Father, Like Son: The Trinity Imaged in Humanity* (Grand Rapids: Eerdmans, 2006), 123.

67. Smail, *Like Father, Like Son*, 123.

and controls the whole Bible," as that which resolves the scandal of particularity in mission. Newbigin's point is that God's intent to bless was always universal but that this was not accomplished "by means of a universal revelation to all humanity." Rather, "there is . . . a process of selection: a few are chosen to be the bearers of the purpose; they are chosen, not for themselves, but the sake of all."[68] Thus, "the one (or the few) is chosen for the sake of the many; the particular is chosen for the sake of the universal." This, says Newbigin, was in keeping with how election is always presented in the Scriptures, that is, a narrowing with a view to expansion. In this regard, Newbigin is in the debt of Karl Barth, whose christological and communal understanding of election[69] does indeed make it the best news of the gospel and a great incentive for engagement with the world of people for whom Christ died. The triune God in his eternal counsels elected to create humanity and to become human for us in the incarnate Son, in order to reconcile and redeem humanity as an ontological whole. This design by God for humanity leads us to take our engagement with humanity with the utmost seriousness. Disengagement is, in other words, a denial of what the incarnation, death, and resurrection mean for all humanity—we call on the unbeliever to realize their destiny as God intends it. We do so by presenting ethics evangelically, since ethics and gospel are inseparable. How we engage is what speaks most loudly! We speak not as "above" humanity but as part of it. Not as legalistic, but as grace-filled. Alexander Solzhenitsyn once commented that the dividing line between good and evil runs through our Christian hearts. We are all as Christians, to use the Lutheran term, *simul iustus et peccator* (simultaneously justified and yet sinners), and our churches and cultures have plenty of darkness and paganism as evidence. We therefore come at things with humility and with full identification with humanity.

Nevertheless, as justified humans in the process of being sanctified, we are receptors of God's self-revelation. That is, as the church we have become those in communion because we have experienced the communion of God. As such, by the new covenant we have the law of God written on our hearts. We have become receptors of the one Word

---

68. Lesslie Newbigin, *The Open Secret: An Introduction to the Theology of Mission* (Grand Rapids: Eerdmans, 1995), 34.

69. Barth does not subscribe to the concept of a mysterious or secret predestinating decree. Barth learnt this from the *Scots Confession* of 1560 and also from Pierre Maury at the International Congress of Calvinist Theology of Geneva in 1936. See Karl Barth, CD II/2, 154–60.

of God (not two, as if gospel and law are two, as Barth said). Therefore, we are that domain where all ethical categories and decisions can and should be decided upon.[70] This has some resonance with the moral vision of Stanley Hauerwas, though it is not mere modelling of *koinōnia*. It is speaking as the *koinōnia* and from the *koinōnia*!

The Uses of the Law

A further rationale for the church to speak in public spaces is the biblical notion of the use of the moral law to instruct society, even if it may not acknowledge this. At least in a formal way, we may appeal to the rational discernment of God's moral order in creation. The theology of the Reformation, emphatic though it was on the inability of human persons to save themselves, nevertheless articulated this use of the law. It was articulated as the first use of the law, the *usus civilus* or *politicus*, the civil use of the law *for all people*, by Philip Melancthon.[71] The civil use is inferred from Paul's discussion of the use of the law in exposing and punishing criminals in 1 Timothy 1:8–11. There are other implications of this concept for institutions that are spoken of as being under the sovereignty of God (1 Peter 2:13–17). There is also a chain of command within the New Testament that relativizes commands to honour the king under the higher sovereignty of God and his law, which may necessitate civil disobedience (Acts 4:19), martyrdom, or immigration. Martyrdom, in the New Testament church experience and into the early church, was an expectation of the early Christians and in a rather sombre way points to the reality of their engagement for the gospel and all that it entailed.

The first use of the law assumes that the state also is a sphere sovereignty under an all-encompassing created order under God (see Calvin, Abraham Kuyper) and that Christ is king of the nation as well as the church, though in a very different manner. Under sphere sovereignty, each sector, or sphere, of life has a distinct authority and competence, which is equal to other spheres of life. It is an alternative to the world-views of ecclesiasticism in the Middle Ages and secularism in modernity. The nation is ruled by the Decalogue, not the Sermon on the Mount (nonretaliation). Within this are the spheres or orders of creation that envelop life and include family and work in science, art, trades and

---

70. Torrance, "On Deriving 'Ought' from 'Is,'" 183–85.
71. Philip Melanchthon, *Loci Communes* (1535).

commerce, agriculture, and so on. In all of this, Christ is Lord. "All authority in heaven and on earth has been given to me," Jesus said in his resurrection power (Matt. 28:18). In contrast with working to create a Christian democracy, however, our task is not to dominate these spheres but to be present in them all, and that must include influencing them in every way. It means praying every day, "Your kingdom come, your will be done, on earth as it is in heaven." Some might say that Kuyper overemphasized sovereignty and that it took Arias Mortimer to correct that and unite the gospel and sovereignty—in that the gospel *is* in fact the annunciation of the kingdom and the invitation to receive it. However, Kuyper's voice needs to be heard in our fragmented world and fragmented church. Kuyper scholar McKendree R. Langley suggests that the church needs to hear afresh today that "Jesus Christ is both the special-grace Head of the universal church and the common-grace Lord over the nations."[72] And within sphere sovereignty, Langley suggests that "Christians, as well as every other societal group, have the right to express their opinions and even to organize in order to influence national life."[73] There is of course a fine line here. How they influence must be in keeping with the kingdom of the Servant King. The mission of God is being worked out in every sphere of society. The Christian seeks to participate in that, knowing that the telos is not political domination but provisional contributions to the new creation, which will have value in the kingdom to come when that creation is fully under the sway of Christ, when every enemy will be the footstool of his feet.

Oliver O'Donovan presents a similar theologico-political ethic. The church should be engaged in the political order as it seeks to live out the implications of the kingdom of God, which has come. God has reaffirmed creation in the resurrection of Jesus, and this includes the reaffirmation of the orders of creation, the basic institutions of family and government.

THE NATURE OF THE CHURCH, THE KINGDOM (*EKKLĒSIA* AND *BASILEIA*), AND THE STATE

There is a tendency within the popular contemporary church to make a large separation between church and kingdom and then sometimes to

---

72. McKendree R. Langley, *The Practice of Political Spirituality* (Jordan Station, ON: Paideia, 1984), 167.
73. Langley, *Practice of Political Spirituality*, 169.

confuse the kingdom of God with the state. The biblical reality depicts a much closer relationship between church and kingdom, as a number of New Testament scholars and theologians have recently shown.[74] The church is in fact the sign, the instrument, and the foretaste of the kingdom, as Newbigin has insisted.[75] A kingdom awareness in the church pulls it toward kingdom engagement with the world, including ethical dialogue. Agents of the kingdom are present in all sectors of public life. A distinction between the church/kingdom and the state also guides the church to avoid triumphalism, which leads to associating the kingdom with any political party, government, or regime. The timely word of Lesslie Newbigin is that when we do this "we are always in danger of defining the Kingdom in terms of some contemporary ideology and not in terms of the manifestation of the Kingdom in the incarnate, crucified, and risen Jesus."[76] A country's liberation from oppression can give rise to another (e.g., Zimbabwe). There may be *signs* of the kingdom in the political sphere, and the church should seek and cooperate with these, but the ultimate sign before the return of Christ is the church itself as the new society in which there is justice, forgiveness, peace, and healing.

Refusal to Capitulate to the Values of Modernity and Postmodernity

To be unengaged in the public square is to capitulate to the values of modernity and the caricature of a monadic God rather than to upend its cherished notions. The despair Newbigin felt is expressed in an eloquent phrase he borrowed from Michael Polanyi. Newbigin "wrote of the 'incandescence . . . of the Christian heritage' burning in the 'oxygen of Greek rationalism' and reaching a position where the 'fuel' is now exhausted."[77] Timothy Yates notes that Newbigin bemoaned "the withdrawal of whole areas of life, such as economics, into autonomy, where

---

74. See Richard Bauckham, who contends that the church is "at the very least the primary sign of the kingdom." Bauckham, "Kingdom and Church according to Jesus and Paul," *Horizons in Biblical Theology* 18, no. 1 (1996): 1–26. Scot McKnight, Ben Witherington, N. T. Wright, Christopher J. H. Wright, David E. Fitch, and Peter Leithart assert the overlap and even identity of church and kingdom.

75. Lesslie Newbigin, *Mission in Christ's Way: A Gift, a Command, an Assurance* (Chester Heights, PA: Friendship, 1988), 12.

76. Lesslie Newbigin, *Signs amid the Rubble: The Purposes of God in Human History* (Grand Rapids: Eerdmans, 2003), 106.

77. Timothy Yates, *Christian Mission in the Twentieth Century* (Cambridge: Cambridge University Press, 1994), 241, with quotes from Lesslie Newbigin, *Other Side of 1984: Questions for the Churches* (Geneva: World Council of Churches, 1990), 21.

moral values are no longer brought to bear on decisions."[78] We might say medicine or sexuality too. So what was the church to do? Newbigin's answer was that "if the church is to recover its nerve and confidence in its message as one of public truth and significance, it has to escape from the private arena, which some of its own leaders have carved out for it as a form of escape from modernity, a path which even a theologian like Schleiermacher encouraged it to take."[79] The modern assumption that Christianity is unscientific—a set of private values grounded in faith, not reason—and therefore not suited for the public square must be upended. In the place of logical positivism, which even scientists no longer claim, critical realism and a "faith seeking understanding" approach in both theology and science must be acknowledged. No one in the public square can claim total objectivity. All knowledge is grounded in faith or interpretation, as postmodernity has shown. Engagement in the public square is a wide and deep missionary encounter that we *must* be and in which we *can* be involved, on the grounds of the historical empiricism of the revelatory events of the life, death, and resurrection of Jesus and the witness of the apostles and the church. To keep our values in the private realm is to capitulate to modernity. But engagement must be done on behalf of and by the power of and in the spirit of the triune God of love, not the God of naked, arbitrary power. Within a democratic society, Christians must exercise tolerance for different viewpoints and defend the right and freedom of all in the public square. Furthermore, as Yates exhortes, Christians must "avoid the 'sacralising of politics' and the 'total identification of a public goal with the will of God,'" whether in the case of the "'religious Right' in the US or in Islamic Iran."[80] For therein lies the "danger of idolatry" with the creation of "false absolutes."[81] Newbigin also warns especially the liberal church of the danger of advocating a form of "Christian" pluralism in which all religions are rationalized by a generic kind of Trinity. Yates concludes that Newbigin has in fact "helped the Western church to realize its

---

78. Yates, *Christian Mission in the Twentieth Century*, 241, citing Newbigin, *Other Side of 1984*, 1–4, 11.

79. Yates, *Christian Mission in the Twentieth Century*, 241, citing Newbigin, *Foolishness to the Greeks: The Gospel and Western Culture* (Grand Rapids: Eerdmans, 1988), 44–45.

80. Yates, *Christian Mission in the Twentieth Century*, 241, citing Newbigin, *Foolishness to the Greeks*, 116–17.

81. Yates, *Christian Mission in the Twentieth Century*, 243, citing Newbigin, *The Gospel in a Pluralist Society* (Grand Rapids: Eerdmans, 1989), 162.

missionary situation,"[82] and his appeal for engagement in light of this is even more relevant today.

THE PROPER CONDUIT (THE "HOW" QUESTION): FROM CHURCH OUTWARD

Much has been said already in this chapter about the need for the public engagement of the church to be *evangelical* and *ecclesial*. Engagement is justified in that the nature of the church as *polis* is the prism through which the world is meant to catch a glimpse of the true *polis*, or the kingdom or new creation community. On this basic assumption there is agreement between theological ethicists such as Stanley Hauerwas, Oliver O'Donovan, and Alan Torrance. Karl Barth once stated that "the hope in which the Christian community has its eternal goal consists . . . not in an eternal church but in the *polis* built by God and coming down from heaven to earth."[83] O'Donovan affirms the truth of this statement in *The Desire of the Nations*, but he asserts that it requires qualification: "It fails to acknowledge the political character of the church itself, veiled and hidden in the time of its pilgrimage, yet always present in its witness to the Kingdom of God."[84] He goes on to affirm:

> The church never was, in its true character, merely the temple of the city; it was the promise of the city itself. . . . If the Christian community has as its *eternal* goal, the goal of its pilgrimage, the disclosure of the church as city, it has as its *intermediate* goal, the goal of its mission, the discovery of the city's secret destiny through the prism of the church.[85]

Where O'Donovan and Hauerwas differ is that the latter is anxious for the church to merely demonstrate this in community rather than engage with society, which is irremediably corrupt. For Hauerwas, the chief motif is peace, which becomes nonviolence. Therefore, the doctrine of retributive justice is compromised, as is any doctrine of

---

82. Yates, *Christian Mission in the Twentieth Century*, 243–44.
83. Karl Barth, "Christian Community," in *Community, State, and Church: Three Essays by Karl Barth* (Eugene, OR: Wipf & Stock, 2004), 19.
84. Oliver O'Donovan, *The Desire of the Nations: Rediscovering the Roots of Political Theology* (Cambridge: Cambridge University Press, 1996), 285–86.
85. O'Donovan, *Desire of the Nations*, 285–86.

judgment meted out at the cross (the *Christus Victor* model prevails), and indeed, salvation is focused purely on liberation from the powers. This means that for Hauerwas the emphasis in engagement with corrupt powers can only be that of martyrdom. Any alternative engagement he finds to involve the politics of domination and violence.

By contrast, the politics of O'Donovan are rooted in God's decisive judgment at the cross, and his account therefore leaves room for those judgments to be applied in the temporal realm. For O'Donovan, God's judgments are the starting point of the New Jerusalem because only through judgment can true peace be established. God's judgment has fallen at the cross, and the resurrection has constituted the church as the fruit of God's judgment of evil and as the new humanity. The ecclesial resurrection community can confidently risk engagement with the corrupt power structures of the world, knowing that in the death and resurrection of Jesus the rulers of this age have already been judged, and knowing that in the fulness of time the decisive judgments will be made, and therefore, in the meantime, judgments can be made. When judgments are made or justice is done now, this gives a foretaste of the complete justice of the age to come.

In conclusion, Peter Leithart has affirmed that if the church is the chief visible, earthly, communal manifestation of the kingdom, as the New Testament suggests, then surely the building up of the church and its life together should be seen as part of the expression and work of the kingdom in the world.[86]

And this, in turn, invites us to consider, circumspectly, how we should engage in the world. Our sense of mission encourages engagement because mission means the Great Commission, the Great Commandment, and the cultural mandate. At the same time, the imperfect and incomplete state of the church and the kingdom in the now but not yet, in the penultimate place where all our ethical judgments are under judgment, urges us against moralizing in a manner that is arrogant or that shows intolerance or the lack of a distinction between the church and the state. Lack of civility is a contradiction of the very nature of our being as people of love.

---

86. Peter J. Leithart, *The Kingdom and the Power: Rediscovering the Centrality of the Church* (Phillipsburg, NJ: P&R, 1993), 96.

Conclusion

Summing up the nature of theological ethics, we may say that, housed within the gospel, flowing from its life in the triune God, the church, as the icon of the Trinity made up of persons-in-relation, is the primary locus of ethics. There is only one sphere in which moral transformation, discernment in ethical inquiry, and courage and power for ethical action can happen—the sphere of participation in the triune God . . . his love, his life, his justice, his righteousness, his holiness. And as the church and its persons live into and out of this union with Christ by the Spirit, they undergo moral formation, discernment, and action imperfectly in a manner that is always in need of forgiveness and redemption, and yet, for all the church's weaknesses, it is still enabled to communicate its inner life and speak humbly and boldly in the public square, both corporately and through its missionally engaged persons in the world.

The primary emphasis has been that ethics is *Trinitarian*. Trinitarian ethics suggests that it is not enough just to be *theological* in one's ethics. It is necessary to be specifically Trinitarian, recognizing that God in the Christian faith is not a generic Creator being that every religion can claim but specifically the God and Father revealed by our Lord Jesus Christ, the one God in three persons, Father, Son, and Holy Spirit. This has repercussions both for the distinctiveness of Christian ethics and for an ethos of love rather than naked divine power, an ethos of humble influence not coercion. God and his Word are indeed our final authority as the sovereign Creator and Redeemer King of the cosmos, but God's way of being and acting in this cosmos may not be described as fate or coercion. God is sovereign, but that sovereignty permits within it creational and human agency. This creates an ethos of freedom for ethics.

The Trinitarian categorization of Christian ethics has a wide scope of meaning, but it includes the transcendence of deontological, utilitarian, and virtue ethics. Thus deontology and utilitarian approaches may be employed within this broad Trinitarian (biblical, christological, pneumatological) framework in ways that are redemptive and teleological.

Considerations of Trinitarian personhood lead by analogy, not univocally, to description of the human agents in ethics as *persons*, with the implication that the category of character or virtue, whilst important, is subsumed within and takes its cue from personhood both with respect to moral formation and the principal virtue of love and with respect to moral decision making or ethical judgments. Whereas the virtue ethicist wishes to speak little of ethical judgments and behaviour, for it is assumed that agents of character will simply discern the good and make good decisions and act as good people, the person-centred ethicist will pursue character and virtue in participation with Christ but still sense the need, in a fallen world of as yet not perfected people, to be desperately dependent on the leading of the Spirit in the moment of ethical judgment, and the Spirit's empowerment for the implementation of the action is required. In other words, there is in the Trinitarian personhood camp a belief that being is not enough on its own and that deciding and doing do matter. To emphasize being but not doing seems to the Trinitarian ethicist to be a gnostic move, one that actually denies a key component of what constitutes the image of God as depicted in Genesis 1 and 2. There is also a lower estimation of what character and virtue mean for even redeemed human persons in the Trinitarian view. Virtue ethicists, following Aristotle, Thomas Aquinas, Alasdair MacIntyre, and Stanley Hauerwas, may appeal to participation in the life or wisdom or holiness of God as the basis for the life of virtue, but it is often not what is heard first. Furthermore, the nature of the participation seems sometimes to be related to the sharing in divine attributes or even divine essence. Such sharing threatens the boundaries of divine and human distinctiveness. Alternatively, participation of the *koinonia* kind averts these problems. Thus participation is first grounded in the incarnational union of God and humanity without confusion. It is then entered into from a human perspective by means of personal and relational union with Christ by the Spirit, from and to the Father. It is thus first a relational union, resulting in the sharing of divine love, holiness, and justice.

A Trinitarian approach values the character formation of persons, but it holds equally the conviction that the command of God (hearing the Word of God outside of ourselves) is crucial in both moral formation *and* ethical decision making and action. That is, there is a recognition of the vital importance of the continual hearing of the Word of God and the continual feeding on Christ in the Lord's Supper for *both* character formation as ecclesial beings formed by the big story of the biblical gospel narrative *and* the hearing of the material that must inform ethical judgment and action. It is not *either* command ethics *or* character ethics; it is both/and. Each is in deficiency if it neglects the other. The question of interpretation of the texts of Scripture and their applicability in light of the authorial intent and cultural placing is, of course, relevant. But the basic commitment of the Christian tradition that Holy Scripture is our final authority is a crucial conviction. Revisioning Scripture to suit current cultural viewpoints in ways that reflect the hegemony of modern, postmodern, fragmented culture and the power of social media cannot be considered an appropriate way of going about things.

Trinitarian ethics involving participative persons also recognizes that ethics is mostly situational, that ethical judgments cannot be given in advance of the situation being experienced, and that, therefore, even with the divine deposit of biblical content, and even though a Christian may be developing as a person of character well-formed, there is a need for the immediate work of the Spirit to lead and to guide in every situation. No person and no church made up of persons of character can decide ethical issues as they come to us afresh in each generation without lived participation in the triune God and specifically without the interpretation and empowerment of the Spirit. This is the vital "inside of ourselves" pneumatic aspect of ethics. Of course, Word and Spirit always go together. This is not an incitement into "pneumatic anarchy," to use a Volfian phrase.[1]

Trinitarian ethics therefore entails a Trinitarian *spirituality*. There is no hope of wise ethical discernment and just decision making apart from transformation of the heart. People do not fail morally because they are unaware of the rules or don't try hard enough; they fail because they have affective knots in their souls and hunger in their hearts. The only hope any of us have of moral transformation is to have souls satiated with the glory of Christ and the love of God and the joy of the Holy Spirit. This is what participation means. It moves us toward having affections that are ordered and satisfied in Christ and that crowd out the lesser affections that stunt our character and cause us to pursue idols, which

---

1. Miroslav Volf, *After Our Likeness: The Church as the Image of the Trinity* (Grand Rapids: Eerdmans, 1998), 234.

can never satisfy. And that life of participation is facilitated by the grace of a committed ecclesial life—feeding on Christ in the eucharist, in the Word, and in community—and personal spiritual practices. Another way to say this is that knowing good and evil, right and wrong, can only come through knowing God, that is, loving God and neighbour, the core of Christian ethics. This is the chief of our affections, and it can only be renewed in us as we receive and live in divine love. In the words of Psalm 23, being led in "the paths of righteousness" flows from a personal, intimate relationship with God characterized by the lived reality that "the LORD is *my* Shepherd."

Trinitarian ethics, because they are ecclesial or communitarian, also means that ethics cannot be done in isolation or individualistically. Persons understood in a Trinitarian way are by nature persons-in-relation. We are morally formed in familial and ecclesial community. And we must consult the deep and wide community of God, the church and its scholars in the past and its experts in the present. For example, although the final authority of the church is the Word of God (*norma normans*) and the creeds and confessions of the church (*norma normata*, the normed norm, the norm normed by the Word), the scholarship of the doctors of the church has a relative authority also, and it has a weight and a value that are significant. Reversing ethical stances on major ethical issues must be undertaken only with great care and wide ecclesial or catholic consultation, a notion sometimes not very well appreciated by evangelicals.

Within this Trinitarian understanding, as we have noted, human agents in ethics are to be described as *persons*, a category greater than character but inclusive of character, a category that is inclusive of both their being *and* their doing. Individual Christian persons, who are by definition ecclesial persons participating in the life and holiness of God in Christ, by the Spirit, and through the church, will pursue the life of wisdom and moral formation for the cultivation of all the virtues under the chief virtue of love, including its moral content summed up in the two aspects of the Great Commandment (love of God and neighbour, summing up the Ten Commandments, not replacing them), and will respond to the situational demands of ethical inquiry and decision making in the following manner: *they will operate participatively through prayer, looking to the triune God from above themselves; they will look for the Word of God that comes to them from outside of themselves* (extra nos); *they*

will seek to hear the promptings of the Spirit of God from within themselves;
they will consult within the community of wisdom in the church and by
researching perspectives in the world around themselves; they will engage in
this discernment and action with a profound sense of dependence and with
an awareness that in the world in which the kingdom has not yet fully come,
our ethical insight is limited, and where there is insufficient revelational
clarity, humility will characterise the Christian ethicist and the regular
practice of confession and absolution.

Within this Trinitarian understanding, we have also established
the church as the primary locus of ethics. What this means for the
church today, minimally, is the necessity of ecumenical dialogue on
all major ethical issues. The witness of a church that is unified around
the essentialist Niceno-Constantinopolitan Creed, in accordance with
its Lord's desires (John 17), must include its ethical witness. Individual
denominations should approach these major issues as a denomination,
and individual Christians must consult ecclesially, but this larger ecumenical witness, which appeals to Word and the doctors of the tradition,
could serve the world with light that may guide it in the moral maze
surrounding global poverty, global warming, bioethics, technology,
sexuality, economics, and many other issues relevant today.

Scripture Index

Subject Index

Author Index